P9-DEH-403

THE LIFE & DEATH OF STARS

THE LIFE & DEATH OF STARS

by Donald A. Cooke

Introduction by Patrick Moore

Crown Publishers, Inc. □ New York

Copyright © 1985 by Donald Alan Cooke.
All rights reserved. No part of this book may be reproduced or transmitted in any form or by any means, electronic or mechanical, including photocopying, recording, or by any information storage and retrieval system, without permission in writing from the publisher.
Published by Crown Publishers, Inc., One Park Avenue, New York, New York 10016, and simultaneously in Canada by General Publishing Company Limited
CROWN is a trademark of Crown Publishers, Inc.
Manufactured in Japan
Book design by Dana Sloan
Original illustrations by Blaise Zito, Associates, Inc.
Library of Congress Cataloging in Publication Data
Cooke, Donald A.
The life and death of stars.

Includes index.
1. Stars. 2. Sun. I. Title.
QB801.C64 1985 523.8 84-4266
ISBN 0-517-55268-X

10 9 8 7 6 5 4 3 2 1
First Edition

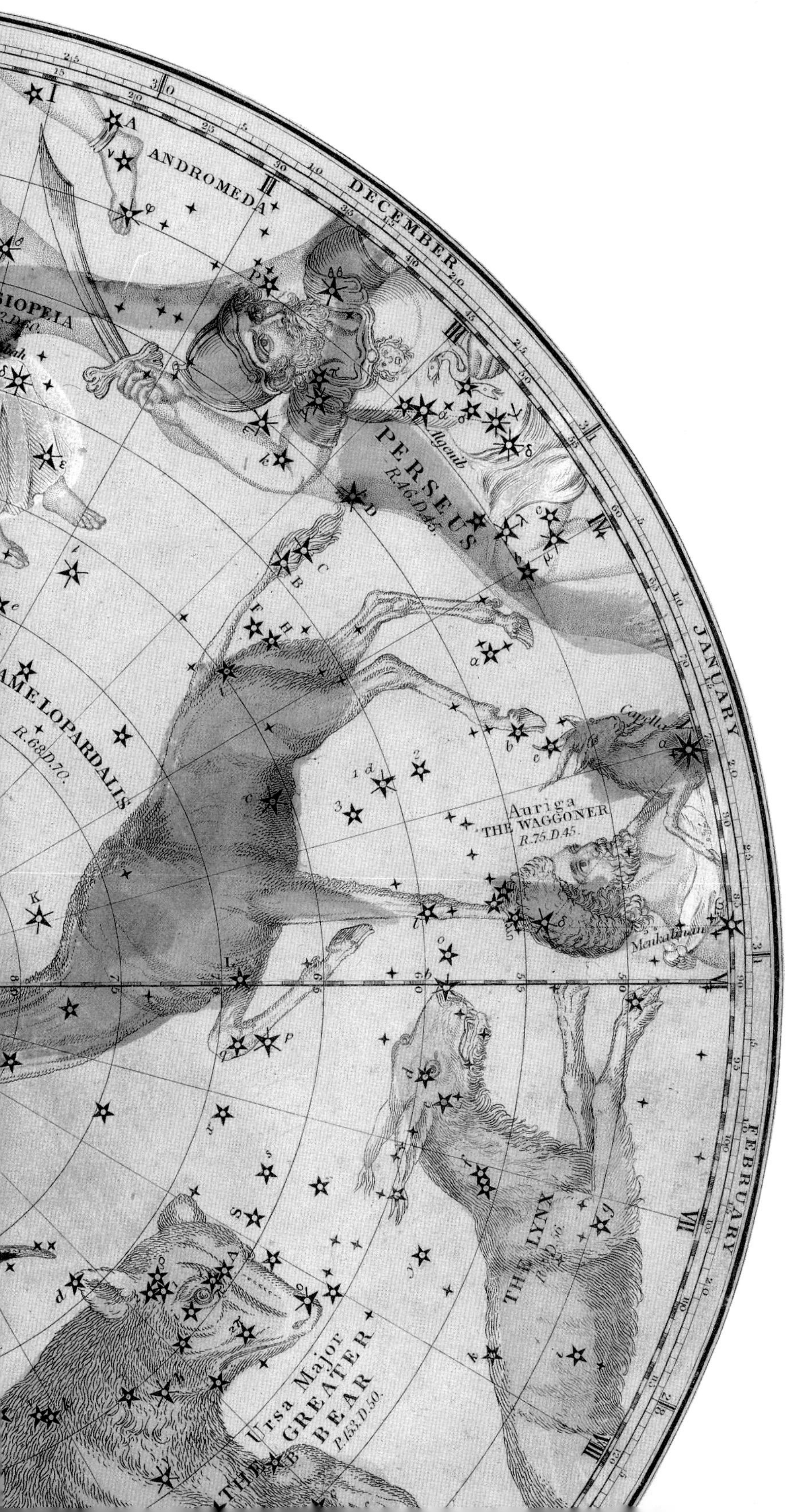
ANDROMEDA
DECEMBER
PERSEUS
JANUARY
Capella
Auriga
THE WAGGONER
R.75.D.45.
THE LYNX
FEBRUARY
Ursa Major
GREATER
BEAR

CONTENTS

To my mother and father,
from whom all inspiration began.

Acknowledgments

There are several people to whom I must express my deep gratitude for their invaluable help in making a dream of mine into this reality. Above all, I want to thank my wife, Sally, for her undying support, tolerance, and for reading and typing the manuscript in its early stages.

The original artwork was prepared especially for this project by my colleague Valentino M. Gonzales, assistant director of the Fels Planetarium, and by the artists at J & R Technical Services, Inc., and Blaise Zito Associates, Inc. It is to their talented hands that I owe much thanks for the visual quality of this book. Other visuals were generously supplied by numerous sources listed in the credits at the end of the book.

Professionally, I am continually indebted to Dr. Jay M. Pasachoff, who not only launched me into a career in astronomy but also supplied several wonderful photographs for this book. I thank George Hamilton for bringing me into the realm of planetaria and the joys of telling the world about astronomy.

Without the help and support of my editor, Jake Goldberg, and the wonderful people at Crown Publishers, not only would this book never have appeared, but it would never even have been conceived.

INTRODUCTION

How old is the universe? How old is the earth, and how were the stars formed? For that matter, how did the universe itself come into being? These are questions that have been asked by humankind for many centuries. Even though we still do not know the full answers, we have at least learned a great deal, particularly over the last few decades. Astronomy today is anything but a static science. New techniques, new instruments, new branches of astronomical study have combined to make a complete change in outlook.

The story of this book is the story of the sun and the stars. We begin with the formation of a star from the almost incredibly thin material spread through space, some of which we can see as the lovely bright nebulae. We follow the story through, but not all stars have the same life histories; some remain dim throughout their long lives, while others, with greater mass, radiate furiously but squander their reserves of energy so quickly that by cosmic standards their life spans are short. Some explode as supernovae, sending material hurtling away into space in all directions; from this material new stars are created. Others, of even greater mass, collapse into what are termed black holes, surely the most bizarre objects in the whole of the universe. Until fairly recently their existence was unknown. Even now they cannot be seen, and we have no idea what happens in their interiors; but we are fairly sure that they must exist.

The old-established idea of astronomers as people who spend all their nights in a lonely observatory looking at the stars could not be less accurate. Modern astronomers spend very little time in an observatory, and to operate a telescope they need not even be on the same continent. By now we have reached the stage in which an astronomer sitting in a control room in, say, Herstmonceux Castle in Sussex can operate a telescope on the summit of Mauna Kea in Hawaii. Anything of the sort would have seemed out of the question not so long ago, but by now it has become accepted fact. Moreover, astronomers are no longer confined to having to study visible light. In fact, visible light makes up only a small part of the total range of wavelengths, or electromagnetic spectrum. At the short-wave end we have ultraviolet, X rays, and then the very penetrative, ultrashort gamma rays; at the long-wave end we have infrared, microwaves, and then radio waves. Although it may come as something of a surprise to the newcomer to learn that radio waves reach the earth from space, it has been known ever since the early 1930s, when an American radio engineer named Karl Jansky discovered, quite accidentally, that his improvised aerial, designed to study static, was picking up radio waves from the Milky Way. Not until after the end of the war did radio astronomy become an important branch of science, but by now it is invaluable. Short-wave astronomy followed later, and in some regions it had to await the development of rockets and space vehicles. For instance, X rays from space cannot be studied from ground level because they are blocked out by layers in the earth's upper atmosphere; the same applies to most of the other wavelengths, apart, of course, from visible light and some radio radiation.

Armed with these new techniques, astronomers have been able to extend their knowledge with amazing rapidity. A book written only five years ago may look decidedly out of date by now; each year seems to bring its quota of new advances.

Although we are still unsure of the origin of the universe, and we cannot trace it back to the moment of creation (if, indeed, there really was a definite moment of creation), we can at least trace the evolutions of the stars. This is the theme of the present book, and it has been carried out with great skill. All the various kinds of stars are described, and we see how each has its own points of special interest and importance. Our sun is no exception. It is an ordinary star that seems so important to us only because it is so near at hand. At a distance of "only" 93 million miles, it is on our cosmic doorstep.

It is also important to remember that astronomy is by no means an isolated science. It has always been the foundation of time keeping and navigation and inevitably is linked with mathematics, but modern astronomy is linked equally closely with physics, chemistry, and many other branches of science. (If we consider space research, we must even include biology; after all, it would certainly be conceited to imagine that we are the only intelligent life in the universe.) This too is brought out here. But for our studies of the sun, for example, we would know much less about the atom than we actually do—and we would probably not have progressed nearly so far in our application of nuclear power for peaceful use.

Great characters flit through the story, great themes are developed, and the end picture is one of absorbing interest. All the results of the most modern research are included. It seems strange now to reflect that even as recently as half a century ago we were still very far from certain just how a star produces its energy.

I recommend this book to you. Clear, concise, and informative, it will hold your interest from the first page to the last. Read it and enjoy it. I did!

PATRICK MOORE

THE LIFE & DEATH OF STARS

1: INTRODUCTION TO THE STARS

As a red hue lingers in the west, the sun disappears beyond the horizon, and the sky grows dark. The crystalline heavens are a radiant blue of unparalleled depth. The first star appears and grows brighter. More stars adorn the evening sky. At last the final traces of twilight slip away, and the sky is dark and deep. There is no moon tonight.

The sky seems boundless in its majesty, and countless stars overwhelm us with joy and humility. We cannot easily comprehend the vast distances in the universe, and we cannot grasp the ages of the stars, but we can revel in the spectacle of their light, and we can wonder what they are.

1.1 In prime locations around the world, observatories have been established so that astronomers can study the wonders of the cosmos. High atop the volcanic mountain Haleakula in Hawaii, the glow of the western sky marks the beginning of a new evening of observation.

This scene is familiar to all who have waited for evening to fall and let starlight and clear air bathe upturned faces. This scene is also the workshop of the observational astronomer. On many mountaintops around the world, observatory domes rub against the sky. The telescope is an instrument, a probe, and an extension of our senses that lets us bridge the ages and distances of the cosmos.

The laboratory of the astronomer is the entire universe, for where else can scientists study matter in all imaginable conditions? The space between the stars is a far better vacuum than scientists can achieve in earthbound laboratories; atoms are stretched to their limits in the hot, dense centers of stars; and the ultimate compression of matter occurs during the formation of a black hole.

Although not always a laboratory of science, the stars have nevertheless been vitally influential in humankind's ascent from the shadowy origins of civilization. The seasonal variation of the fixed stars and the five "wandering stars," or planets, as we know them, were seen as signs of supernatural powers that ruled human life and fate. There is evidence of this dependence on astrological prediction in literature from the fifth century B.C., and even during the Renaissance the primary reason for observing the sky was to make accurate astrological predictions.

These same motions of the heavenly bodies were used to establish the first calendar. The cyclic changes of the sun, moon, and planets told people when to sow seeds and harvest crops. Once farming was practicable, settled communities developed and cities and culture flourished. We still tell time by the stars. Our 24-hour day is based on the time it takes for the sun to make one complete passage around the sky. Of course, we know that our planet spins on its axis, so that the sun appears to go around the earth once each day.

As the earth orbits the sun, the seasons change because of the tilt of the earth's axis. In summer, the northern hemisphere is more directly illuminated by the sun's warming rays (Figure 1.2a). In winter the axis is pointed away from the sun so the rays hit the earth obliquely and spread their energy over a larger area than in the summer (Figure 1.2b). The fact that the earth's axis is tilted 23.5 degrees from the perpendicular to the earth's orbit around the sun is simply a matter of chance. The material that formed the solar system, including our planet, coalesced and was spinning with various local orientations. Each planet has a unique tilt to its rotation.

Imagine this planet with an axis that was perpendicular to the orbit's plane. We would have no seasonal variations in the temperate zones, and the sun would always lie above the earth's equator. With no seasons, the temperature at our latitude would be more or less constant through the year, similar to that of the spring and autumn. Snow would fall only at the highest latitudes. Once early people understood the cycles of the heavenly bodies, they were able to plan their lives around a calendar. It was such settled agricultural communities that eventually led to today's technological and cultural society.

From the earliest human who set out on a journey far from home, people have used the stars as navigational beacons. The ancient Greeks noticed as they sailed the Mediterranean Sea that the north star would change its position in the sky depending on where they sailed north or south. They and other nautical societies used this fact to help them determine their position at sea.

The instruments we use to navigate today are different from those of the ancient Mediterranean communities that took to boats for trade and conquest, but the fundamentals of navigation remain the same. Our most sophisticated machines to date, the two Voyager spacecraft that explored the outer planets, use stars to guide them through the solar system.

As practical as the stars have been, it is natural to wonder what they are, and elegant and fanciful notions have arisen out of imaginative and superstitious minds.

Religious beliefs played an important role in peoples' understanding of the night sky. The planets, which slowly change position with respect to the fixed stars, were named for Roman gods, for who else would move so majestically and eternally among the points of light? The fastest-moving planet was named Mercury, after the winged messenger of the gods, and the planet that appears so beautiful as an evening star was called Venus.

The Eskimos believed that stars were round holes in the sky that glowed like fire. The Babylonians held that the stars were suspended on strings that were simply pulled up in the daytime, and some American Indians said that the stars and the Milky Way were campfires of those who are on their way to their final resting place.

Today, the stars are all of these things to us because they are a part of our heritage and of our ascent to civilization. The 88 constellations into which the starry sky is divided are named after characters of bygone times, and we still pass on their myths from one generation to the next. The stars are timekeepers, navigational lighthouses, and subjects of poetic thought and art; and they are scientific laboratories.

Walt Whitman wrote: "Over all the sky—the sky! Far, far out of reach, studded, breaking out, the eternal stars." We know the stars are not eternal. Each star begins its life, feeds off its own body of hydrogen, and dies when its usable fuel is exhausted. In the history of astronomy, the understanding of the life and death of stars is a new and very exciting field of science. The last century has witnessed the discovery of pulsars, black holes, and stellar factories in glowing nebulae.

The stars are important to us because we are made of stuff that has come from stars that have exploded. This book explores the life cycles of the stars, from their births in cold clouds of dust and gas to their violent deaths and reunion with the space between the stars. We should know about stars to fully appreciate our existence in the universe.

Stellar Distances and Brightness

On any clear night, it is obvious to an observer of the sky that the stars are not all the same. Some stars appear brighter than others, which gives the quality of depth to the beauty of night. If all the stars are the same distance away from us, they must shine with different brightnesses. This was a widely accepted belief of natural philosophers in ancient Mediterranean civilizations because the sky does indeed look like a dome on which the stars are placed.

On the other hand, if we think that all stars give off the same amount of light, surely the observed variation from star to star is due to varying distances among them. In fact, the stars are both different distances away and possess different intrinsic brightnesses, so the night sky has a variety of depth and brilliance. The determination of a star's distance and brightness is a very important observational aspect of the astronomer's job.

There are several ways in which astronomers define the brightness of a star. The simplest is to consider how bright the star appears to us in the night sky. As mentioned before, the apparent brightness of a star is dependent on how bright the star actually is and its distance from us. This observed brightness is called *apparent magnitude* and really does not say much about the star itself, since it only classifies it by appearance.

The apparent magnitude of stars was first described by Hipparchus in ancient Greece some 2,000 years ago. The great astronomer Ptolemy improved on Hipparchus's classification scheme, which divided the visible stars into six distinct classes of brightness. The brightest stars were said to be first magnitude, fainter stars second magnitude, and so on down to sixth magnitude.

In the nineteenth century, astronomers began making more precise determinations of the relative brightness of stars, and they found that the brightest stars in the night sky were about 100 times brighter than the faintest stars. On Hipparchus's magnitude scale the modern measurement of 100 times corresponded to the difference between first magnitude and sixth magnitude, so today we consider any difference of five magnitudes to be equal to a difference of 100 times in intensity.

The intermediate magnitudes, then, represent differences in intensity of 2.5, because $2.5^5 = 100$, where 5 is the number of magnitude jumps that equals the 100-times difference in intensity. The difference between third magnitude and fourth is a brightness of 2.5 times, with the fourth-magnitude star being fainter. What about a difference of two magnitudes? $2.5^2 = 6.25$, so two magnitudes equals a difference in intensity of 6.25.

1.2a The tilt of the earth's axis is toward the sun in the summer for the northern hemisphere.

1.2b In winter in the northern hemisphere, the earth's axis tips away from the sun.

The stars in Hipparchus's catalog were transferred into the newer, more accurate measurement scale. Incidentally, we still say that sixth-magnitude stars are the faintest we can see with the naked eye. A difficulty arose, however, when astronomers, using optical aids, realized that some of the brightest stars are actually *more* than 100 times brighter than the faintest stars. These became classified as zero-magnitude stars. Sirius, which is the brightest star in the sky other than the sun, has an apparent magnitude of -1.4 on the modern scale. Had Hipparchus realized just how bright Sirius really is, perhaps he would have used it as a standard starting value for his scale, but the naked eye is not as discerning as the instruments of the nineteenth century, so we have become accustomed to a list of positive and negative magnitude values.

The sun is the brightest object in the sky: its brightness corresponds to an apparent magnitude of -26.8. We must remember that the brightest stars have the lowest values on the magnitude scale.

The sun, however bright it appears to be, is by no means the most luminous star in the sky. It appears to be so bright only because it is so close by. Intrinsically, the sun is an average star. To fairly compare the true brightness of stars, astronomers established another brightness classification related to the apparent magnitude scale, called *absolute magnitude*.

To determine the absolute magnitudes of stars, astronomers removed the distance dependence of apparent magnitude by determining the brightness of stars as if they were all the same distance away from the earth. To perform such transformations, however, we must know something about the true distance to each star we are measuring. We must know whether the star should be "moved" away to our standard distance or drawn closer to reach our standard distance.

Astronomers know the distance to nearby stars through a trigonometric method that is commonly employed in range-finder cameras. It is done by sighting an object from two different locations a known distance apart and measuring the change in viewing angle to sight the object.

For example, hold your thumb out with your arm extended. Close one eye and notice a distant object in the room that your thumb is covering. Now without moving, close that eye and open the other one. Your thumb will no longer be covering the same thing it was in the first part of the experiment. Your thumb appears to move across the background.

The closer you position the thumb to your face when doing this experiment, the more your thumb will seem to move. Astronomers use this technique by sighting nearby stars in relation to more distant ones, which appear fixed because they are so far away. As we look from different locations, the close stars change their position much more than the distant stars, and we measure the angle in the sky that the local stars seem to move. Astronomers want to use sighting locations that are as far apart as possible to maximize the displacement of the target star's position; they actually

1.3 Telescopes gather light and focus it into an image that the observational astronomer can photograph or analyze with other equipment to learn about starlight.

make measurements at different times of the year, after the earth has traveled several million kilometers in its orbit around the sun.

Applying trigonometry to the measured angle, and knowing how far apart the observations were made, we can accurately calculate the distance to the star. Astronomers have developed their own units of length because even the nearest star is so far away that it becomes tedious to talk of its distance in kilometers or miles. A *light-year* is one such unit of length. It is the distance that light travels in one year, and it amounts to about 10 trillion kilometers (more than 70,000 times as far away as the sun from the earth).

Astronomers have also defined a unit of length called a *parsec*. The word is made up of parts of two words—*parallax* and *second*. The *parallax* of a star is the angle in the sky through which the star seems to move when observed from the earth after our position changes by one *astronomical unit*, or 93 million miles, which is the distance from the earth to the sun. *Second* refers not to a time interval but to an angle. A second of arc is 1/3,600 of a degree. Thus, a star whose *parallax* is one *second* of arc is defined to be one parsec away. One parsec equals 3.26 light-years.

Unfortunately, parallax measurements can be accurately made for only about 10,000 of the nearest stars, since the farther the star, the smaller the angle. The closest star to us is Proxima Centauri, whose parallax angle is only three-quarters of a second of arc. Parallax measurements can be made on stars as far away as 300 light-years (less than 100 parsecs), but this is only about one-third of 1 percent of the diameter of the Milky Way Galaxy, in which our sun resides.

Once we have measured the distance to the nearby stars using the parallax method, we can determine the absolute magnitude of each star. For example, Proxima

The Inverse Square Law

There are two notable examples of the inverse square law that illustrate its principles. Both radiation and gravity decrease proportionally to the square of the distance as you move away from the source. For instance, if we move twice as far from a star, its light will appear only one-fourth as bright.

Similarly, if the moon were three times as far from the earth as it is, the earth's pull on the moon would only be one ninth as strong.

In both cases, the result is written in terms of $1/r^2$, where r is the distance to the source. Naturally, as you approach a source of light or gravity, the opposite holds true. The strength of the light or gravity increases, following the inverse square law.

The inverse square law is used by astronomers to determine how much light a star a given distance away produces. When the distance of that star is determined through parallax, we can determine its absolute magnitude. Light, like all electromagnetic energy, radiates outward uniformly in all directions from its source, like an expanding sphere, and in fact the inverse square law is derived from geometrical arguments about the rate at which the surface area of a sphere increases as its radius increases. The total radiated energy must pass through this sphere, and consequently the amount of energy at any one point on the sphere—the point through which we observe a star, for example—decreases as the radius and surface area of the sphere increase.

Centauri is 1.3 parsecs from the sun. The standard distance astronomers use to determine absolute magnitude is 10 parsecs, so we must calculate how bright Proxima Centauri would appear if it were more than seven times farther away at a distance of 10 parsecs. Proxima Centauri's apparent magnitude is 11.05, too faint to be seen with the naked eye. If we could move it back to 10 parsecs, it would be even fainter; 15.5 is then its absolute magnitude.

Table 1 shows the distance, apparent magnitude, and absolute magnitude of the nearest 25 stars. Notice that the sun, which is extremely bright because it is so near, has an absolute magnitude of only 4.85, which from 10 parsecs would be visible with the naked eye but would not be one of the brightest stars in the sky.

Table 2 lists the brightest stars in order of apparent magnitude. Sirius is the brightest star, excluding the sun, and is seen in the winter sky. Comparing absolute magnitudes among these 25 brightest stars, however, we can quickly see that Canopus and Arcturus, with absolute magnitudes of −3.1 and −0.3, respectively, are *intrinsically* brighter than Sirius. They simply give off more light; the reason they appear fainter is that they are considerably farther away. Distances in Table 2 are given in both parsecs and light-years.

It is possible to measure, very accurately, the amount of light that reaches the earth from stars. Astronomers use photometry, which is simply the measurement of the amount of light from an object, to find how much energy falls on a very small area on earth, say a square centimeter. If we also know a star's distance, we can determine the total amount of energy the star emits.

For convenience, the luminosity of stars is usually written in terms that compare their true brightness to that of the sun. In other words, $L_{\odot} = 1$, where the circle with a dot in it indicates the sun. Thus, a star with an intrinsic brightness that is 1,000 times that of the sun is written L = 1,000L. The luminosity of the sun in actual units of energy output is 3.8×10^{33} ergs per second (ergs are a unit of energy). To fathom the incredible energy output of the sun, it is instructive to know that it takes 10^9 ergs each second to light a 100-watt light bulb. The sun is 10^{24} times brighter.

Colors of the Stars

It is obvious to the casual observer that the stars not only have different magnitudes but that they shine with different colors. Some stars are a brilliant blue-white, whereas others appear reddish. The colors of the stars are directly related to the temperature of the surface layers, where the light we see is emitted.

Perhaps you have heard the terms *white-hot* and *red-hot.* They describe the appearance of metal when it is heated to different temperatures. White-hot metal is

Scientific Notation

In dealing with very large or very small numbers, as we must in the sciences, we find it convenient to use a special shorthand notation called scientific notation. When large strings of zeroes are attached to numbers, we can simplify and shorten them by counting the number of zeros and writing that quantity as a superscript over a 10.

For example, 1,000 may be written as 10^3 (three zeros), and 1,000,000 is represented by 10^6. Thus, such numbers as the speed of light, which is about 299,792,458 meters per second, are often rounded off as if the last several digits were zeros and rewritten in scientific notation as 2.99×10^8 meters per second.

The mass of the electron is a very small number and might be written in scientific notation as 9.1096×10^{-28} grams. To translate this into standard notation, you would write a decimal point, 27 zeros, and then 91096. It would look like this: .00000000000000000000000000091096.

Clearly, scientific notation is a convenient way to manipulate large numbers, and today most calculators and computers that allow scientific computations have input and output capabilities using scientific notation.

hotter than red-hot metal. We can think of stellar color in the same way. Astronomers accurately determine a star's surface temperature by measuring the color distribution of the light it emits.

Stars, incandescent light bulbs, burning charcoal, and numerous other objects emit radiation because they are hot. Radiation consists of a broad range of wavelengths of which visible light is only a small portion. White light from lamps and the sun is really the result of all the colors of the spectrum put together. Raindrops and prisms can separate light into its component colors; rainbows are the most commonly known manifestations of this effect.

The stars too emit light in all colors of the spectrum, and astronomers can measure how much light at each wavelength is emitted by using special filters that pass only specific wavelength ranges. In comparing these measurements, we find that the intensity of the radiation is not constant across the visible spectrum but is actually a curve if plotted as a graph.

At some wavelength along the graph of color intensity the curve peaks, and the wavelength of the peak is dependent only on the temperature of the material emitting the radiation. The color of a star, then, is dominated by that part of the spectrum where the intensity is greatest.

Temperature Scales

Three scales are generally used in the measurement of temperature. Fahrenheit and Centigrade (Celsius) are probably the most familiar of the three and are used by nonscientists. Celsius is based on the freezing point of water at 0 degrees and its boiling point at 100 degrees. Compare this to the Fahrenheit scale, which has a freezing point of water at 32 degrees and a boiling point at 212 degrees. A simple equation relates the two scales. It may be written in either of the following ways:

$$F = 9/5C + 32$$
$$C = 5/9(F - 32).$$

Kelvin measurement is closely aligned with Celsius, but in degrees K, 0 degrees refers to absolute zero, the point at which all matter stops moving. The freezing point of water in Kelvin is 273 degrees and the boiling point is 373 degrees. The relationship between Kelvin and Celsius measurements is thus

$$K = C + 273 \text{ or } C = K - 273.$$

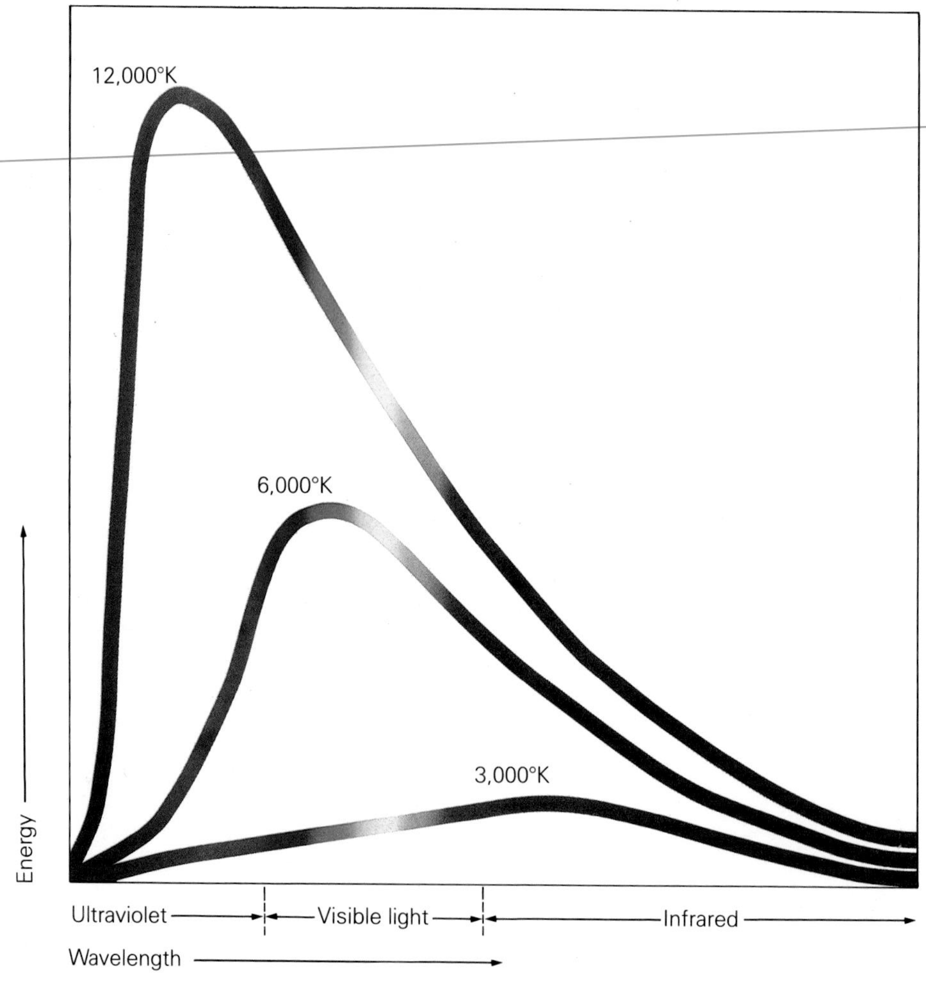

1.4 Stars with different temperatures have different distributions of energy as a function of wavelength. Notice that the hotter stars have distributions that peak farther into the ultraviolet. Also note that hotter stars are brighter at all wavelengths.

Table 1
The Twenty-five Nearest Stars

No.	Star	Distance (Parsecs)	Apparent Magnitude	Absolute Magnitude
1	Sun		−26.72	4.85
2	Proxima Centauri	1.30	11.05	15.49
	Alpha Centauri A	1.33	−0.01	4.37
	Alpha Centauri B		1.33	5.71
3	Barnard's Star	1.83	9.54	13.22
4	Wolf 359	2.38	13.53	16.65
5	BD +36° 2147	2.52	7.50	10.50
6	Luyen 726-8 A	2.58	12.52	15.46
7	Sirius A	2.65	−1.46	1.42
	Sirius B		8.30	11.20
8	Ross 154	2.90	10.45	13.14
9	Ross 248	3.18	12.29	14.78
10	Epsilon Eridani	3.30	3.73	6.14
11	Ross 128	3.36	11.10	13.47
12	61 Cygni A	3.40	5.22	7.56
	61 Cygni B		6.03	8.37
13	Epsilon Indi	3.44	4.68	7.00
14	BD +43°44 A	3.45	8.08	10.39
	BD +43°44 B		11.06	13.37
15	Luyten 786-6	3.45	12.18	14.49
16	Procyon A	3.51	0.37	2.64
	Procyon B		10.70	13.00
17	BD +59° 1915 A	3.55	8.90	11.15
	BD +59° 1915 B		9.69	11.94
18	CD −36° 15693	3.58	7.35	9.58
19	G 51-15	3.60	14.81	17.03
20	Tau Ceti	3.61	3.50	5.72
21	BD +5° 1668	3.76	9.82	11.94
22	Luyten 725-32	3.83	12.04	14.12
23	CD −39° 14192	3.85	6.66	8.74
24	Kapteyn's Star	3.91	8.84	10.88
25	Krüger 60 A	3.95	9.85	11.87
	Krüger 60 B		11.30	13.30

Table 2
The Twenty-five Brightest Stars

No.	Name	Star	App. Mag.	Abs. Mag.	Distance (Lt.-Yrs.)	Distance (Parsecs)
1	Sirius	α Canis Majoris A	−1.46	+1.42	8.7	2.7
2	Canopus	α Carinae	−0.72	−3.1	98.0	30.4
3	Arcturus	α Boötis	−0.06	−0.3	36.0	11.2
4	Rigil Kentaurus	α Centauri A	0.01	+4.37	4.2	1.3
5	Vega	α Lyrae	0.04	+0.5	26.5	8.2
6	Capella	α Aurigae	0.05	−0.6	45.0	13.9
7	Rigel	β Orionis A	0.14	−7.1	900.0	279.0
8	Procyon	α Canis Minoris A	0.37	+2.6	11.4	3.5
9	Betelgeuse	α Orionis	0.41	−5.6	520.0	161.2
10	Achernar	α Eridani	0.51	−0.23	118.0	36.6
11	Hadar	β Centauri AB	0.63	−5.2	490.0	151.9
12	Altair	α Aquilae	0.76	+2.2	16.5	5.1
13	Aldebaran	α Tauri A	0.86	−0.7	68.0	21.1
14	Spica	α Virginis	0.91	−3.3	220.0	68.2
15	Antares	α Scorpii A	0.92	−5.1	520.0	161.2
16	Fomalhault	α Piscis Austrini	1.15	+2.0	22.6	7.0
17	Pollux	β Geminorum	1.16	+1.0	35.0	10.9
18	Deneb	α Cygni	1.26	−7.1	1,600.0	496.0
19	Beta Crucis	β Cygni	1.28	−4.6	490.0	151.9
20	Regulus	α Leonis A	1.36	−0.7	84.0	26.0
21	Acrux	α Crucis A	1.39	−3.9	370.0	114.7
22	Adhara	ϵ Canis Majoris A	1.48	−5.1	680.0	210.8
23	Shaula	λ Scorpii	1.60	−3.3	310.0	96.1
24	Bellatrix	γ Orionis	1.64	−4.2	470.0	145.7
25	Elnath	β Tauri	1.65	−3.2	300.0	93.0

Figure 1.4 shows radiation curves caused by stars at different temperatures. Notice that a star with a surface layer at a temperature of 3,000° K emits most of its radiation in the red and infrared regions of the spectrum. To the naked eye, such a star appears reddish. A star with a temperature of about 6,000° K emits strongly in the blue range and takes on the blue-white brilliance characteristic of hot stars. The hot stars with temperatures as high as 12,000° K emit most of their radiation in the ultraviolet part of the spectrum. Ultraviolet radiation cannot be seen by our eyes, and ultraviolet light from the stars is absorbed in the ozone layer of the earth's atmosphere, but such stars *are* visible at optical wavelengths and are very bright because radiation is emitted at all parts of the spectrum, not just at the peak. Even though peaking in the ultraviolet, the intensity curve for a 12,000° K star is still brighter in the visible portion than a 6,000° K star whose intensity reaches a maximum in that region.

Atoms and Light

Virtually all of the information we can gather about the stars is contained in the radiation they emit. Looking up into the night sky, observing with telescopes, and using satellites to view the heavens from above the earth's atmosphere are activities that developed because starlight is our one link to the universe.

For more than 200 years, scientists had realized that sunlight consisted of component colors that could be separated by passing the light through a prism. Figure 1.6 illustrates the order in which the colors appear every time we disperse the radiation into a spectrum. Rainbows display the same colors when raindrops act like tiny prisms in the air.

In the early 1800s two scientists studying the spectrum of the sun found that dark gaps exist at certain positions in the artificial rainbow they had created with prisms. William Wollaston and Josef von Fraunhofer were working independently when they discovered these dark gaps of missing color, called spectral lines.

Through trial and error in laboratories around the world, scientists found that some of the patterns of dark lines in the solar spectrum can be reproduced by heating gases of various chemical elements. If a gas of a specific element is heated, it gives off spectral lines, in color, that fill in the unique pattern of some dark lines in the sun's spectrum. Each chemical element has its own unique pattern of wavelengths at which spectral lines fall. Thus, spectral lines can identify each element, as a fingerprint might identify a criminal. Today, we refer to dark lines against a rainbow background as absorption lines, and bright lines against a dark background are called emission lines.

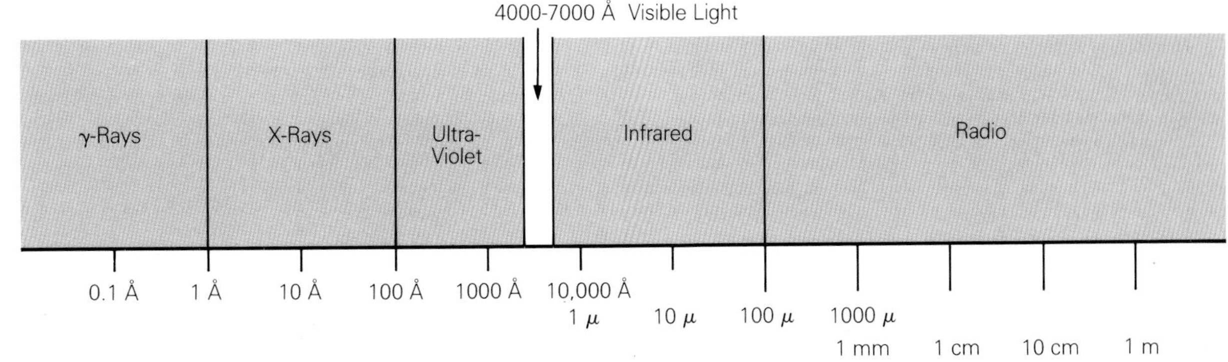

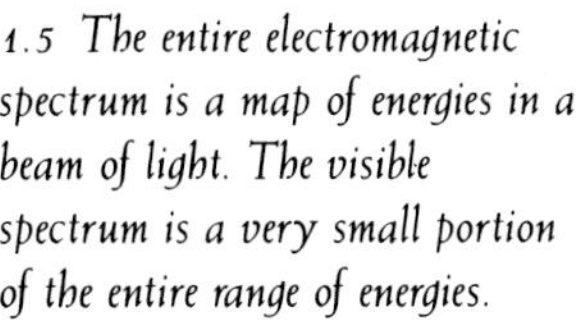
1.5 The entire electromagnetic spectrum is a map of energies in a beam of light. The visible spectrum is a very small portion of the entire range of energies.

The visible light we see from the sun and stars is only a small fraction of the total map of energies produced by atoms. Radio waves, infrared radiation, ultraviolet light, and X rays are other portions of the electromagnetic spectrum. Figure 1.5 shows the entire range of energies, including visible light. Notice that the shorter the wavelength, the higher the energy required to excite the atoms that emit the radiation. For example, it takes much less energy to broadcast a radio signal than to take an X ray of a broken bone.

The elucidation of how a gas emits or absorbs radiation is one of the great triumphs of modern physics, and it occurred because a handful of imaginative scientists worked together, synthesizing previous experience and exploring a new reality about the atom.

The atom absorbs and emits light to form continuous spectra and spectral lines. We cannot see inside an atom, but the spectrum forms a kind of stained-glass window through which we can infer what is going on inside. Let us consider an atom of hydrogen, the simplest in structure of all. A lone electron rapidly orbits the single-proton nucleus. The electron moves so quickly about the nucleus that we cannot determine its position at any one instant. We might define energy as

1.6 The spectrum of radiation that can be seen with the human eye. This band of color was produced by passing light through a prism, which breaks the light apart into its component colors.

mass in motion, and even though the electron has a very small mass (about 9×10^{-28} grams), its high orbital speed gives it a lot of energy. We can make an analogy with some familiar experiments. When we tie a string to a rock and swing the rock about our head, we impart energy to the rock. The planets also have energy as they orbit the sun. If we supplied more energy to the earth, it would move farther from the sun. Conversely, were we to remove some of the earth's energy, it would move closer to the sun. The atom reacts in a similar manner to additions and subtractions of energy, although the nucleus and electron are bound by electrostatic forces, while the earth-sun system is gravitationally bound. An increase of energy moves the electron farther from the center, and a decrease of energy moves the electron closer to the nucleus. At this point, however, we discover the first obstacle when applying traditional physics to atoms. Only specific values of energy are capable of affecting the electron's orbit when added or subtracted. This discovery led scientists to develop a new theory of physics, one based on the notion that energy exists in discrete packets called quanta.

The modern theory of light explains that an atom is very selective in the values of energy absorbed or emitted by electrons. Atoms of specific elements absorb or emit light only at specific wavelengths, which is what we observe when we see spectral lines.

A heated solid will produce all ranges of radiation, which will appear as a continuous spectrum of color. An atom, however, will emit only certain selected amounts of energy, which appear as single colors at different parts of the spectrum. A sodium atom, for example, emits photons that have energies corresponding to a specific portion of the spectral map in yellow light. Mercury emits green light. When the radiation from atoms such as these is passed through a modern spectroscope, the bright monochromatic light appears as spectral lines. The atoms of each element have characteristic spectral lines because no two atoms of different substances have the same configuration of electronic energy levels. This means that no two elements will produce spectral lines in the same pattern and positions in the spectrum, and thus the spectrum is a "fingerprint" of the element emitting the light we observe.

A fingerprint in a criminal laboratory, however, yields only identification of the suspect. The spectrum of radiation yields identification of the elements emitting the light, but with further analysis can also suggest temperatures and densities of the emitting region. We can already see the ramifications of spectral analysis. By studying the light emitted by the stars, we can recognize chemical elements present in the star, the temperatures in the star, and the amount of material that forms the star. Further study often yields information about motions and various violent events that occur in the known universe.

The Doppler Effect

Not only does the spectral analysis of radiation reveal the processes going on inside atoms due to temperatures and densities of the gas, but a special property of radiation also allows us to explore the large-scale dynamic motions of radiating regions such as the surface of stars or diffuse clouds of gas. We call this property the Doppler effect.

The Doppler effect is the shifting of wavelengths of light due to motions of the body that is emitting the radiation. If a star, for example, is moving toward us, all its radiation will be shifted toward the high-energy end of the spectrum. This is called a blue shift. If a star is receding from us, the light will be shifted toward the red, and thus called a red shift, a term widely used in explaining the expansion of the universe as galaxies fly away from one another.

It is easy to measure Doppler shifts if they are recognizable spectral lines of which we know the wavelengths. When we analyze an emission or absorption spectrum, we can detect any shift in the spectral lines from the position they would occupy if the source of radiation were stationary. The faster a source is moving toward us, the greater the displacement of the spectral lines to the blue. The faster the object is moving away, the greater the red shift. Using Doppler shifts, we can calculate the velocities with which stars, galaxies, and nebulae are moving toward or away from us. We will see in subsequent chapters how important the ability to measure motions of objects in space has been to astronomers.

The Spectra of Stars

Astronomers apply the principles of atomic physics and radiative processes to their only connection with the cosmos—starlight. The wealth of information carried within the radiation from the stars is so great that spectroscopy, the study of the spectrum, must be considered to be one of the most powerful scientific methods yet devised.

The visible spectra of normal stars consist of a bright background of color, called a continuous spectrum, that is crossed by dark absorption lines. Absorption lines are formed when hot radiation passes through a cooler gas, allowing the unexcited atoms in the gas to absorb radiation at specific wavelengths. The outer layers of a star form absorption lines the same way, as hot gas radiates a continuous spectrum and cooler overlying layers absorb light at particular wavelengths.

The white light we see from the sun and stars, which is really all of the colors put together, is formed in an outer layer of the stellar atmosphere. We cannot see into the interior of any star because the gas layers are too thick, so the nature of the radiation we observe is dependent on the physical conditions in these outer layers, and the spectra of stars vary depending on the temperature of this emitting region.

For example, the sun's spectrum is full of spectral lines produced by absorbing atoms such as iron and silicon. A solar spectrum exhibits other elements including hydrogen, sodium, and ionized calcium (an ion is an atom that has lost one or more of its normal constituency of electrons). The sun is a relatively cool star, where the temperature in the radiating layers is about 5,500° K.

Hotter stars exhibit fewer spectral lines of neutral atoms because the temperature in these stellar atmospheres is hot enough to strip electrons away from nuclei (Figure 1.7). On the other hand, stars that are cooler than the sun have spectra with many more absorption lines, including some caused by molecules (Figure 1.8).

In the late nineteenth century, hundreds of thousands of stellar spectra had been photographed, and the differences just explained were thoroughly investigated. Some stars had very dark spectral lines caused by hydrogen absorption, while others showed practically no hydrogen lines at all. A classification scheme was set up to categorize stars by the darkness of hydrogen lines in their spectra, and the stars were labeled alphabetically: A for the strongest hydrogen absorption, B for slightly weaker absorption, and so on.

These classes of stars are called spectral types. Scientists later took the same classification scheme but reorganized the letters to express the fact that differences among spectra of various stars are due to temperature differences in stellar atmospheres. The letter categories were reordered to reflect this new understanding of stellar spectra, and the new spectral type of classification is, from hot stars to cool stars, O, B, A, F, G, K, M.

In addition to the letter categories, the spectral types are subdivided by number, such as B0, B1, B2, . . . B9. Simple inspection of a stellar spectrum often yields the spectral type of the star. The sun, incidentally, is a G2 star.

The Hertzsprung–Russell Diagram

Early in the twentieth century, two astronomers independently plotted a new type of graph that has become a valuable tool in understanding stellar evolution

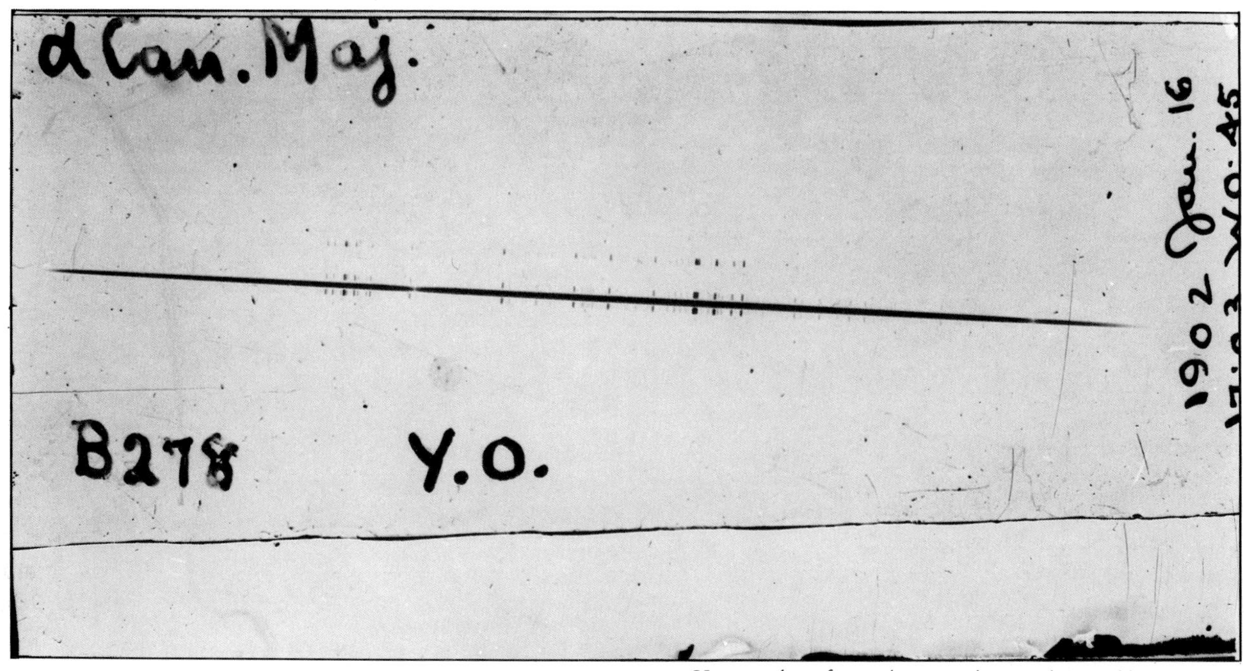

1.7 Hot stars have fewer absorption lines in their visible spectrum than cool stars. Figures 1.7 and 1.8 are actual photographic plates taken in the early part of the century at Yerkes Observatory in Michigan. Also known as Sirius, α Canis Majoris is the brightest star in the night sky.

1.8 Cool stars have spectra that indicate the presence of many complex atoms and even molecules. Antares is a red giant star.

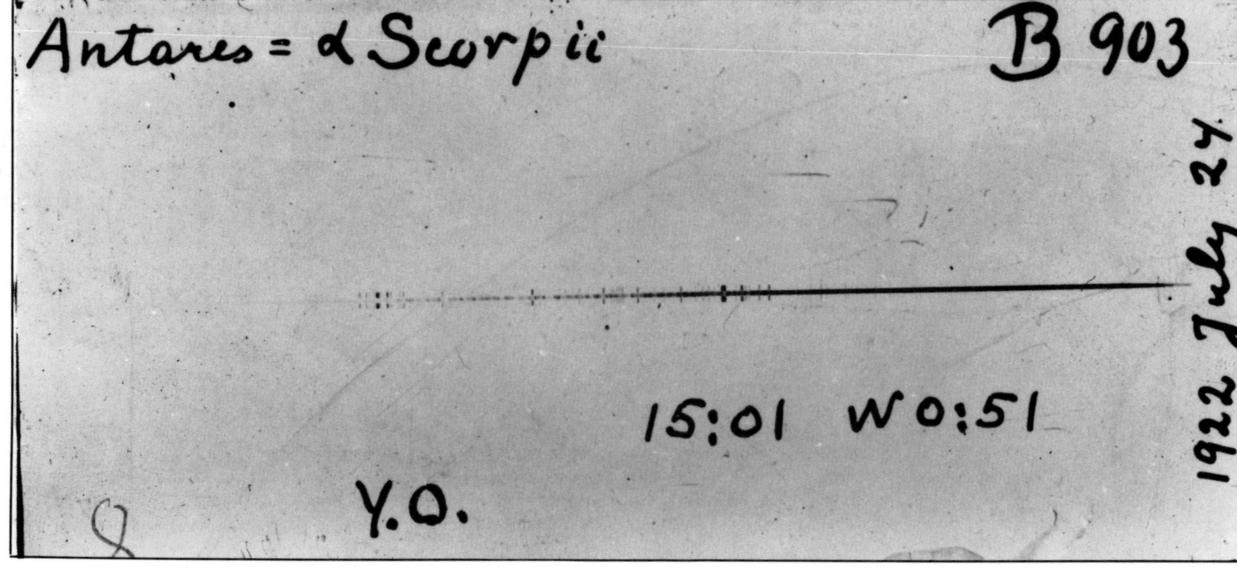

and stellar distances. Ejnar Hertzsprung and Henry Norris Russell plotted the temperatures of nearby bright stars as a function of absolute magnitude.

The two scientists plotted the spectral type of the stars, which is equivalent to knowing their temperatures. They used nearby stars with known distances so that the absolute magnitude of the stars was well known.

Hertzsprung and Russell discovered that the stars fall in specific regions of the graphs, not at random. Figure 1.10 is a composite of the nearby and the brightest stars. Most ordinary stars in the prime of life lie on a diagonal band called the *main sequence*. This band runs from hot, bright stars in the upper left to cool, faint stars in the lower right. In the upper right of the H-R diagram are stars that are cool but very luminous. These are red giant stars. Stars that are very hot but faint are called white dwarfs (lower left). Explorations of non–main-sequence stars appear later in this book, as do stars in the prime of life, but the H-R diagram immediately yields a great deal of information about stars being observed.

For example, if we perform parallax measurements on a nearby bright star and determine that its absolute magnitude (i.e., its apparent magnitude from 10 parsecs away) is −5, and we recognize numerous lines in its spectrum and categorize the star as a K5 spectral type, we can immediately plot the star on the H-R diagram and know that we are observing a red giant.

The H-R diagram also assists astronomers with distance measurements of more remote stars. If, for example, we observe an F2 star on the main sequence with an apparent magnitude of +6, we can convert this brightness to a distance since we already know the absolute magnitude of F2 stars. F2 stars have absolute magnitudes of +2, so the star appears to us to be 4 magnitudes fainter. Thus the star is really more than 36 times (2.5^4) fainter than if it could be moved to 10 parsecs. This is equivalent, by use of the inverse square law, to being six times farther away, or 60 parsecs from the earth.

This method of finding stellar distances has become known as *spectroscopic parallax*, because of its analogy with true parallax measurements, described earlier in this chapter.

The H-R diagram is an extremely useful tool in the understanding of stellar evolution as well. We can label types of stars on the basic H-R diagram (Figure 1.10). White dwarfs, red giants, and stars on the main sequence are types of stars we observe easily on a clear night, but they are also stars at different stages of their lives (subsequent chapters will explore each phase of a star's lifetime). H-R diagrams of model stars have helped theorists understand the sequence of size and spectral type each star passes through from stellar birth to stellar death. We will also see when and why a star, during its life, becomes a red giant, white dwarf, or blue supergiant.

1.9 The solar spectrum is a classic absorption spectrum that is full of dark lines marking the presence of chemical elements that are in the outer layers of the sun.

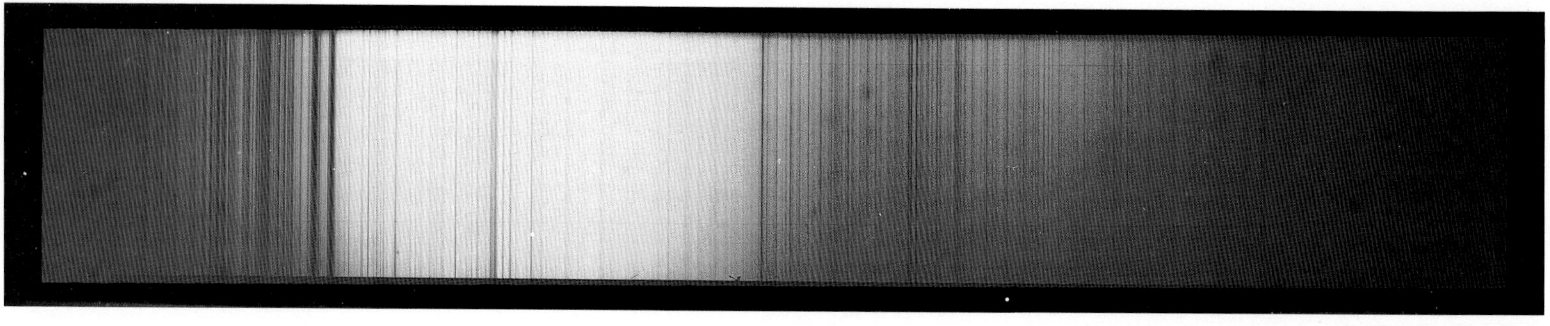

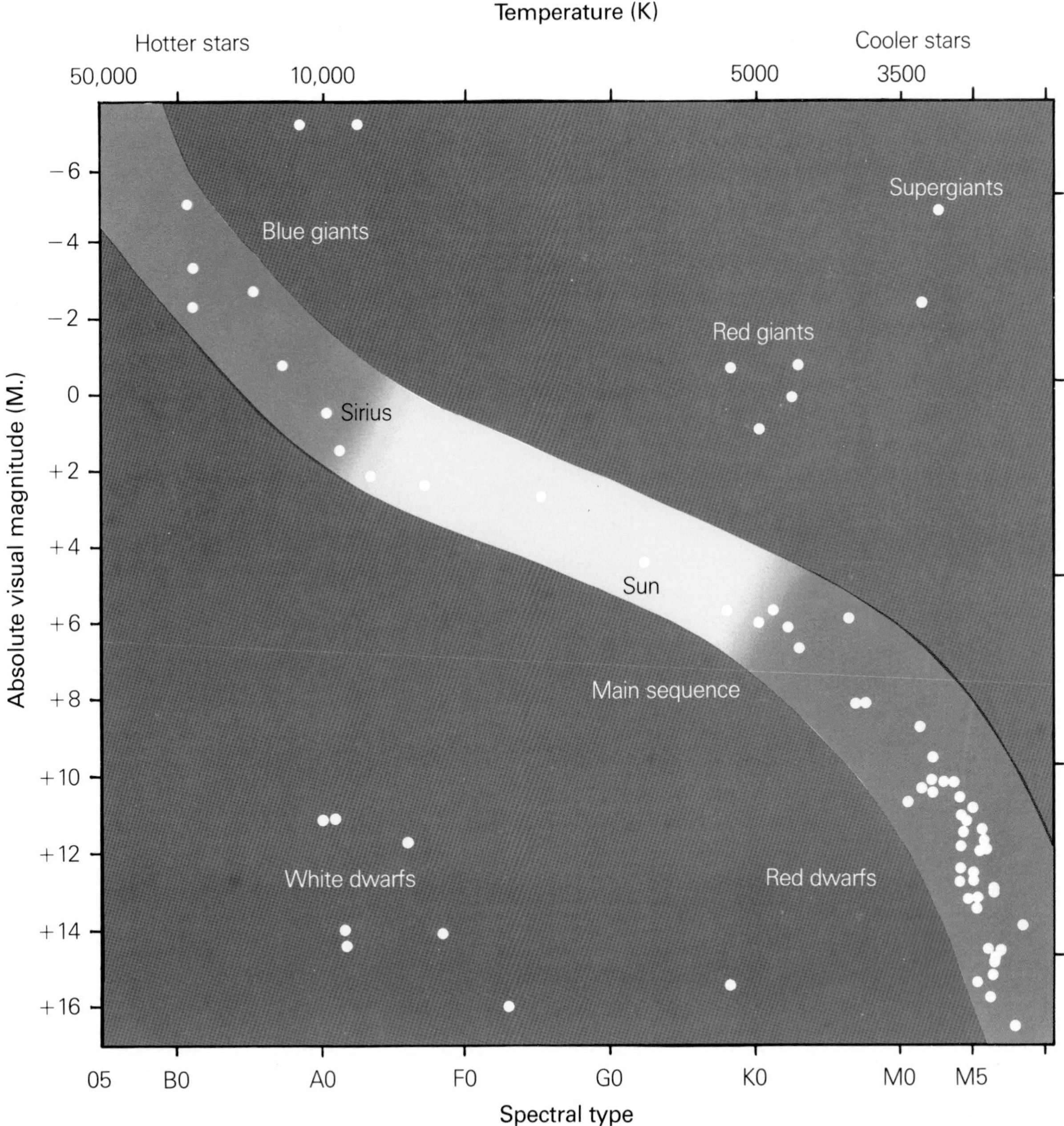

1.10 A Hertzsprung-Russell diagram onto which both the nearest and brightest stars have been superimposed.

Masses and Size of the Stars

The sun is the only star whose size we can directly and accurately measure. We know the distance to the sun, and we know the angle the sun takes up in the sky; with geometry, we can calculate its diameter.

All of the other stars, however, appear to the naked eye as points of light against the dark background of space. Through large telescopes and on film, the nearest and brightest stars take on a fuzzy disk appearance that is the result of turbulence in the earth's atmosphere distorting incoming starlight. The atmosphere's shimmering causes the stars' twinkling appearance as well, but for astronomers, it prohibits observation of a star's size and surface features.

Astronomers use several methods to make direct measurements of a star's diameter, but the results are only approximations. One method relies on the ever-changing position of the moon. As the moon orbits the earth, it regularly passes in front of stars, obscuring them at the lunar edge. The stars do not quite blink off instantaneously, however, because it takes a fraction of a second for the moon to cover a star's entire surface. The moon's limb (rim) provides a sharp edge, enabling astronomers to study the starlight during the brief period of time that the moon eclipses the star. We call such an eclipse a *lunar occultation*, and we can deduce the size of the star if we know its distance. Unfortunately, the moon passes over only about 10 percent of the entire sky during one year, so we cannot use this technique for very many stars.

Most stars exist in pairs or in multiple groupings (see Chapter 2) in which one star actually eclipses another as they orbit their common center of gravity. As a star is eclipsed, it is possible to measure the decrease in light emitted by the stellar system. With this and other relevant information, such as characteristics of the orbit, we can determine the size of the occulted star.

There is an indirect method of deducing stellar diameters that involves the absolute magnitude and surface temperature of stars. We can estimate the amount of surface area a star has by comparing its brightness with the temperature. For example, a very bright cool star must be bright because it has a lot of surface area emitting light. On the other hand, a faint hot star must be small because it does not have much surface area radiating. Of course the surface area of a sphere is dependent on its radius, so this gives us an estimate of its size.

Some exciting new methods of measuring stellar diameters have been developed since 1960. The principle of interferometry, which is a technique that combines two signals emitted by one object but received at two separate observing positions, has been used to measure the diameter of a few of the closest and brightest stars. This technique simulates the high resolving power of a hypothetical telescope with an aperture or mirror diameter equivalent to the distance between the two receivers. Interferometry is also widely used in radio astronomy and overcomes difficulties in resolution both intrinsic to telescopes and caused by the earth's turbulent atmosphere.

A fascinating new method, called speckle interferometry, gives astronomers a chance to "see" the surface features of some nearby red giants stars. Speckle interferometry takes advantage of the turbulence in the earth's atmosphere by making a series of extremely short exposures of a star's image as it jumps around through air currents of different densities. The data are usually stored in a computer after they are received by a photometer, an electronic device that measures the amount of radiation hitting a small area of light-sensitive material. The computer then synthesizes the information and actually forms a picture of the star's surface, including star spots and stellar explosions called flares. The diameters of stars analyzed with speckle interferometry are easily determined. Figure 1.12 illustrates the surface of Betelgeuse, a nearby red giant star that has been seen for the first time with the aid of the speckle interferometric method.

The mass of a star is extremely difficult to measure; for stellar sizes, binary star systems yield the best results with direct observations. The orbit of gravitationally bound stars about their center of mass is dependent on the individual masses of the stars themselves. By observing the detailed characteristics of the binary orbits, astronomers can calculate the minimum mass of the two stars. There are several dozen binary systems of which we know the masses, and astronomers have plotted on a graph their masses versus the intrinsic brightness of the stars. This graph is called the mass-luminosity relation (Figure 1.11) and shows that the more massive a star is, the brighter it is. This relation holds true, however, only for stars on the main sequence (that is, in the stable prime of life).

Stars generally range from 50 times more massive than the sun to about 25 times less massive. It turns out that the mass of a star is the dominant characteristic that determines a star's evolution, a fact we will examine in later chapters.

The Lives of Stars

In a sense, stars are but one manifestation of a cosmic evolution that began some 10 to 20 billion years ago with the big bang. The stars are neither the beginning

1.11 The mass-luminosity relation.

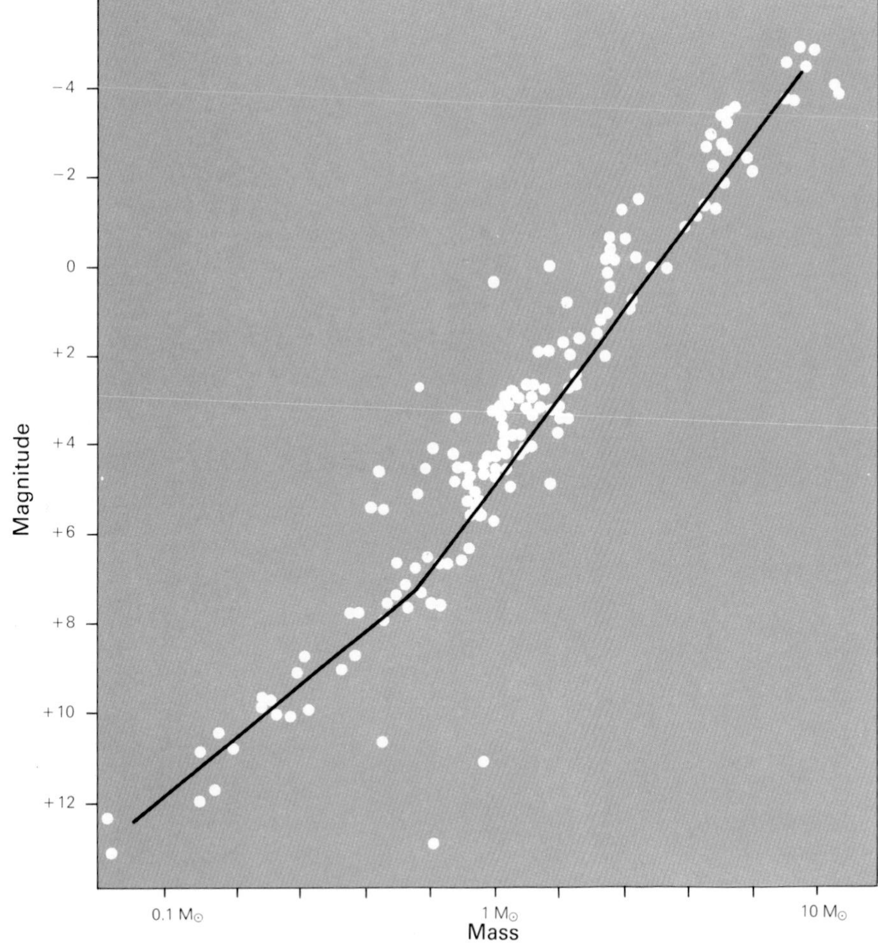

nor the end of the story, and the variety of stars, nebulae, and other astronomical objects is the thread that weaves the ageless tapestry of time.

This book is devoted to the life and death of stars because stellar life cycles are the keystone between the way the universe was and the way it will be. Stars change the way the cosmos appears. They alter the mix of chemical elements by converting nuclear fuel into other types of atoms. They lead to the formation of life, which, in our experience at least, can ponder itself and its origins.

As we reach farther into the universe with satellites and new telescopes, we will undoubtedly learn more about the stars. For now we must realize that we have come from them, and in addition to the valuable science we can learn from studying them, we can discover a sense of why we are here and whence we came.

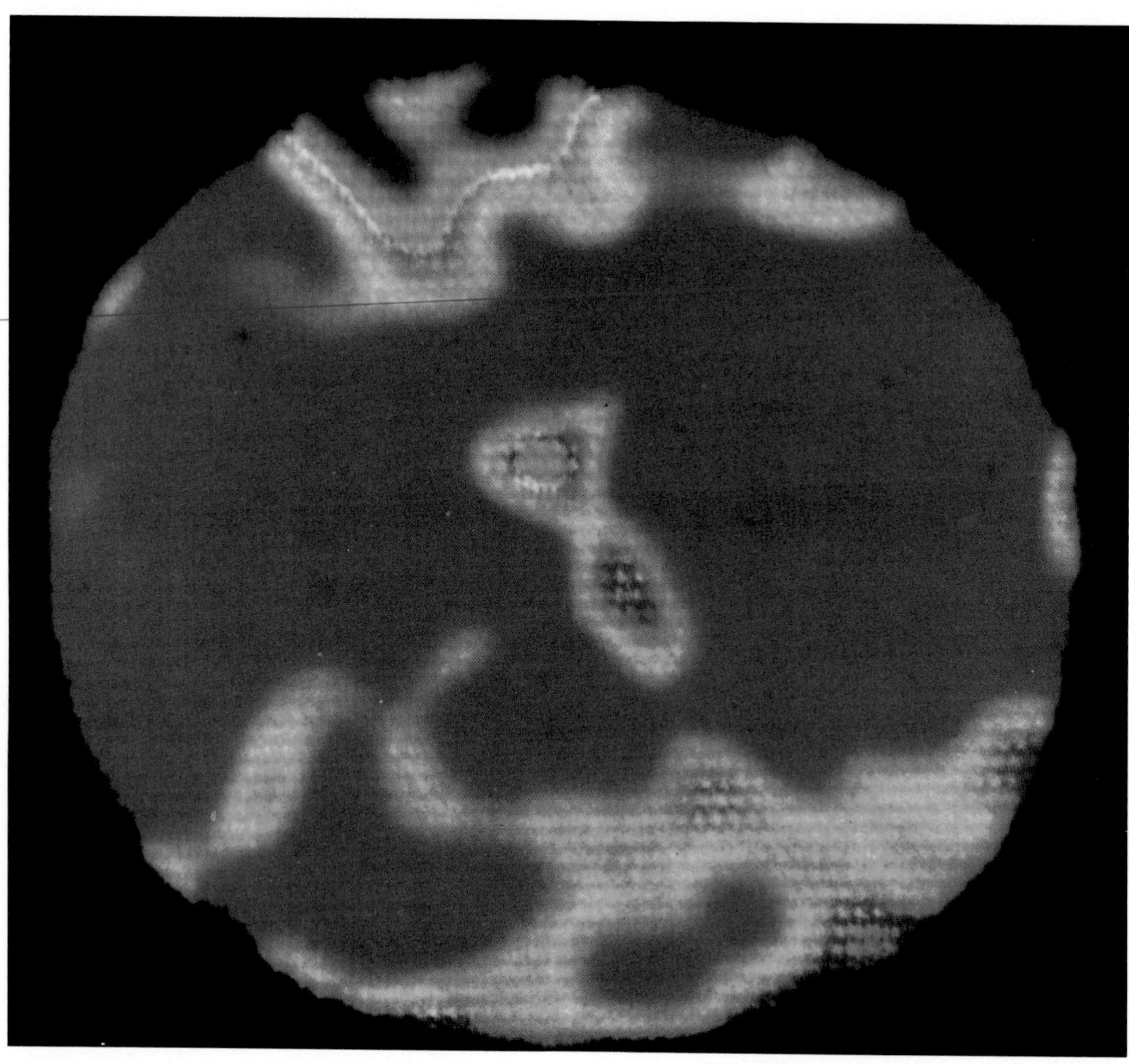

1.12 Left: *The surface of a giant star that is only 520 light-years away. This is the first star that was analyzed with speckle interferometry techniques.*

1.13 Opposite: *With the tools outlined in this chapter astronomers probe the secrets of our galaxy and of the distant galaxies beyond. Temperatures, colors, distances, luminosities, and sizes are all pieces of the tapestry that enable us to understand the universe.*

2: STELLAR GROUPINGS & VARIABLE STARS

Binary and Multiple Star Systems

On a clear night when thousands of brilliant stars fill the dark sky, an observer might point to the individual specks of light and think that each, like the sun, stands alone in space. In fact, our sun is an exception; with large telescopes astronomers have been able to determine that some 90 percent of stars on the main sequence have companion stars in orbit with them.

The naked eye and small optical aids such as binoculars and small telescopes do not have the resolving power necessary to separate most multiple stars that appear to be one star. As larger telescopes were developed in the nineteenth century, more and more stars were recognized to have stellar companions.

True binary stars have two stellar components held in orbit by gravity. There are even stars that appear single to the naked eye but have six or more constituent stars orbiting a

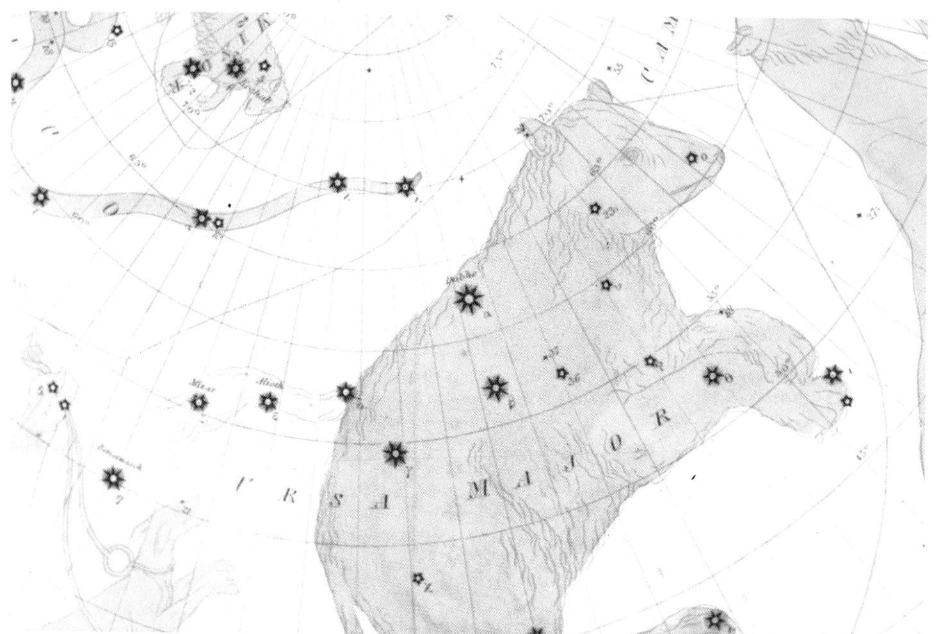

2.1 *The Big Dipper consists of the seven brightest stars in the constellation called Ursa Major (Latin for great bear). Mizar is the middle star in the Dipper's handle.*

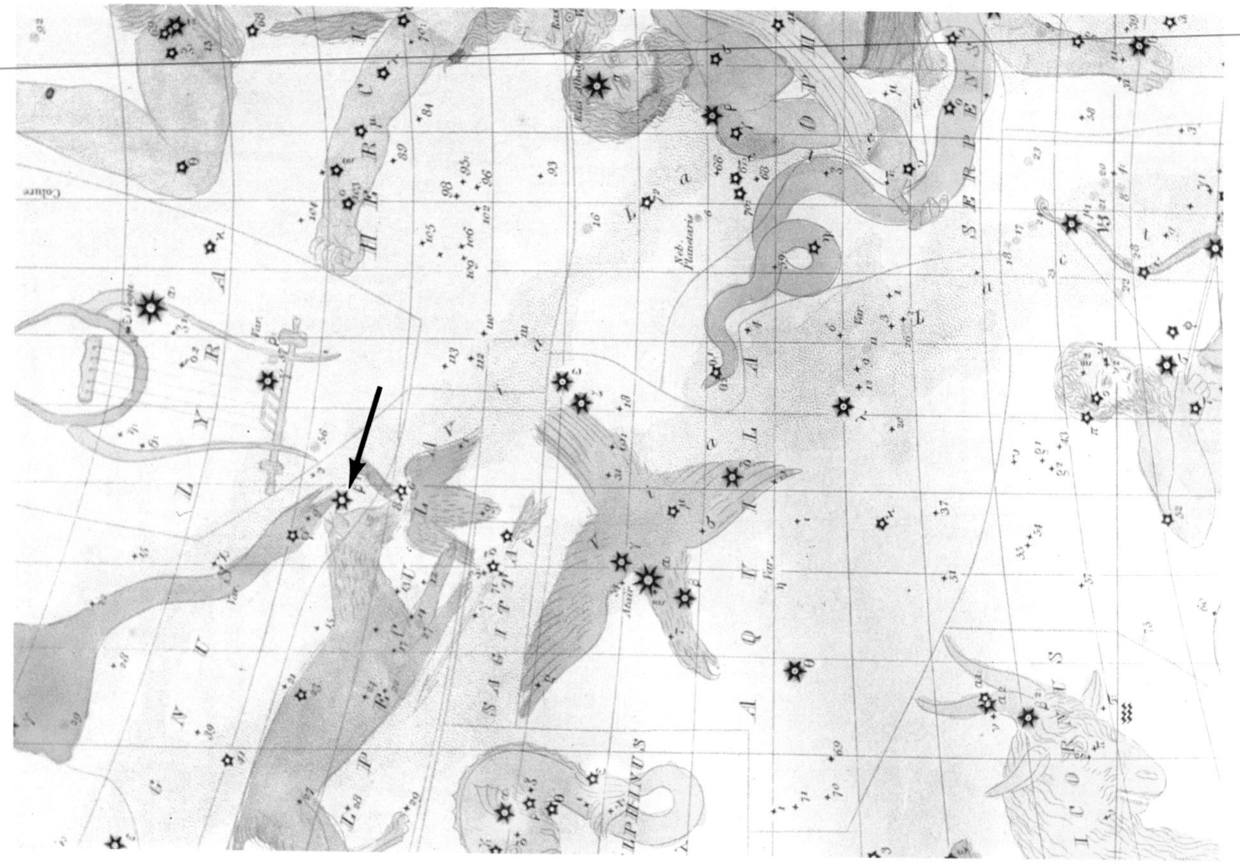

2.2 *The constellation Cygnus. Albireo is the star in the head of the swan. This constellation is also called the Northern Cross.*

common center of gravity. A few stars might appear to be binary stars because they lie along the same line of sight, but they might be very different distances from us. Such false binaries can be confusing to casual observers.

An interesting case in point is the middle star of the Big Dipper, called Mizar. Figure 2.1 shows the position of this famous system. Mizar's most evident companion is Alcor, and many people can see them both with the naked eye. Alcor, although appearing to be a neighbor of Mizar, is much farther away, and their proximity in the sky is just a coincidence. A telescope, however, reveals that Mizar does indeed have a faint companion star that can be resolved with a modest optical aid.

Another interesting binary system is Albireo in the constellation Cygnus, the swan (Figure 2.2). One of the two stars is a hot star of spectral type B and the other is spectral type K, cooler than the sun. A small telescope shows this strikingly beautiful pair—the hotter star is blue, the cooler star is golden.

Not all multiple stars are separated by enough space to be seen. Many stars are too close together for even the most powerful telescopes to resolve into distinct components. Astronomers have devised other means to determine the existence of binary stars. One method of discovering multiple star systems is to analyze the spectrum of light from the object. Often, it is clear from the spectrum that two or more distinct stars have contributed characteristics to the emitted radiation. The spectrum might be a composite of the spectra of both stars. Mizar, in the handle of the Big

2.3 *This photograph shows a field of variable stars near the center of the Andromeda Galaxy. Two variables are marked.*

Dipper, is a spectroscopic binary as well as a visual binary. Both visual components of Mizar have other components that are other companion stars, both discovered spectroscopically.

Sometimes the alignment of the orbits of binary stars is such that from our vantage point one star periodically passes in front of and behind the other star. In Chapter 1 we mentioned that such eclipsing binary stars aid us in determining the sizes and masses of stars, but by studying the varying levels of light emitted by the stellar system first, we can detect the presence of both stars.

Over a period of time, astronomers observe the variation in radiation output of an eclipsing binary and they generate a light curve. Figure 2.4 is an example of the light curves from the eclipsing binaries shown. The changes in intensity of the light curves are dependent on the sizes of the stars and the angle from which we view the orbit. In Chapter 1, we discovered that binary star systems enable astronomers to measure the mass of many nearby stars, as well as stellar sizes, but as we shall see in subsequent chapters, we are very dependent on binary and multiple systems in the search for black holes and other stellar corpses.

Since scientists began launching satellites aimed at studying X-ray emissions from outer space, they have discovered that many of the strongest X-ray sources may be attributed to binary star systems. Figure 2.5 shows such an X-ray telescope. X rays are emitted from binary stars when the two components are very close and the more massive one is pulling material from the other. As this matter hits the surface of the more massive star, it heats up and emits X rays. If this is happening in an eclipsing binary, the X rays will appear to pulse, because sometimes the hot spot is on the far side of the system and sometimes it is on our side.

Galactic Clusters and Globular Clusters

There are other gravitationally bound systems of stars that exist on larger physical scales than multiple stars.

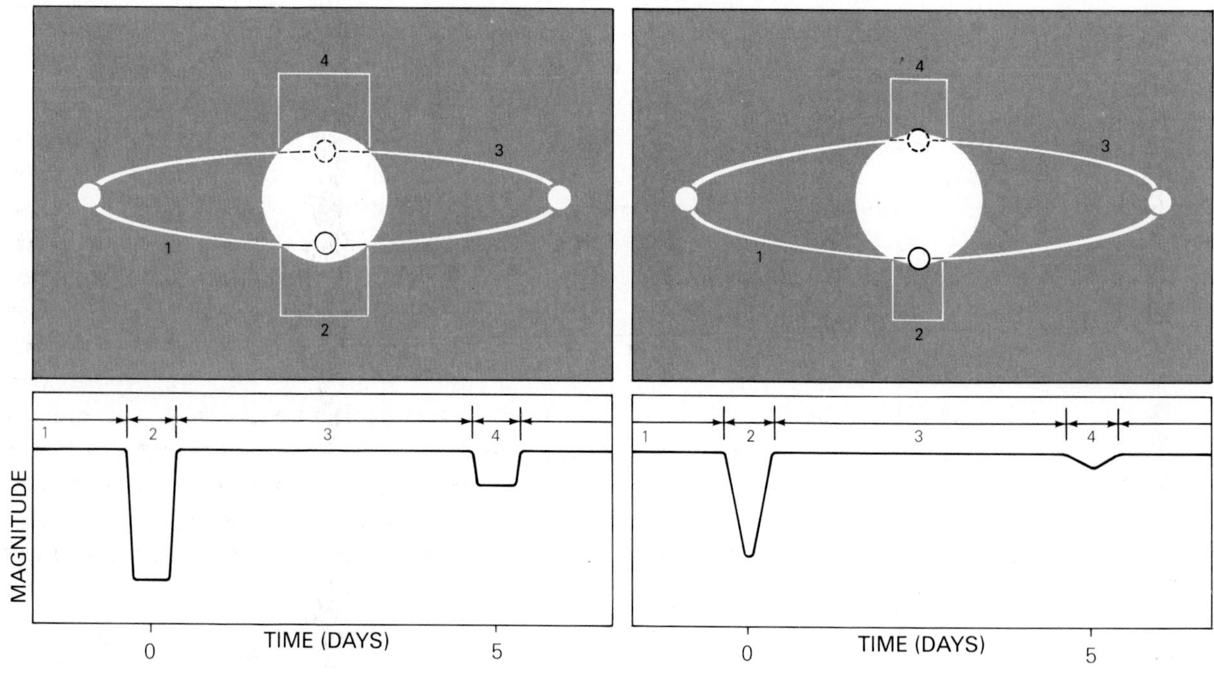

2.4 The light curves of eclipsing binaries change in relation to the positions of the orbiting stars.

These are called galactic and globular clusters.

Galactic clusters are large, loose conglomerations of approximately 1,000 or fewer stars. The appearance of this type of cluster (see Figures 2.6 and 2.7) has caused astronomers to call them "open clusters" as well.

The most famous galactic cluster is the Pleiades, found in the constellation Taurus, the bull. Figure 2.7 shows that this group, often called the Seven Sisters, actually consists of dozens of stars. Analysis of their distances suggests that they are all approximately the same distance from us.

Another famous galactic cluster also resides in the constellation Taurus. This cluster forms the *V*-shaped nose of the bull. It is called the Hyades, and it occupies a much larger region of the night sky than do the Pleiades (see Figure 2.8).

We can study the actual motions of the stars that form the Hyades by analyzing the Doppler shifts in their spectra. In Figure 2.9 it is clear that the cluster is expanding despite the force of gravity of each star on its neighbors. The stars of the Pleiades are young, hot stars, and some of the gaseous nebula from which they collapsed is evident as a blue glow in Figure 2.7.

More than a thousand galactic clusters are known, but only a handful can be seen without telescopes.

When we analyze the spectra of stars making up the galactic clusters, we find that they have a relative abundance of the chemical elements similar to those found in our sun. Such stars have been labeled *Population I* stars and consist of approximately 90 percent hydrogen, 9 percent helium, and 1 percent other elements heavier than helium. This is typical of stars in the spiral arms of our Milky Way Galaxy, of which the sun is a member, and the spiral arms of other galaxies.

Population II stars have considerably less abundance of the elements heavier than helium than Population I stars. We shall see later that this fact is due to differences in their birth. Population II stars are found in another type of stellar conglomeration, called a *globular cluster*.

Globular clusters are tight concentrations of 10,000 to 1 million stars. Figure 2.10 shows one globular cluster. Globular clusters seem to be distributed around the center of our galaxy in what we call the galactic halo. There is too much dust and gas in the plane of the galaxy for us to see any globular clusters in the spiral arms.

Figure 2.11 shows a graphic representation of the distribution of galactic and globular clusters. The symmetrical position of globular clusters enabled astronomers early in the twentieth century to measure accurately the size of the Milky Way Galaxy.

Globular clusters played an important role in the determination of just where in our galaxy we are. In 1917 Harlow Shapley noticed that globular clusters were distributed mostly in one direction from our standpoint, in the direction of the constellation Sagittarius. This led him to realize that they are actually centered around the core of the galaxy and that we are far out along the edge of this spiral city of stars. Before Shapley's discovery, scientists thought that the sun was in the center of the galaxy, but the sun is only an average star that has no claim to a privileged location.

X Rays and Globular Clusters

In recent years astronomers have been able to study X-ray emission from celestial objects because satellite technology has developed to a point where telescopes can be carried aloft and controlled remotely from the earth. Globular clusters have been a notable source of X rays in outer space.

Some of the X-ray emission from globular clusters appears as intense fluctuations of emission lasting only a few seconds but changing in intensity by as much as 25 times. These X-ray sources have become known as bursters, and several bursters have since been discovered away from globular clusters as well. Some bursters vary on a regular basis, while others seem to turn on and off randomly. An X-ray burst is shown in Figure 2.12.

The theoretical framework now used to explain

2.5 The Einstein Orbiting Observatory, here seen being prepared for launch, records X-ray emission from many different celestial objects. The data are sent from the satellite to earth stations by radio telemetry and then converted into pictures by a computer.

2.6 *An example of an open, or galactic, cluster in the constellation Cancer. Notice that the stars are spread out in a rather large region of the sky. This object is M44 in Messier's catalog of nebulae.*

2.7 *The Pleiades is a galactic cluster consisting of dozens of young stars in the constellation Taurus. The blue glow around the brightest stars is a reflection nebula of material left over from the stars' formation.*

2.9 *A map of the Hyades showing the direction of motion of each of the major stars. In a very real way, these stars are leaving their stellar nursery.*

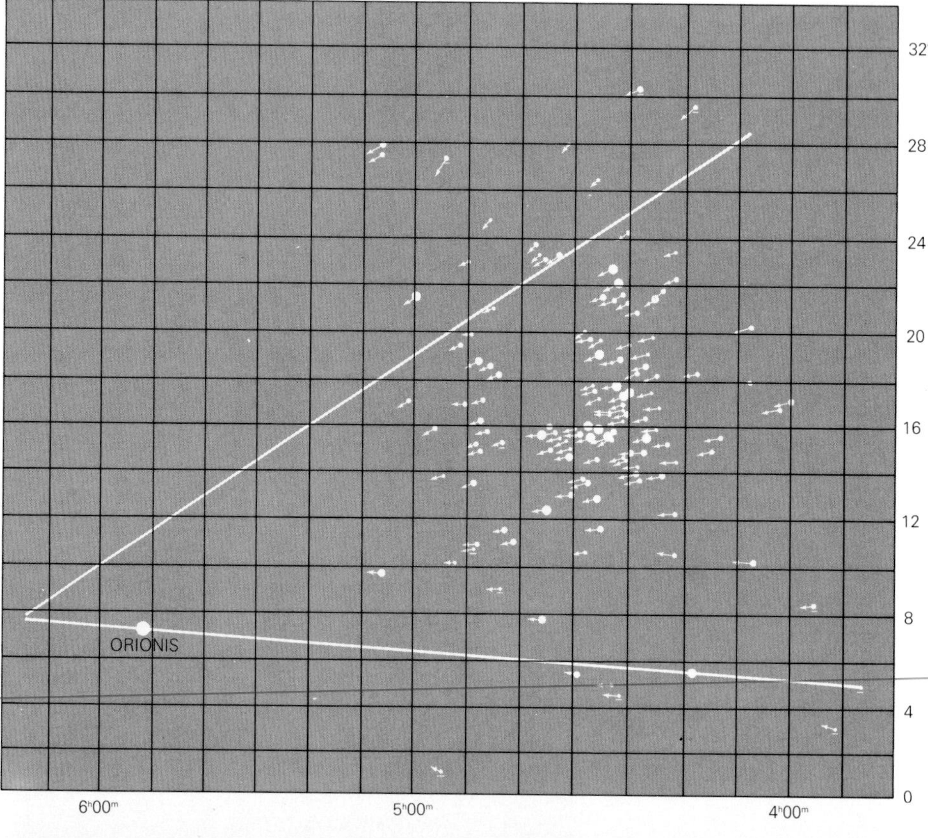

2.8 *The Hyades is an old galactic cluster in Taurus.*

2.10 *A globular cluster is a dense region of thousands of stars located around the center of the Milky Way.*

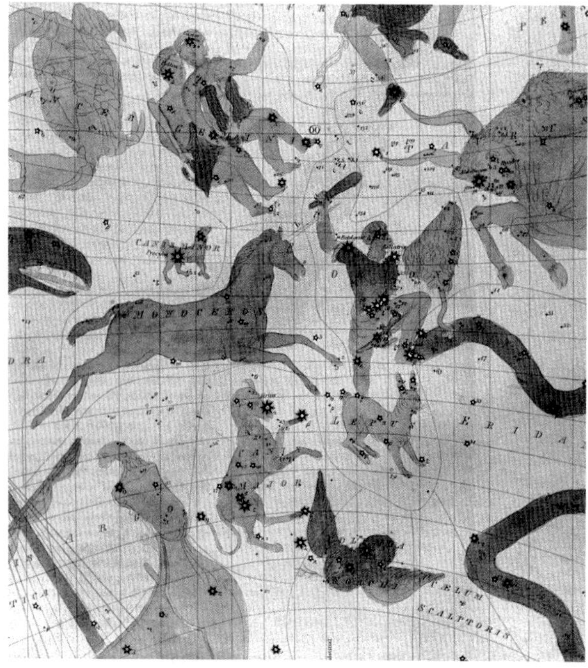

bursters involves some of the most fascinating and unusual notions in modern science. Bursters may be caused by stellar binary systems, in which one of the stars is a neutron star or black hole. We will discuss the processes of stellar evolution that lead to neutron stars and black holes later in this book, but both are end points of stellar lives after stars have exhausted their nuclear fuel and collapsed to a highly compact state.

If a neutron star were in a binary system, its high gravitational force would pull material from a companion star onto its surface. This matter explodes when it hits the neutron star, giving off X rays. That X rays appear in bursts is caused either by something interrupting the flow of matter onto the neutron star or by an eclipsing orbit of the binary system. Another explanation of bursters has been proposed, involving black holes. Some scientists have suggested that giant black holes reside at the center of globular clusters. As matter is pulled into the black hole, it heats up and emits X rays. Figure 2.13 shows an X-ray burster photographed by the Einstein Observatory, a special satellite equipped to measure X-ray radiation from space.

The Hertzsprung–Russell Diagram and Stellar Clusters

When we introduced the H-R diagram in Chapter 1, we noted that after determining a star's spectral type or temperature and its absolute magnitude, we can locate the star on the diagram and determine what kind of star it is. An H-R diagram can also be used to analyze the evolution of stars as they go from normal, main-sequence stars to red giants and so on. The dynamics of stellar evolution can be graphed on an H-R diagram.

We must necessarily make a couple of assumptions when we analyze a cluster in this way. We assume that all of the stars in the cluster were born about the same time from the same cloud of gas in the galaxy. Thus they have similar chemical compositions and ages. Only the masses of cluster stars are different. Stars lie on the main sequence most of their lives, so we believe that non–main-sequence stars, such as those lying to the right, have evolved off the main sequence as they

2.11 The distribution of galactic and globular clusters in the Milky Way Galaxy.

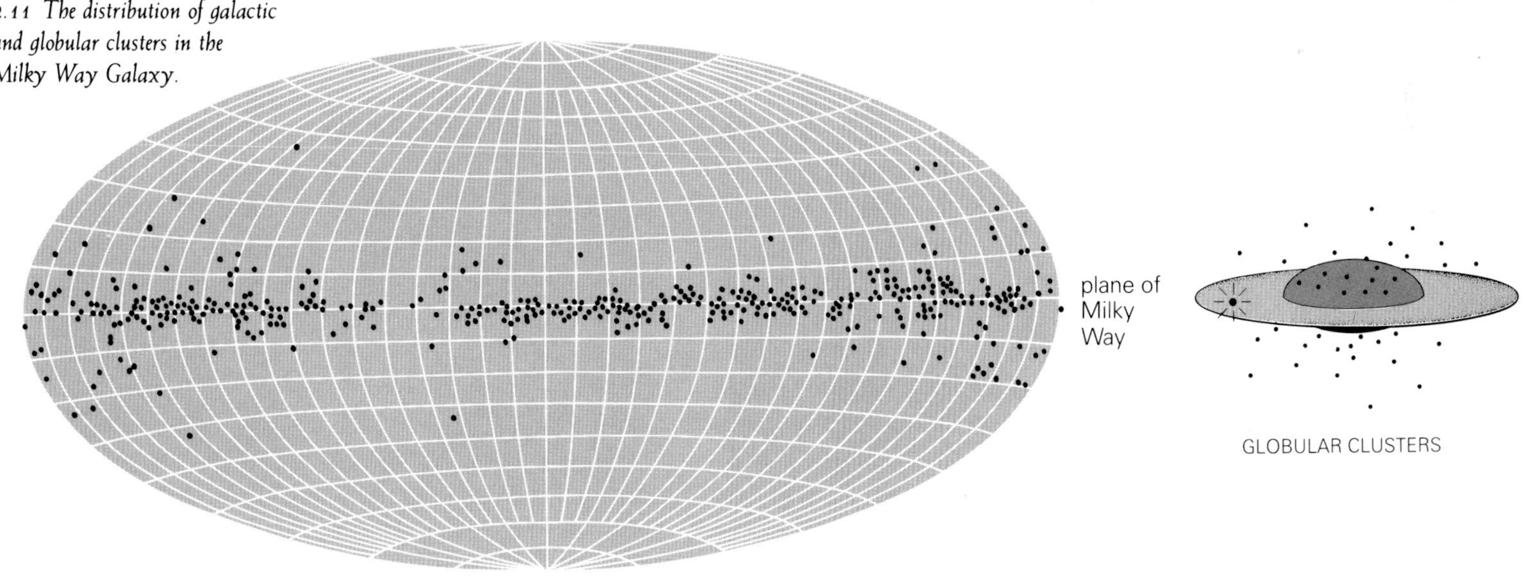

aged. If we combine this with the mass-luminosity relation (Figure 1.11), we learn that the brighter stars are the more massive and tend to evolve faster than low-mass stars by using up their fuel more quickly. This explains why the more luminous stars evolve off the main sequence before the fainter stars do.

At this point we make a large jump to using H-R diagrams of clusters as a valuable tool for determining the ages of clusters. The farther down the main sequence the stars begin to move off to the right, the older the stellar cluster must be. Figure 2.14 is an H-R diagram of a galactic cluster cataloged as M67. It is older than the cluster plotted in Figure 2.15, which is the double cluster in Perseus labeled Persei η and χ.

If we plot several galactic clusters at one time, we see, as in Figure 2.16, that the young Pleiades cluster contains brighter stars that are still on the main sequence than the Hyades does, and so on. Thus the point where the cluster turns off the main sequence can be read like a clock.

We can do the same analysis for globular clusters: M3 is graphed in Figure 2.17. Note that the turnoff is very low. This means that the globular cluster has existed long enough for many of the fainter stars to begin evolving away from the main sequence. Globular clusters are very old.

We need a yardstick, though, to measure absolute ages of clusters by this method, and astronomers use theoretical calculations of how long stars of certain masses should stay on the main sequence to gauge a cluster's age.

Globular clusters are so old that they exhibit one additional feature that no galactic cluster has. It is called the horizontal branch, and it represents stars that are moving to the left of the H-R diagram *after* they have existed as red giants. At this point they do not change their luminosity (thus the branch is horizontal), but their temperatures increase drastically. No stars in galactic clusters are as old as these. Astronomers have pegged the age of various galactic clusters to be between 10 million years and 10 billion years. Some globular clusters may be more than 12 billion years old. This is an interesting age, since astronomers think the universe is between 10 billion and 20 billion

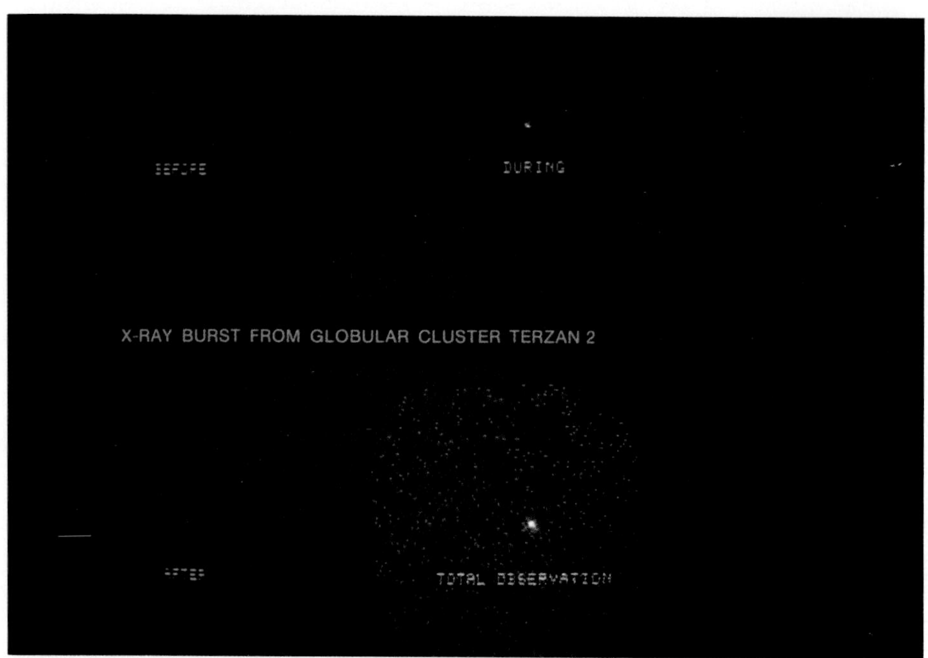

2.12 *Comparative X-ray images showing the brightening of a burster.*

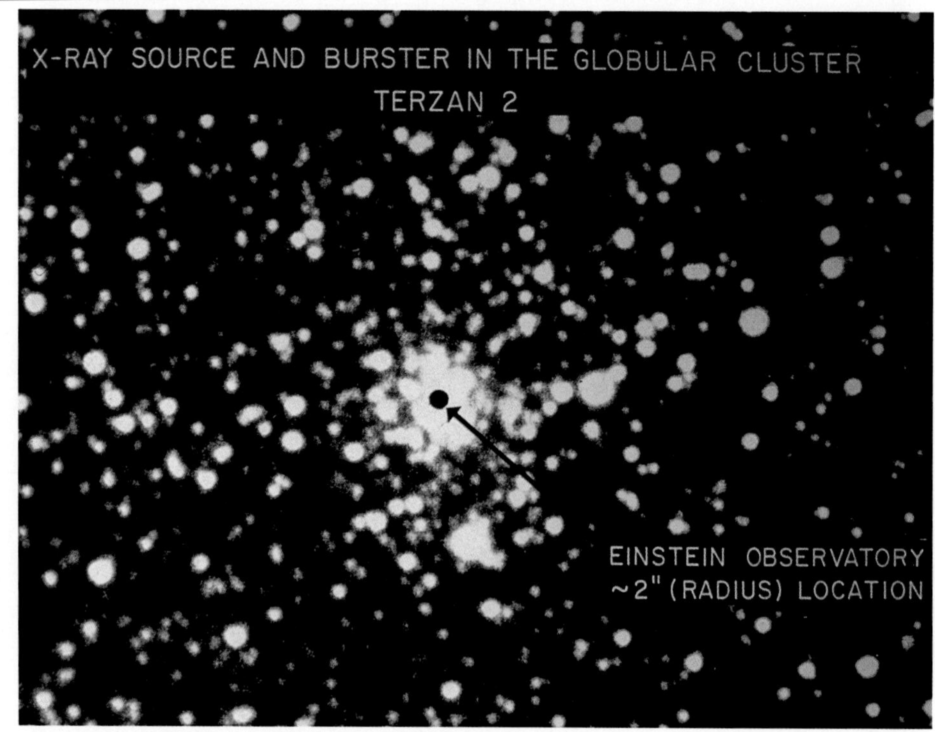

2.13 *An example of an X-ray burster in action, photographed by the Einstein Observatory in space.*

years old. Obviously, the oldest galactic clusters must still be younger than the cosmos.

Variable Stars

As one star in a binary system eclipses another, the total light received on earth diminishes. We see this as a drop in intensity, and a graph of this brightness variation as a function of time is called a light curve. Such variability in the brightness we observe is not due to the star's energy output itself, but to its orbit. This is an extrinsic cause for variability. Individual stars may themselves vary in brightness because of internal mechanisms that are not yet well understood. These intrinsically varying objects are called variable stars.

There are several types of variable stars, each named after the first of its kind discovered. The periods of fluctuation of the different variable stars may range from several years to only a few seconds, and some of the brighter variables make wonderful targets for amateur astronomers to chart. A group named the American Association of Variable Star Observers (AAVSO) has an international membership of amateurs and professionals who are dedicated to observing and plotting the intensity changes of variable stars.

Cepheid Variables

One of the most important types of variable stars is known as a Cepheid variable. These variable stars can have periods of fluctuation of between 1 and 100 days. Cepheid variables are giant stars whose intensities vary by about a magnitude. The fluctuations in intensity are caused by pulsations in the star, during which the star is larger when brightest and smaller when faintest. We do not understand the cause of the pulsation, but we know that Cepheids have one characteristic that is very important to astronomers: the longer the period of the intensity fluctuation, the more light an individual Cepheid emits. Figure 2.18 illustrates the light curve for two Cepheid variable stars. The brighter star has the longer period of fluctuation. This characteristic seems to hold for all Cepheids, and *any* Cepheid that is as bright as 2,000 suns will have a period of 10 days.

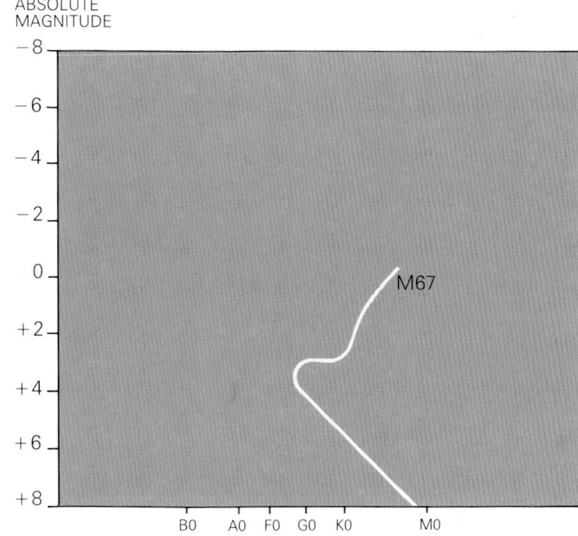

2.14 The stars of the galactic cluster M67 in the constellation Cancer, plotted on an H-R diagram.

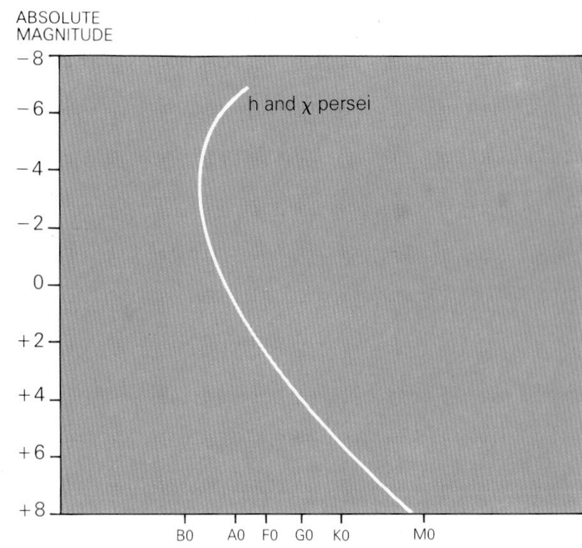

2.15 An H-R diagram of the double cluster in Perseus. Note that most of the stars are still on the main sequence, so that the cluster is very young.

This is called the *period-luminosity relation,* and with it scientists have unlocked the secrets of the size of our galaxy and the distance to nearby galaxies. If we plot the absolute magnitude of several Cepheid variables against their periods, we can draw a smooth line through the dots that represents the relationship between period and luminosity.

During the early years of the twentieth century, Henrietta Leavitt, a famous astronomer at the Harvard College Observatory in Cambridge, Massachusetts, pioneered the work with Cepheid variable stars by studying a few dozen Cepheids in the Large and Small Magellanic Clouds. She worked out the period-luminosity relation in 1912 after doing years of careful analysis of the light curves of her target Cepheid variables.

The Large and Small Magellanic Clouds are two small, irregularly shaped galaxies near the Milky Way. Fortunately, Cepheids are bright enough so that we can see many of them individually in the Magellanic Clouds. When scientists compared the light curves of Cepheids in our galaxy with those in the Magellanic Clouds, there was no doubt that they were similar in nature. The only difference was that the ones in the Magellanic Clouds were much fainter.

During the early years of the twentieth century, astronomers used indirect measurements of the distance to local Cepheid variables to determine their absolute magnitude. Knowing the period of brightness fluctuation of a Cepheid variable star gives us its absolute magnitude directly from the period-luminosity relation. Observation of the star's apparent magnitude is then compared to the absolute magnitude, from which we can infer the distance to these stars.

2.16 Plotting several galactic clusters on an H-R diagram illustrates the use of this sort of graph as a way of figuring out the relative ages of clusters.

2.17 Hertzsprung-Russell diagram for a globular cluster, M3, showing the turnoff from the main sequence, the horizontal branch, and the red giant region.

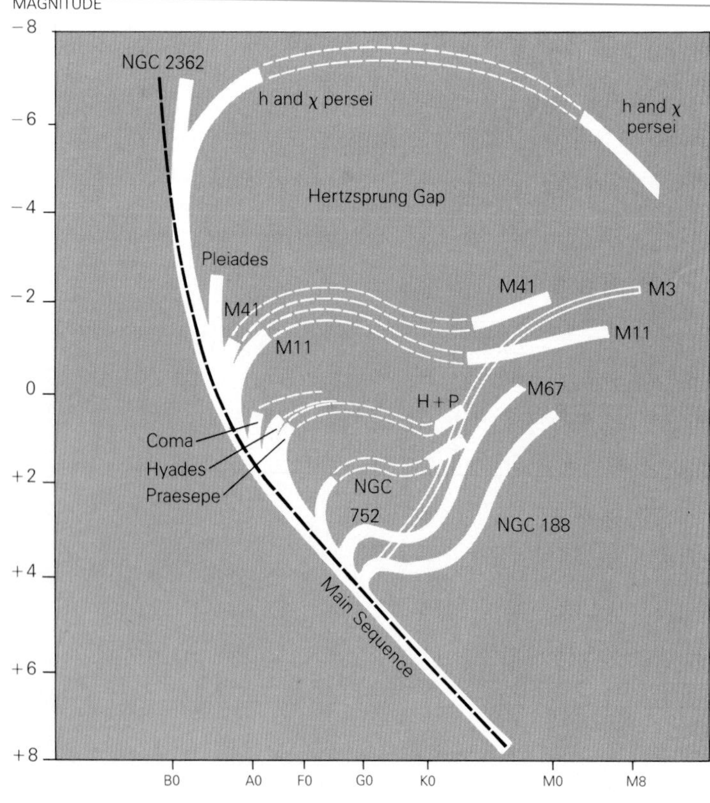

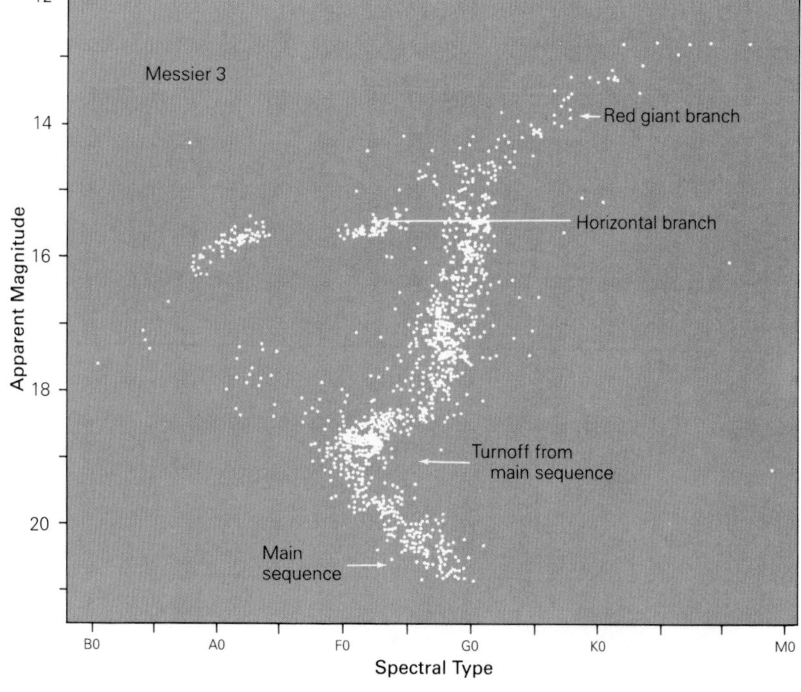

Cepheid variables were used in this manner to determine the distance to the Magellanic Clouds. Although only about 700 Cepheids are known in our galaxy and a few others have been observed in other galaxies, they remain a powerful indicator of distance, since it is relatively simple to determine how bright they really are by measuring their intensity fluctuations.

Cepheids are examples of variable stars that are pulsating in tempo with their changes in brightness. Cepheids may change in size by 5 to 10 percent; the spectral type of a Cepheid also varies with its luminosity.

RR Lyrae Stars

Another class of variable stars was first found in globular clusters. The double R in the name refers to a complex notation astronomers have developed to identify variable stars. Because RR Lyrae is one of the brightest and best known of this class of stars, the entire group has become known by this name. Figure 2.19 shows Lyra's position.

RR Lyrae stars were first called cluster-type variables because of their original discovery in a stellar cluster.

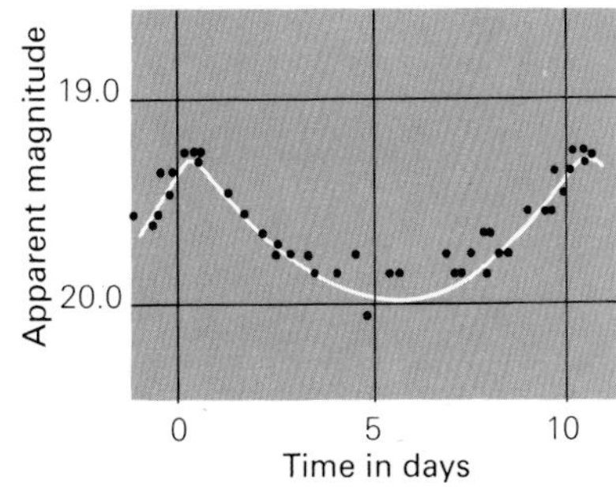

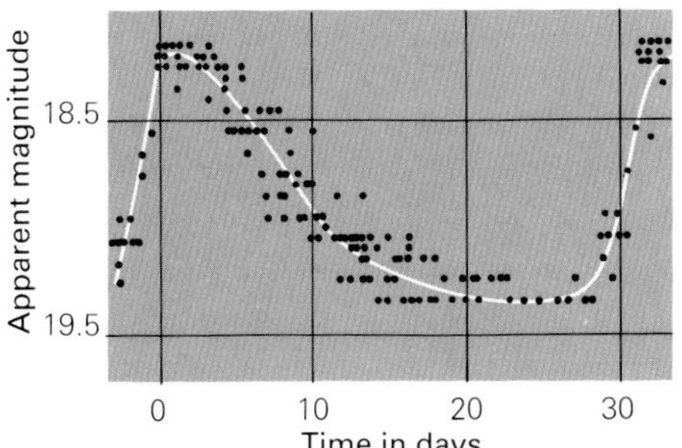

2.18 *Light curves from two Cepheid variable stars show that the brighter the star, the longer the period of variability.*

Astronomical Catalogs and Notation

Astronomers have developed a notation for nonstellar objects observed in outer space. Specific cataloging began with the work of Charles Messier, a French astronomer of the late 1700s who cataloged 101 fuzzy objects he saw through a telescope. Messier listed these objects because they were permanent and not to be confused with comets, which is really what he was on the lookout for. The 101 objects are listed with the letter M and the appropriate number in his catalog, such as M31, M44, and so on.

More recent works include the New General Catalogue, listing thousands of celestial objects recorded by J. L. E. Dreyer in 1888. Messier objects are found in the NGC, but they are designated with the letters NGC and the corresponding catalog number. Newer catalogs exist, including the 3rd Cambridge Catalogue of quasars and other unusual objects.

Astronomers have a specific nomenclature of star identification as well. Some stars have names, such as Betelgeuse and Rigel, but *all* stars that are visible are designated by a Greek letter and the possessive form of the Latin name of the constellation in which the star resides. The brightest star in a constellation is labeled α, the next β, and so on. For example, the brightest star in the constellation Canis Major (the great dog) is known as α Canis Majoris. The second brightest star in Orion is written as β Orionis.

They have periods of fluctuation that are shorter than Cepheids, usually less than a day, and they are not very bright stars. RR Lyrae stars have been identified in only the nearest galaxies, most of them in the Milky Way.

RR Lyrae variables are pulsating stars whose intensity varies by about one magnitude. All RR Lyrae variables exhibit approximately the same luminosity. This enables astronomers to use them as standard beacons with which to measure distance. Comparing apparent magnitudes with intrinsic luminosity, we can determine the distance to these stars with relative ease. This has been particularly helpful in calculating the distance to globular clusters. RR Lyrae stars tend to be old, evolved stars often located on the horizontal branch of the H-R diagram of globular clusters.

Mira Variables

Mira variables are long-period variable stars. The light curve of Mira in the constellation Cetus, the whale, has brightness fluctuations that peak every 11 months,

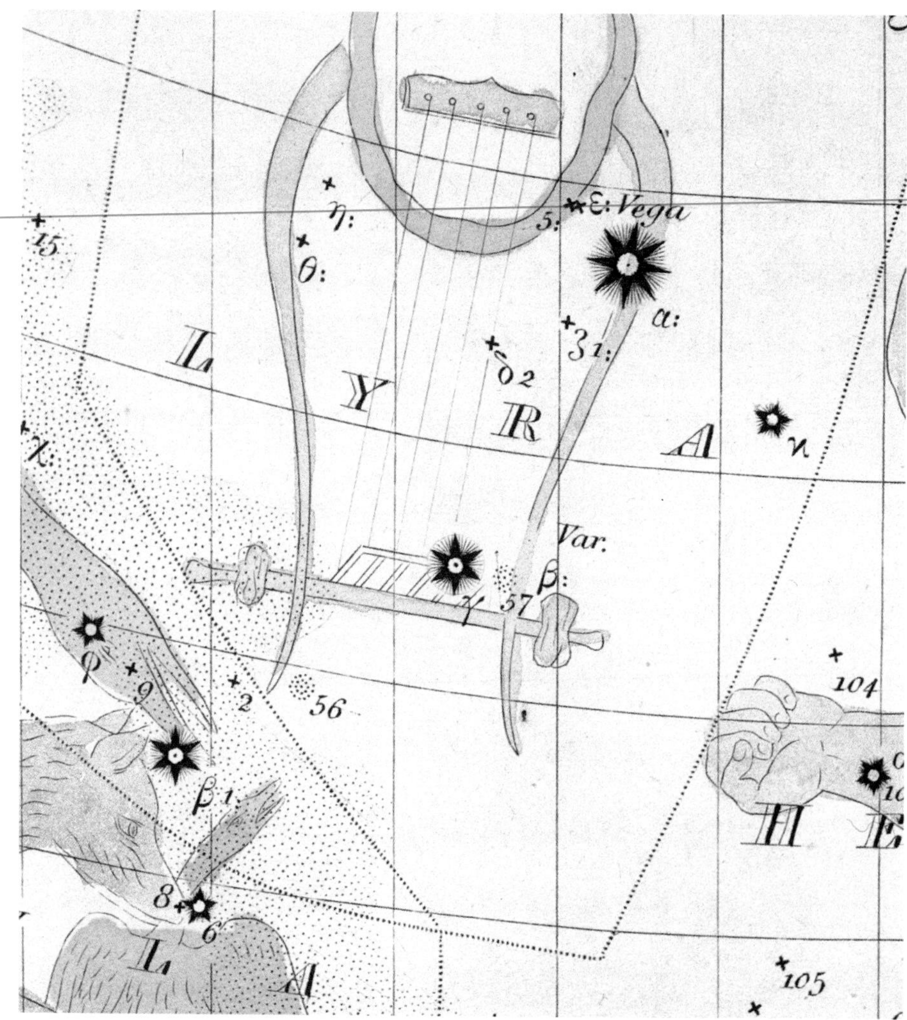

2.19 *The constellation Lyra.*

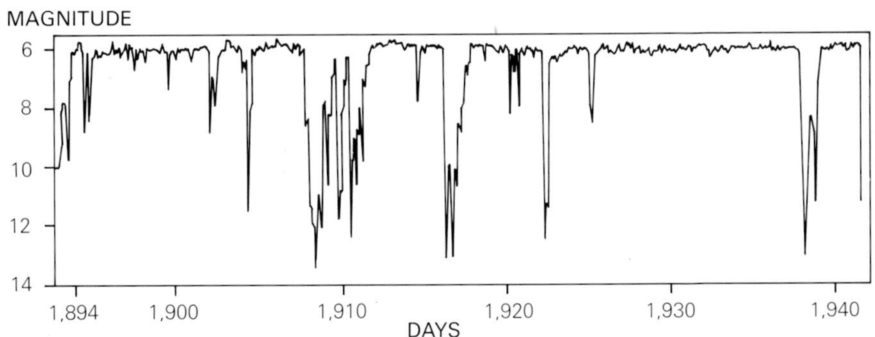

2.20 *The light curve of an irregular variable called R Coronae Borealis.*

and the intensity changes by about six magnitudes, or by a factor of 250. Mira is the name given to this entire class of variable stars, of which our galaxy may contain as many as 100,000.

Mira variables are giant stars of cool spectral classes, mostly type M. Such red giant stars are several hundred times larger than the sun. As these stars do not seem to be changing size, however, some other mechanism must be heating the surface, making them more luminous.

Other Periodic Intrinsic Variables

Several other types of periodic variable stars exhibit long and short periods of fluctuation. RV Tauri variables and W Virginis stars have periods similar to the Cepheids, but have different spectroscopic properties. The similarity, however, has led astronomers to refer to these two classes of variable star as type II Cepheids.

There is a class of variable star that consists of hot stars of spectral type B. They bear the designation β Canis Majoris, after one of its most familiar members. These stars exhibit small, rapid fluctuations in brightness that indicate that they are pulsating, although astronomers do not yet know why.

Irregular Variables

Some stars change intensity in a totally irregular or random fashion. Figure 2.20 shows the light curve of R Coronae Borealis. The most drastic changes in intensity are not increases, but rather drops in brightness. The spectra of R Coronae Borealis stars show that they are rich in carbon and very bright (bright enough to have been spotted in the Magellanic Clouds).

T Tauri stars are another class of erratic variables that may be a combination of intrinsic and extrinsic variable stars. They lie in nebulae that probably interact with the star itself. Some astronomers have proposed that T Tauri stars are actually being born (see Chapter 4) from the material of the nebula. This is supported by evidence that these stars appear in very young regions and in galactic clusters.

The Sun and Flare Stars

Our own star undergoes some minor fluctuations in intensity, although anything more drastic would be very hazardous to life on earth. The sun goes through periods of magnetic activity that operate on a 22-year cycle (see Chapter 6). When the sun is at its peak magnetically, large explosions called solar flares erupt on the surface. These flares increase the total energy output of the sun.

Such behavior has been seen in other stars as well, including our nearest stellar neighbor, Proxima Centauri. Some flare stars actually have flares several times as intense as those on our sun, although any periodicity of flare outbursts on other stars is not well documented. Flare stars all seem to be on the main sequence.

Novae

The term *nova* means new star, but astronomers have learned that novae are not new, just newly visible. Novae are stars that increase in brightness so dramatically that they are often seen by the naked eye for the first time. The brightness of novae may increase by hundreds or even millions of times.

Astronomers have deduced with spectroscopy and the light curves of novae that they are stars that actually expel part of their outer atmosphere. They brighten in a few days and fade over several months or years. The gas that is thrown outward eventually thins to the point that it becomes transparent and detectable by the presence of emission lines in the star's spectra. Years after a nova fades, the gas shell may be visible in large optical telescopes.

Stars do not give off much of their mass during nova outbursts, so there is no reason that such ejections cannot happen several times during a stellar life. In fact several novae do repeat; they are called recurrent novae.

A recent theory holds that most, if not all, novae occur in binary star systems when one star is approaching the red giant stage and the other has evolved into a white dwarf. The expulsion of matter may occur if part of the red giant's outer atmosphere falls on the white dwarf, heating up and generating nuclear reactions. The energy from the reactions blows off the infalling material, and recurrent novae may operate on the same basis, since matter from the red giant could continuously fall on the white dwarf star. Figure 2.21 shows two pictures of the same region of the sky. Note the new star in the photograph on the left.

Putting Variables in Perspective

When we look at the different types of variable stars by plotting them on a H-R diagram, it seems clear that they have some relationship to stellar evolution. Cepheids, RV Tauri stars, and Mira variables are red giant

stars that have left the main sequence. RR Lyrae stars are globular cluster stars that are returning to the main sequence on the horizontal branch, since they are very old. Thus stars that are constant in brightness for much of their life may evolve into variable stars later on, and instabilities, including pulsation, may develop as a star evolves into old age.

The Sun, Almost a Binary Star

The sun is alone in space; at least it has no other stars orbiting it. Its system of planets is probably not a unique entity in the universe, but the sun actually came fairly close to being a binary star during its formation about 4.5 billion years ago.

The material that did not become the sun went into building the planets, asteroids, and comets. Jupiter is the most massive of the planets in the solar system, but had it been only 10 times more massive when it was formed, thermonuclear fires would have ignited and instead of the beautiful gaseous planet with its giant red spot, a small yellow star would be glowing in our night sky. Naturally, the orbits of the planets that did form would have been different from those we know, and the planets would have evolved lifeless and hot.

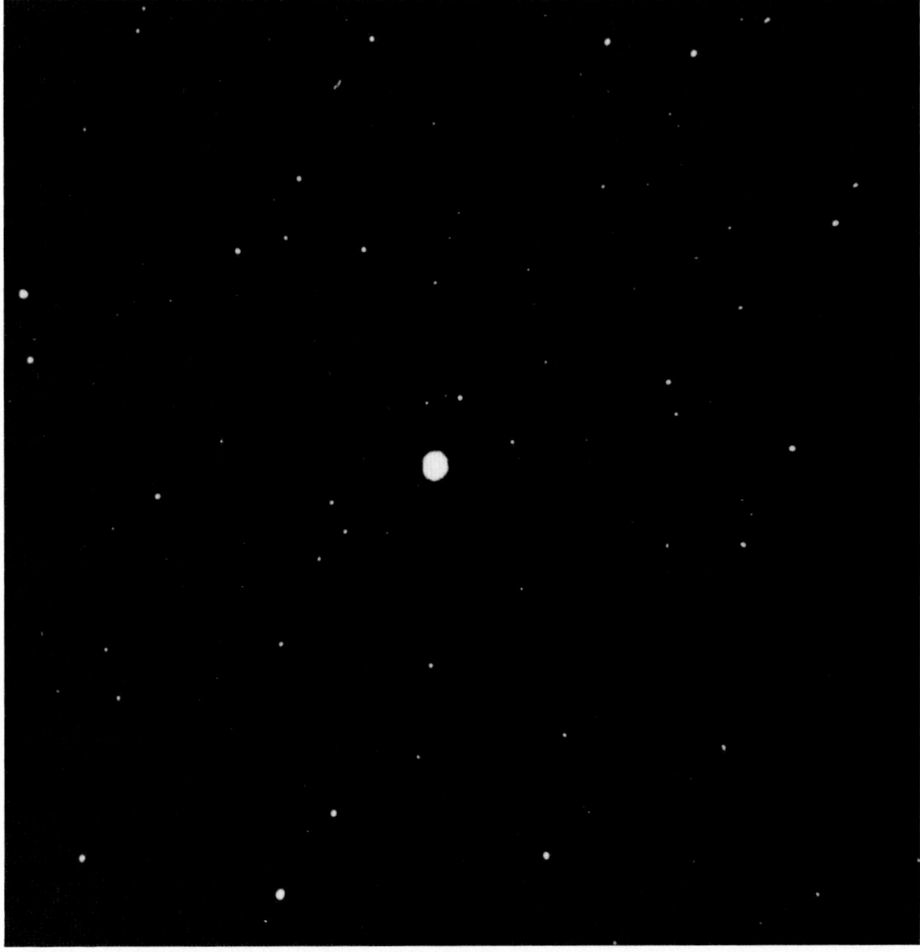

2.21 *Two pictures of the same region of space photographed years apart. The new star in the photograph on this page is a nova.*

3: THE SPACE BETWEEN THE STARS

The Interstellar Medium

It is no wonder that until the late eighteenth century, people thought that the space between the stars was an empty void. Just look at the night sky. By terrestrial standards the interstellar medium is empty because it is far more devoid of matter than is the best vacuum achieved in earth's laboratories.

Space is full of material, however. Just because we cannot always see it does not mean it does not exist. With the application of fine optical telescopes, it became clear that large clouds of glowing gas exist in space. These were called *nebulae* (Latin for clouds), a name still applied to the beautiful and tenuous clouds in the realm of the stars.

In the eighteenth century, astronomers also noticed that some areas of the sky appear totally devoid of stars. William Herschel observed that even along the Milky Way there are large dark areas. The nineteenth-century Italian astronomer Angelo Secchi may have been the first to realize that these dark regions were not voids, but areas where clouds of dust are blocking more distant stars. Dark clouds are also called nebulae. We will explore both bright nebulae and dark nebulae because they play important roles in the formation of stars. The gas and dust between the stars is generally called the interstellar medium.

An understanding of the interstellar medium is important to astronomers because, as we shall see in Chapter 4, the material from the space between the stars eventually forms new stars and planets. In addition, stars at the end of their lives eject material into interstellar space to complete the cycle of stellar evolution.

Emission Nebulae

Bright nebulae are also called emission nebulae because they give off radiation. In general, the density of the interstellar medium is about one atom per cubic centimeter, but there are large volumes where the density of space is considerably greater. These areas are the nebulae, whose density is closer to 300 atoms per cubic centimeter.

The Great Nebula in Orion is perhaps the best known of all emission nebulae. The American Indians called the region "the smoking star" because this small hazy patch in the middle of Orion's sword is visible to the naked eye on very clear nights. Figure 3.1 shows several nebulae in Orion and Figure 3.2 shows the position of the Great Nebula.

Ninety percent of the universe is hydrogen, and nebulae have the same proportion of this atom, which consists of one electron electrically bound to a proton. This configuration is called neutral hydrogen, or HI. When the atom absorbs a sufficient amount of energy, the electron escapes, and we say the atom has been ionized. We call ionized hydrogen HII. Since so much of the universe is hydrogen, astronomers have used HI and HII to describe regions in space where hydrogen clouds exist either in the neutral state or in the state of ionization.

HI and HII regions can exist side by side if the conditions are right. HII regions form around a hot star that is embedded in the nebula. The ultraviolet radiation that the star emits ionizes the hydrogen atoms

3.1 Several nebulae are associated with the young hot stars of the lower part of the constellation Orion, the hunter. The bright gas clouds are areas where stars are being born.

3.2 The constellation Orion. The middle "star" in the sword is M42, the Great Nebula.

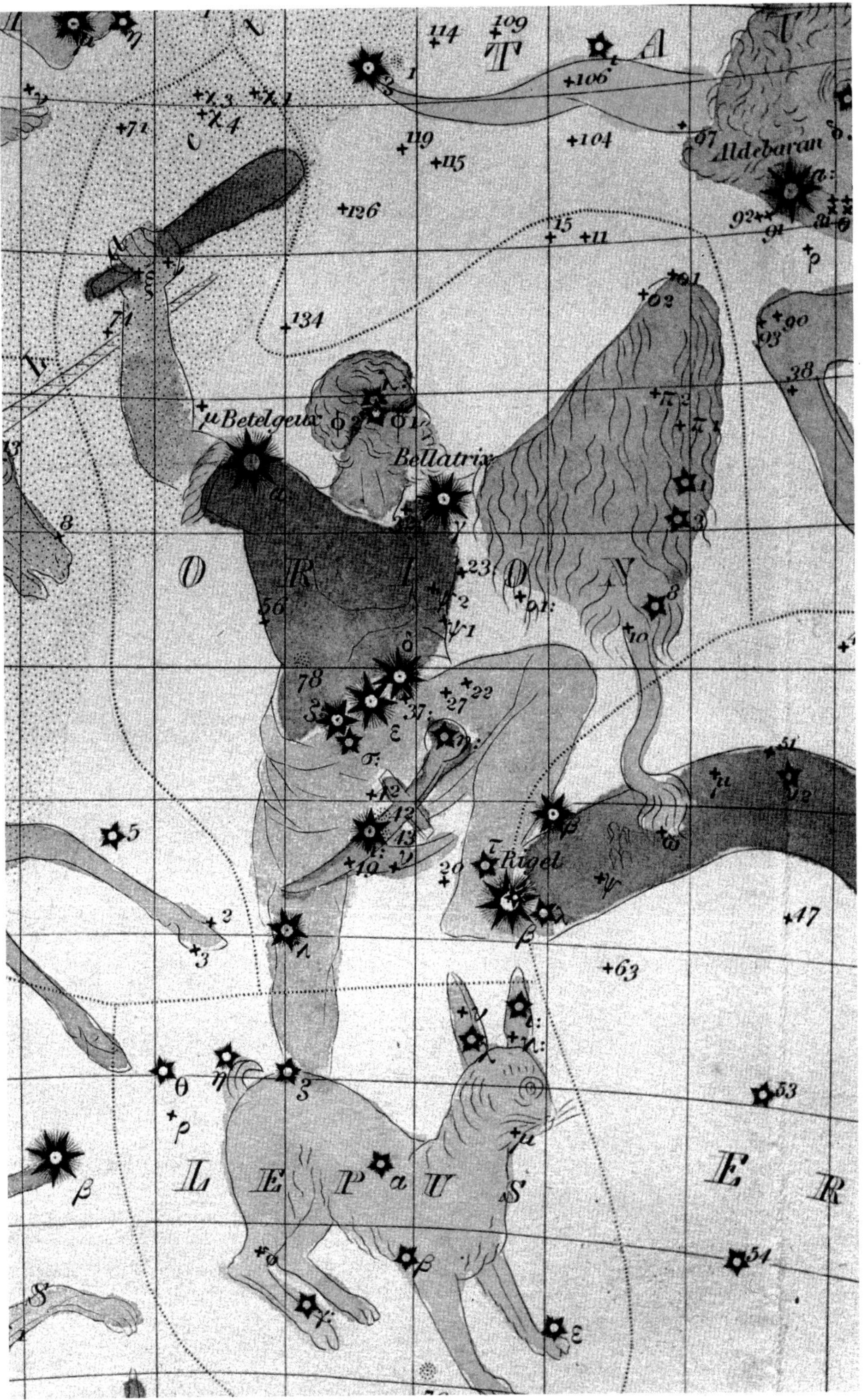

in the vicinity of the star and it becomes an HII region (Figure 3.5). The size of this volume is dependent on the density of the nebula (the denser it is the less the radiation from the star can penetrate, so the smaller the HII region) and the luminosity of the star. The boundary of the HII region is very distinct, and an HI region surrounds it. Where no star is present, only HI regions exist.

Often, HI regions are full of hydrogen molecules that have formed from the bonding of two atoms. HI regions are cold, about 100° K (−270° F) and mostly nonluminous.

HII regions are hot because of the excitation of protons and electrons by the ionizing radiation from the nearby star; the temperature in HII regions reaches 10,000° K. HII regions actually *are* the emission nebulae we see, because as fast as electrons are stripped away they recombine with other protons in the nebula and emit spectral lines that we can analyze with spectroscopic methods. A spectrum of a nebula shows bright emission lines from hydrogen, as well as helium, oxygen, and nitrogen.

Figure 3.3 shows the Lagoon Nebula in the constellation Sagittarius. The red glow is caused by hydrogen atoms that are fluorescing and emitting a spectral line in the red that dominates the other emission lines. The North America Nebula (Figure 3.4) and most other emission nebulae, or HII regions, appear red in many photographs, and we can usually see the hot star that is ionizing the gas in the interstellar medium. Emission nebulae are among the most beautiful objects in the sky.

Absorption Nebulae

In addition to gas clouds that form HI and HII regions, a component of the interstellar medium consists of dust grains that occasionally occur in dense clouds that we call dark nebulae or absorption nebulae. These nebulae are seen as dark regions against a starry background or against emission nebulae.

3.3 *The Lagoon Nebula. The dark lanes are formed by obscuring dust clouds between us and the HII region.*

3.4 The North America Nebula is given its name because dark dust clouds block some of the HII region so that it appears in the shape of the North American continent.

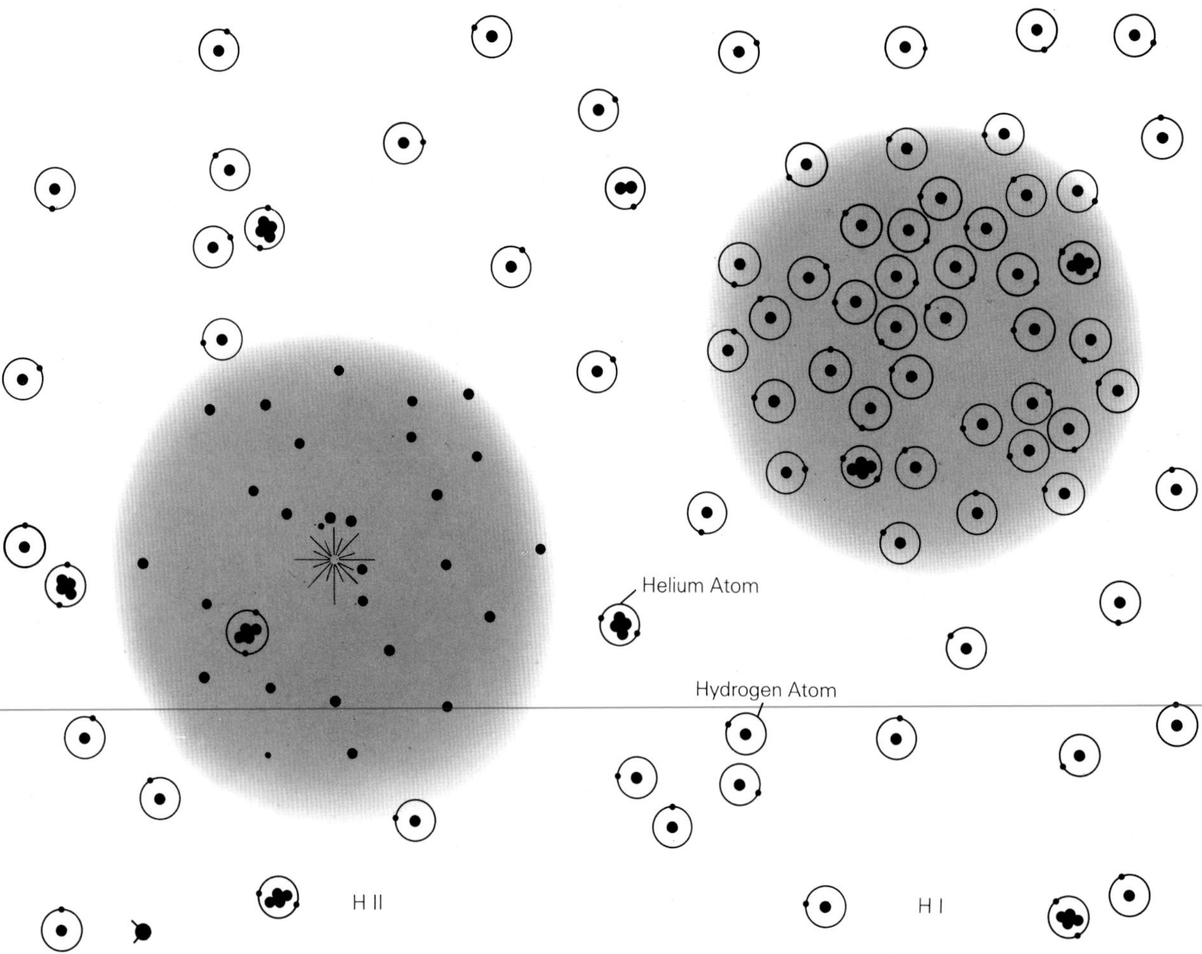

3.5 *Diagram of a spherical HII region around a hot star. A region of un-ionized hydrogen gas that is of higher density than normal is an HI region.*

One of the most famous examples of obscuring clouds of dust is what is called the *dark rift* (Figure 3.6), which runs along the Milky Way and appears to split it in two. The dark rift is actually made up of several smaller clouds, but the obscuration of stars behind it is so great that ancient astronomers described the dark rift as being a hole or tunnel in the sky.

The Horsehead Nebula (Figure 3.7) and the Coal Sack (Figure 3.8) are fine examples of dark nebulae that are blocking light from nebulae or stars on the other side.

Reflection Nebulae

Although dust grains in interstellar space actually absorb some radiation, they mostly scatter or redirect light in all directions. A small percentage of this scattered light comes to us, so dark nebulae are not really completely black but actually have a faint luminosity.

When a dense region of dust surrounds a very bright star, the cloud may scatter enough radiation so that it can be seen. Since such a cloud is reflecting starlight, we call it a reflection nebula.

Figure 3.9 shows Merope, one of the stars of the

3.6 One section of the Milky Way that shows the dark absorption clouds that block light from more distant stars. Entire lanes of dust at times seem to divide the galaxy in two.

3.7 A dark cloud in the shape of a horse's head in the constellation Orion is blocking light from the more distant HII region. Because of its shape, this object has become known as the Horsehead Nebula.

open cluster the Pleiades, surrounded by extreme nebulosity. Reflection nebulae are primarily blue due to the color of the hot star. Figure 3.10 shows an interesting celestial object called the Trifid Nebula. The Trifid is actually the HII region that is seen emitting red light. Dark lanes of obscuring dust seem to divide the HII region into three parts, and a blue reflection nebula surrounds the neighboring bright star. The Trifid Nebula, then, exhibits all three types of nebulosity.

Interstellar Reddening and Absorption

Although thick absorption nebulae are responsible for the very dark regions in the galaxy, dust grains permeate all interstellar space and cause a slight darkening of all celestial objects. This is much the way a fog dims the headlights of oncoming cars.

The existence of this diffuse obscuration by interstellar dust was not known until the 1930s, so distance measurements to stars and clusters made before 1930 were in error. You will recall in Chapter 1 that astronomers compute the distance to objects by comparing their apparent magnitude with their absolute magnitude. If starlight is dimmed by passing through the interstellar medium, its apparent brightness is underestimated and its distance is overestimated. Figure 3.11 shows why we see more dust when we look toward the galactic center than up out of the plane of the galaxy.

Astronomers thought that the stars in our galaxy thinned out so that the Milky Way was only a few thousand light-years across and that the sun was near the center. When corrections were made for the intervening dust, astronomers realized that the sun is about two-thirds from the galaxy's center—we do not even see as far as the center—and that if dust were not blocking the galaxy's starlight, we would be able to read at night under the stars.

In addition to dimming starlight by reflecting it in all directions, the dust is more efficient at scattering short wavelength radiation (blue light) than long wavelength radiation (red light). This is true of the earth's

3.8 Below left: *The Coal Sack is an absorption nebula that blocks out the light from distant stars, so that at first glance, this region of the sky appears devoid of stars.*

3.9 *A blue reflection nebula surrounds the young hot stars of the Pleiades.*

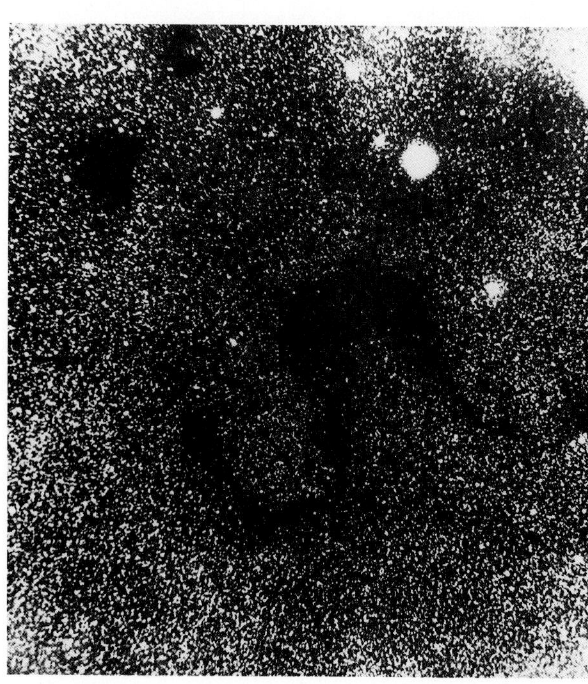

atmosphere and explains why the sky is blue and sunsets are red. Figure 3.12 shows the geometry of sunsets and the blue sky at noon. Notice that by the time the sunlight at sunset reaches our eye, most of the blue light has been removed from the beam, so the sun appears orange or red. That same blue light removed from our sunset is redirected to form someone else's blue sky.

The same geometry holds true for interstellar reddening. As starlight travels through the interstellar medium, the blue light is scattered in other directions, so the stars appear reddish. The farther the star, the redder it appears (and dimmer as well). Astronomers were puzzled by the fact that some stars whose spectra exhibit characteristics of hot B- and A-type stars appear to be cooler. Of course, when the laws governing interstellar reddening were worked out, this discrepancy in observational data made sense.

3.10 *The Trifid Nebula in Sagittarius is the red emission nebula that is divided by dark lanes of dust. The blue reflection nebula is nearby, but not associated with the Trifid.*

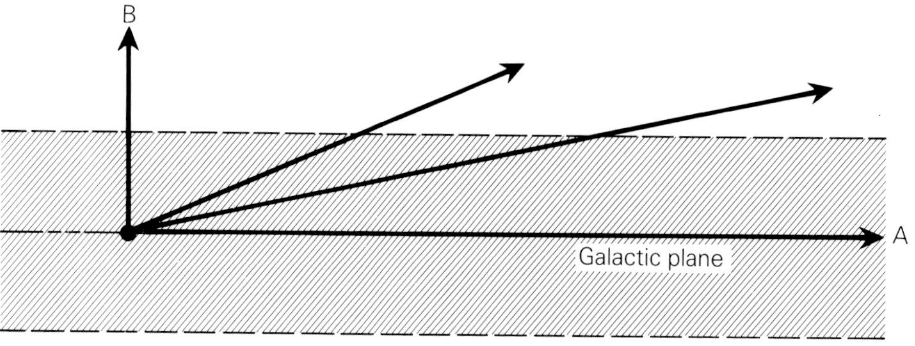

3.11 As the gas that formed the galaxy flattened out into a disk due to rotation, more and more matter became visible along the plane of the galaxy (direction A) than perpendicular to the plane (direction B). Thus we can see more dust lying in lanes when we observe the Milky Way, particularly toward the galactic center.

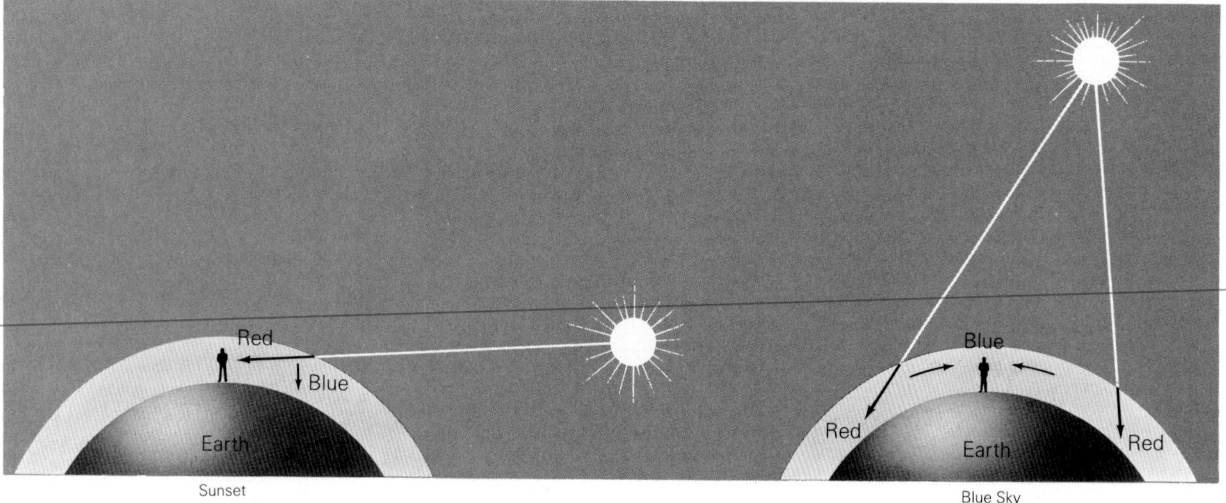

3.12 The geometry of sunsets and blue skies is related to the scattering of atmospheric molecules. Blue light is redirected by molecules, while red light passes through the air unscattered from the sun to the observer.

Observations of the Interstellar Medium

With the exception of emission and reflection nebulae, we cannot directly observe the interstellar medium in visible light. We can see what effects it has in terms of absorption and reddening, but the gas and dust not concentrated in nebulae are not dense or hot enough to emit visible radiation.

This cool, tenuous gas does emit radio waves, however, and the serendipitous discovery of this background radio noise was the beginning of radio astronomy. We have learned that all of the stars, although they emit some radiation in the radio portion of the spectrum, do not emit enough energy in radio waves to account for the intensity astronomers observed. The radio emission comes from the gas in interstellar space.

The Hydrogen Radio Spectrum

As has been mentioned, hydrogen makes up about 90 percent of the cosmos and exists primarily in the neutral state (i.e., the electron is bound to the nucleus) in diffuse clouds spread throughout the galaxy.

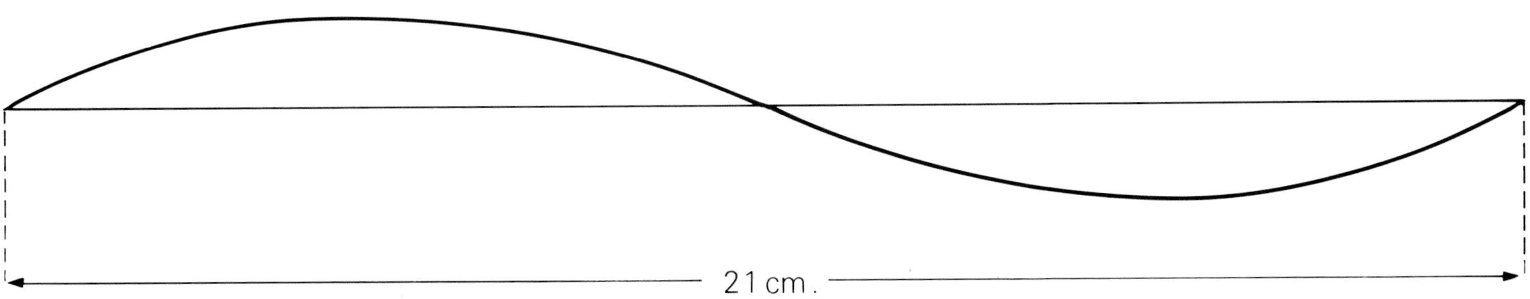

3.13 The actual length of the 21-centimeter wave.

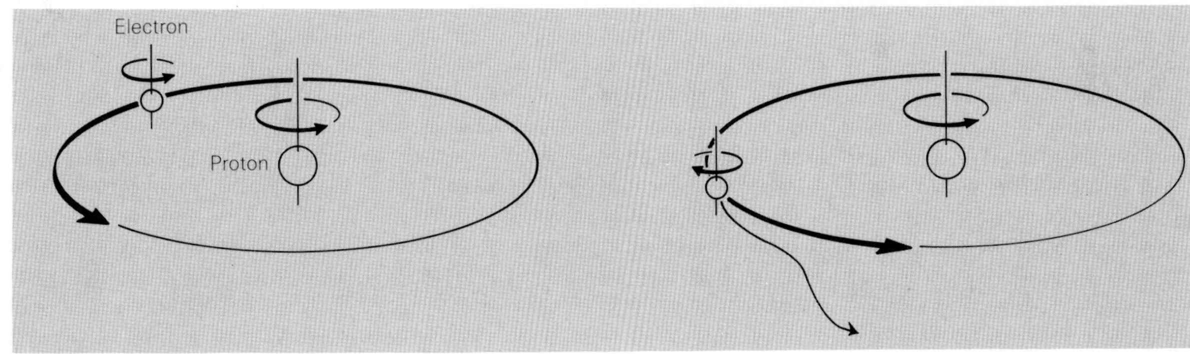

3.14 The 21-centimeter radiation from hydrogen results when the electron, which is spinning in the same direction as the nucleus, flips to the opposite spin, and the atom loses a small amount of energy in the form of radiation.

As in spectroscopy of visible light, radio astronomers can also observe spectral lines at specific radio wavelengths, and with hydrogen the most prevalent atomic species by far, it is no wonder that the first spectral line to be discovered in the radio range is caused by hydrogen. The wavelength of this spectral line is 21 centimeters (see Figure 3.13) and has a frequency of 1,420 megaHertz. Each hydrogen atom has a small amount of energy because the proton and the electron both spin about their axes as the electron orbits the proton. Depending on the relative directions of the particles' spin, they may either add energy if the spins are in the same direction or subtract energy if the two spins are in opposite directions. The spins usually *are* in opposite directions, but occasionally a collision with another particle will align the spins of the proton and electron, so the total energy of the atom is slightly higher than normal. The excited atom emits a low-energy spectral line at a wavelength of 21 centimeters. Figure 3.14 illustrates the principle behind this "spin flip" emission of neutral hydrogen.

In 1944, the Dutch astronomer H. C. van de Hulst proposed that enough interstellar hydrogen atoms would be radiating at 21 centimeters to make the emission observable by radio astronomy techniques.

The detection of 21-centimeter radiation was a great triumph for astronomy, because it enabled astronomers to locate the distribution of neutral hydrogen in our galaxy. Recall that the interstellar dust and gas dim and redden the more distant stars to the extent that we cannot optically view the central region of the galaxy. Radio waves penetrate the gas and dust, so we can "see" in radio light far beyond the horizon of visible astronomy.

Mapping Our Galaxy

As we look past our own galactic collection of stars, gas, and dust, we see other galaxies that exhibit a spiral structure (Figure 3.15). Most of the stars and interstellar material is concentrated along the spiral arms of such galaxies, but the absorbing dust in our own galaxy prevents us from seeing in visible light the shape of the Milky Way.

The nearby structure of the galaxy can be deduced from optical observations of nebulae and young stars, but Figure 3.16 shows just how limited these deductions are. We can see small segments of three spiral arms. That is all.

With 21-centimeter radiation, however, we can observe all the way across the galaxy, and Figure 3.17 illustrates an early map of the Milky Way Galaxy based on motions of HI regions about the galactic center. If we assume that all of the regions of neutral hydrogen orbit the galactic center in uniform circles, then with measurement of the Doppler shifts of these clouds (some are approaching us and others are receding) we can deduce a map such as in Figure 3.17. Unfortunately, HI regions have considerably more complex motions than assumed by astronomers in the 1950s and 1960s. Besides orbital motions around the center of the galaxy, gas clouds also move randomly in other directions about which we have little information. Thus we cannot take the map too seriously. It clearly shows, however, that a spiral structure is inherent in our galaxy.

3.15 The Whirlpool Galaxy is an example of a spiral galaxy consisting of some 100 billion stars.

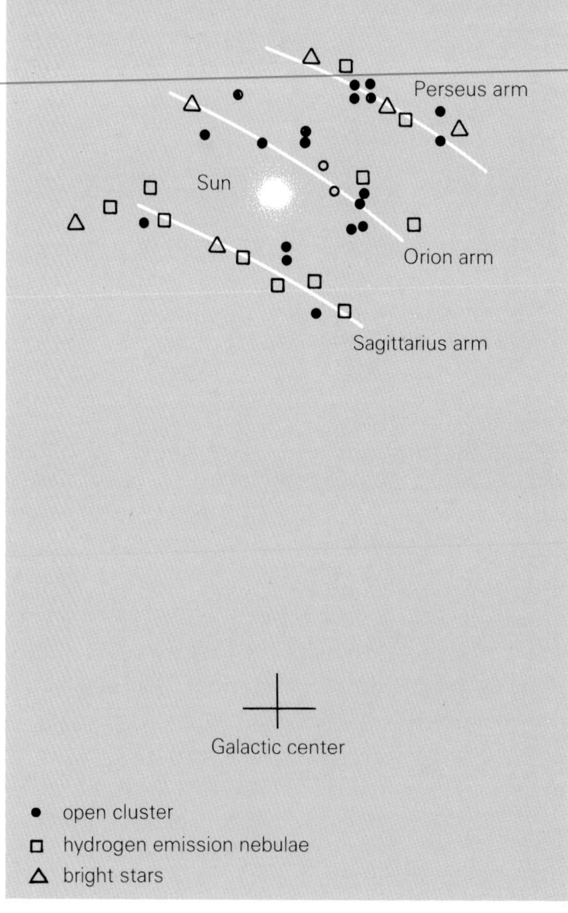

3.16 Based on optical observations of the galaxy, our knowledge of the Milky Way system is extremely sketchy. We can only deduce the nearby structure of the nearest spiral arms.

Chemistry in Interstellar Space

When we think of chemistry, we visualize a high school classroom or perhaps an industrial laboratory where people make compounds and molecules in test tubes or beakers. In fact, chemical processes are occurring all around us, from rusting hinges on a gate to

3.17 An artist's rendition of the spiral structure of the Milky Way Galaxy. The dark channel from the galactic center expanding outward reflects our ignorance of the distance to hydrogen clouds in these spiral arms because the clouds are neither moving toward nor away from us, and thus have no Doppler shift from which to deduce distances.

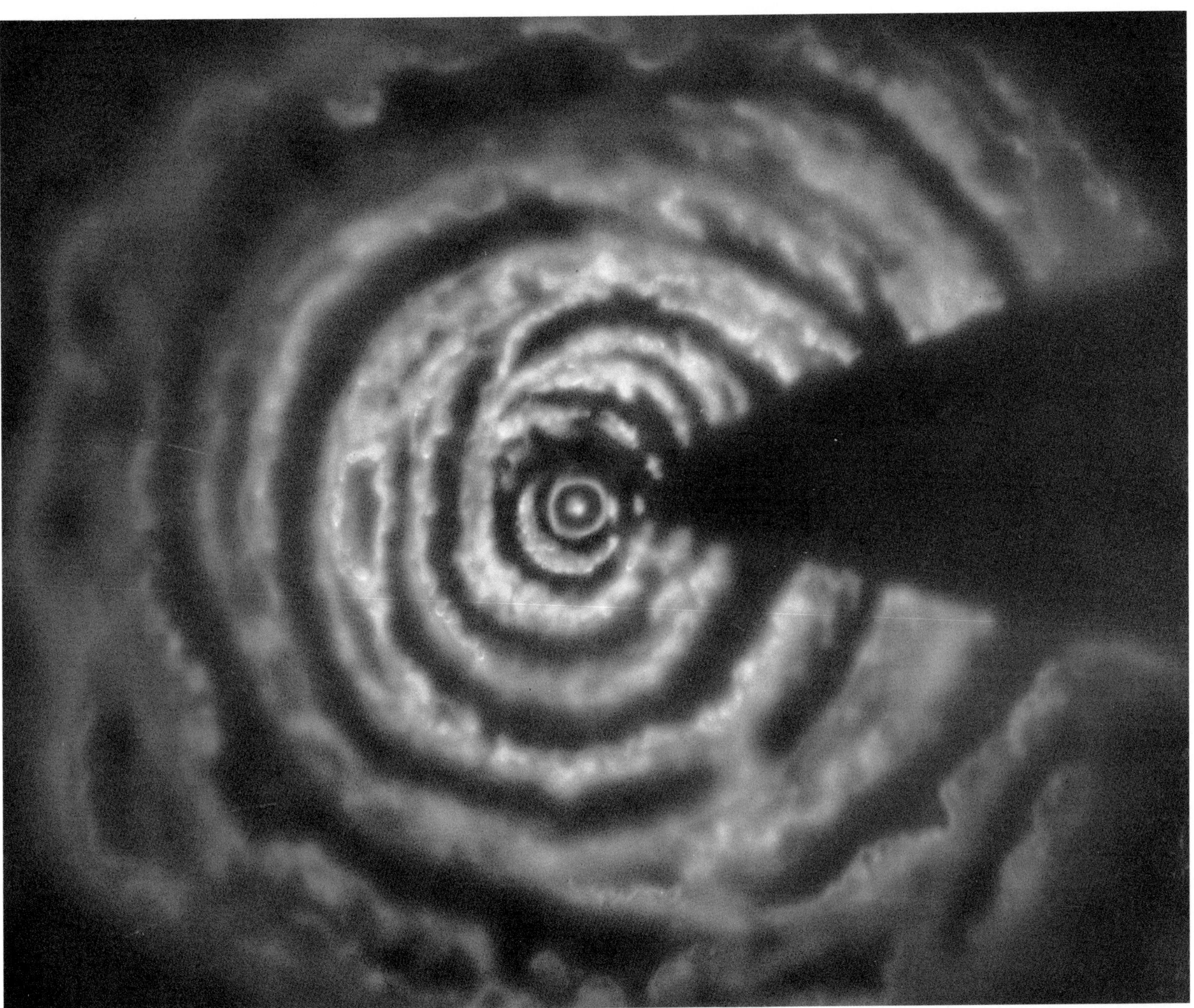

the ozone layer 60 miles above the surface of the earth.

Chemistry is going on in space as well, although it is an unusual laboratory because the temperatures and densities are so low that they cannot be duplicated on earth.

Most of the material in the universe, as we have noted, is hydrogen, and although astronomers have observed neutral and ionized hydrogen spectra in the interstellar medium, the study of emission from hydrogen *molecules* (H_2) has been accomplished only in recent years. The reason that H_2 emission was not observed before 1970 is that the radiation occurs in the far ultraviolet part of the electromagnetic spectrum, which is absorbed by the earth's atmosphere. Astronomers had to wait until satellite technology took astronomical instruments above the atmosphere and opened new windows on the universe. In 1970, scientists at the Naval Research Laboratory in Washington, D.C., successfully observed absorption lines of H_2 by using a rocket to lift an instrument package. A star, emitting all wavelengths of light, is more distant than the absorbing material. As the light passes through a cloud of gas, radiation is absorbed by atoms and molecules, and absorption lines appear at the appropriate wavelengths in the spectrum.

Hydrogen molecules dissociate easily when exposed to ultraviolet radiation, so astronomers were not surprised that H_2 was not observed in every direction. To

Table 3
Molecules Discovered Optically

Name	Chemical Notation	Year of Discovery
Methylidyne	CH	1937
Cyanogen radical	CN	1940
Methylidyne ion	CH^+	1941

Table 4
Radio Discoveries of Interstellar Molecules

Name	Chemical Notation	Year of Discovery	Wavelength
Hydroxyl radical	OH	1963	18.0 cm
Ammonia	NH_3	1968	1.3 cm
Water	H_2O	1968	1.4 cm
Formaldehyde	HCHO	1969	6.2 cm
Carbon monoxide	CO	1970	2.6 mm
Hydrogen cyanide	HCN	1970	3.4 mm
Cyanoacetylene	HC_3N	1970	3.3 cm
Methanol	CH_3OH	1970	36.0 cm
Formic acid	HCOOH	1970	18.0 cm
"X-ogen"	HCO^+	1970	3.4 mm
Formamide	NH_2HCO	1971	6.5 cm
Carbon monosulfide	CS	1971	2.0 mm
Silicon monoxide	SiO	1971	2.3 mm
Carbonyl sulfide	OCS	1971	2.7 mm
Methylcyanide	CH_3CN	1971	2.7 mm
Isocyanic acid	HNCO	1971	3.4 mm
Methylacetylene	CH_3C_2H	1971	3.5 mm
Acetaldehyde	CH_3CHO	1971	28.0 cm
Thioformaldehyde	CH_2S	1971	9.5 cm
Hydrogen isocyanide	HNC	1971	3.3 mm
Hydrogen sulfide	H_2S	1972	1.8 mm
Methanimine	CH_3N	1972	5.7 cm
Sulfur monoxide	SO	1973	3.0 mm
(No name)	N_2H^+	1974	3.2 mm
Ethynyl radical	C_2H	1974	3.4 mm

Name	Chemical Notation	Year of Discovery	Wavelength
Methylamine	CH_5N	1974	3.5 mm
Dimethyl ether	$(CH_3)_2O$	1974	9.6 mm
Ethyl alcohol	CH_3CH_2OH	1974	2.9 mm
Sulfur dioxide	SO_2	1975	3.6 mm
Silicon sulfide	SiS	1975	2.8 mm
Acrylonitrile	H_2CCHCN	1975	22.0 cm
Methyl formate	$HCOOCH_3$	1975	18.0 cm
Nitrogen sulfide (rad)	NS	1975	2.6 mm
Cyanamide	NH_2CN	1975	3.7 mm
Cyanodiacetylene	HC_5N	1976	3.0 cm
Formyl radical	HCO	1976	3.5 mm
Acetylene	C_2H_2	1976	2.4 μ
Cyanohexatryne	HC_7N	1977	3.0 cm
Cyanoethynyl radical	C_3N	1977	3.4 mm
Ketene	H_2C_2O	1977	3.0 mm
Nitroxyl	HNO	1977	3.7 mm
Ethyl cyanide	CH_3CH_2CN	1977	2.6 mm
Methane	CH_4	1977	3.9 mm
Molecular carbon	C_2	1977	1.0 μ
Butadinyl radical	C_4H	1978	3.0 mm
Cyanoethylyne	C_3N	1978	3.0 mm
Cyanooctatetra-yne	HC_9N	1978	3.0 cm
Nitric oxide	NO	1978	2.0 mm
Methyl mercaptan	CH_3SH	1979	4.0 mm
Isothiocyanic acid	HNCS	1979	3.0 mm
Ozone	O_3	1980	1.0 mm

survey the sky, Copernicus, NASA's third orbiting astronomical observatory, was launched, giving astronomers the opportunity to point the ultraviolet telescope at any direction in the heavens. No H_2 radiation was observed near hot blue stars, but in the direction of cooler red stars, more than half of the hydrogen in clouds was discovered to be in molecular form. Presumably, interstellar dust helps protect the molecules from any ultraviolet light that would break them apart. We shall see soon that this dust plays a major part in the chemistry of the interstellar medium as well as shielding the molecules once they form.

Absorption lines from a few other interstellar molecules and atoms have been observed in the optical region of the spectrum. They include cyanogen (CN), sodium (Na), calcium (Ca), and iron (Fe). Table 3 lists such molecular absorbers observed in the optical spectrum.

The most exciting discoveries of molecules have occurred with radio telescopes. Since the first detection of molecules in 1937, more than 50 other molecules have been observed in the interstellar medium.

At a wavelength of 18 centimeters, astronomers observed four spectral lines in 1963. They were attributed for a while to a molecule labeled "mysterium," reflecting its uncertain origin. Mysterium turned out to be a radical (not quite a molecule) made of one oxygen and one hydrogen atom, OH. In 1968 H_2O (water) and NH_3 (ammonia) were observed, and not long afterward, formaldehyde (CH_2O) was discovered absorbing at a wavelength of 6 centimeters. Astronomers discover the spectral line first and then identify it by researching all possible emitters that radiate at the observed wavelength. Laboratory physicists produce enormous volumes of lists of emitters and wavelengths. Sometimes more than one atom or molecule radiates at almost the same wavelength, and the scientists must make some reasonable choice among the possible emitters.

Among recent discoveries are carbon-based molecules such as formic acid (CH_2O_2), methyl alchohol (CH_4O), and even the drinking alcohol, ethyl alcohol (C_2H_6O). Table 4 shows the molecules discovered in the interstellar medium, the chemical notation of the molecule, and the year discovered. Also included in Table 4 is the wavelength of the observed radiation; although some of the first molecules were observed in centimeter radiation, most have been recorded in millimeter wavelengths by small radio telescopes, such as the one illustrated in Figure 3.19.

The Formation of the Interstellar Medium

Observations of molecules and of the distribution of the interstellar medium are very important in understanding the evolution of stars. There are two reasons that material exists in the space between the stars. First, matter was left over from the formation of the stars and galaxy. Second, old stars throw matter into space that has undergone nuclear transformations. This second component is, in a sense, recycled material.

The study of molecules is crucial in determining the physical characteristics of the interstellar medium. The density of various clouds is revealed by the presence of certain molecules. For example, after performing laboratory studies of molecule formation, we know that gas clouds composed of carbon monoxide (CO) must be at least 10 times less dense than a cloud in which formaldehyde (CH_2O) has formed.

Of great significance to scientists is that the same chemistry with which we have become familiar on

3.18 Left: *The 210-foot-diameter telescope at Parkes, Australia. The sun does not interfere with radio astronomy, so observations can be made at all hours of the day.*

3.19 Opposite: *The radio telescopes at Owens Valley, California, including this 130-foot-diameter dish, have been used to search for molecules in interstellar space. One of the molecules sought from this site is deuterium, which has been around in the universe since the big bang.*

earth is active throughout space. The fact that chemical processes are universal, as are physical laws and physical constants (the speed of light, gravitation), makes it possible for us to understand the universe. If everywhere we look, different rules applied to nature, we would have no way of developing a comprehensive description of the universe. We would not even be able to discern what the physical laws are! It is reassuring to be able to extend our local knowledge of physics and chemistry to the rest of the cosmos.

Scientists base theories of star formation, the beginning of the universe, and even the possible existence of life elsewhere on theoretical and observational science performed in laboratories, offices, and with the help today of large computers. The dust clouds in outer space are a kind of laboratory also, where densities are far lower than can be created artificially on earth, but our knowledge of molecule formation on earth must be used to explain the presence of molecules in such a remote laboratory.

Perhaps the most accepted current theory of molecule formation in interstellar space involves the direct use of dust grains as a medium where chemical processes take place. We have already suggested that the dust particles shield molecules from destructive ultraviolet radiation from stars, but now appears that they play a fundamental role as catalysts among atoms.

The hydrogen in the interstellar medium is generally considered to be leftover material from the formation of the galaxy. Hydrogen was formed during the early phases of the big bang and permeates all space. Some helium was also created, according to the big bang theory, and this explains its presence in HI and HII regions. The elements that make up the dust grains, however, are not accounted for in any big bang theory, and so we must think of mechanisms that would produce dust.

The probability that gas condensed into dust particles is rather small since the densities of HI regions are incredibly low. Scientists now think that dust forms from matter that is ejected from the surface layers of red giant stars. Dust grains probably consist of an amalgam of silicates, carbon, magnesium, aluminum, and other elements that were not created during the big bang, but rather in the nuclear fires of stars and in explosive stellar deaths. These heavy atoms condense and form dust clouds that we see obscuring more distant stars and nebulae. Indeed, there is a lot of dust in the galaxy; there is a lot of material that has been recycled through stars and returned to the interstellar medium. A type of nebulae that we will examine in Chapter 7 and Chapter 8 originates from stars at the end of their lives. This type of glowing nebula should not be confused with emission nebulae (HII regions), but as we shall see, it is vital to the formation of new stars, including our sun.

The role that the dust grains play in the formation of molecules in interstellar space is one of interaction with the surrounding gas. Dust grains are probably about 10^{-5} centimeters (0.00001 cm) across, and they are made of rocky material, including iron. Covering this hard interior may be a layer of ice covered by hydrogen atoms that have hit and stuck to the surface. Atoms come and go, colliding with the grain in interstellar space. Sometimes chemical reactions occur on the surface and OH, H_2O, and other more complex molecules may form and further interact to produce the long chains of organic molecules.

We do not observe these molecules while they are stuck to dust grains, however, and somehow they become released and float freely in space. Perhaps some ultraviolet radiation from a star supplies the molecule with enough energy to escape from the grain, but since scientists are unable to reproduce the physical conditions of the interstellar medium, we are still unclear about all the processes taking place in the cold, vacuous space among the stars.

One thing is certain: the interstellar medium eventually forms stars, and the material of stars returns to space at the end of their lives. In the next chapter, we will examine the formation of stars as they collapse from the clouds of interstellar gas and dust that provide all astronomers with beautiful shapes and colors to study, photograph, and wonder about.

3.20 *The interstellar medium is full of graceful gas clouds that are slowly collapsing to form new stars. The Trifid Nebula is one such region in the space between the stars.*

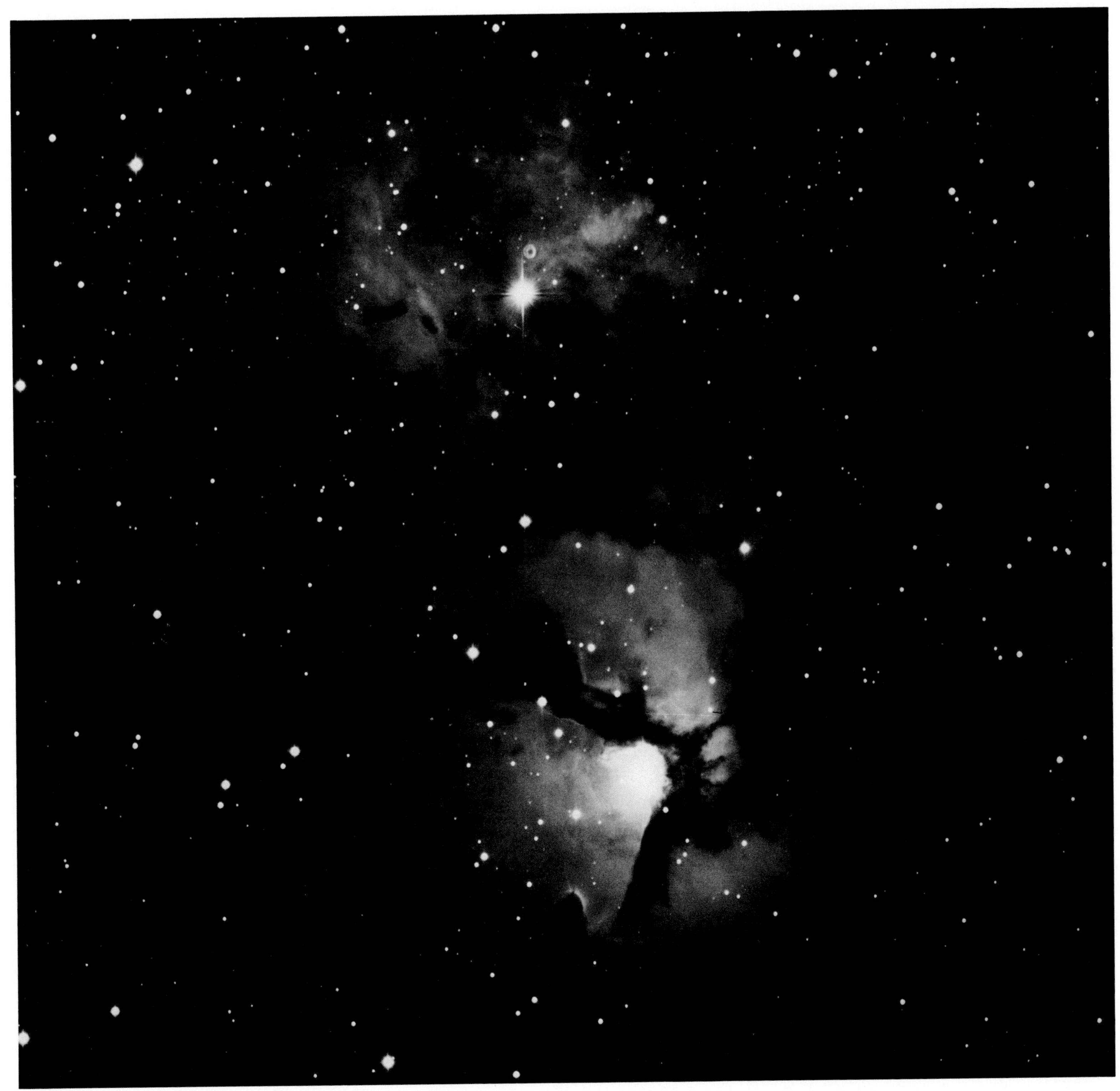

4: THE BIRTH OF STARS

Infrared Astronomy

The depths of molecular clouds have been probed by radio astronomy techniques, and scientists have determined the physical conditions in these regions of space. Collisions among molecules tend to slightly heat up these cold clouds of gas and dust so that, in addition to radio waves, they emit infrared radiation.

Infrared radiation consists of wavelengths that are longer than visible red light and shorter than radio waves. Infrared radiation is generally identified with warm objects, and several infrared devices are used on earth to measure heat radiation for a number of purposes. Infrared detectors, sometimes called sniperscopes, allow people to "see" in the dark as long as warm bodies are in view. Other devices measure heat loss from houses for analysis of energy conservation, and several satellites have used infrared cameras to record climate, vegetation, and even fish populations on earth. Figure 4.2 shows such an infrared photograph. The red regions are vegetation, and the black bodies are lakes, rivers, and bays.

Astronomers have studied stars and planets with infrared techniques for several years, but they have had to overcome some substantial obstacles in trying to observe this part of the spectrum. The major problem is that water vapor in the earth's atmosphere absorbs most incoming infrared radiation. Astronomers have used balloons to carry infrared instrument packages above the rather low-lying water vapor. The tops of tall mountains can also provide good observational bases for infrared observations, since some peaks both are higher than much of the water vapor and may be in locations of low water-vapor density. This has led to the construction of several earth-based infrared observatories. Figure 4.3 shows the Multiple Mirror Telescope (MMT) in Arizona, and the Infrared Telescope Facility on Mauna Kea, Hawaii, is pictured in Figure 4.4.

The newest technological development in astronomy has been the application of satellites as celestial observatories. For infrared studies, this has culminated with the Infrared Astronomical Satellite (IRAS), launched early in 1983, which systematically mapped the sky in infrared radiation. Figure 4.1 is a photograph of this satellite.

Astronomers have had to develop special infrared detectors for satellites, but even the ground-based telescopes require electronic recorders because only a few types of film emulsions are sensitive to infrared radiation. Infrared radiation detectors are very difficult to make, however, because they themselves give off infrared radiation if they are the least bit warm. Radiation from their own system would pollute any incoming celestial radiation, so the detectors have to be cooled to extremely low temperatures with liquid nitrogen or liquid helium.

The great contribution that infrared astronomy has made has been to serve as a probe into the dust clouds that are stellar nurseries. We now look into the interstellar medium, where stars are being born.

Building Star Models

Up to this point, we have been discussing characteristics of stars that are determined observationally by astronomers using a wide range of techniques. Observations are only half the astronomical story, however; theory must also be developed to give us a complete understanding of the physical processes going on in space. In general, observation and theory go hand in hand. A valid theory requires observational evidence as support, and observations demand a theory to give us the entire picture. The field of stellar evolution is no exception to this rule.

Astronomers observe stars in a variety of positions along stellar evolutionary paths. Some are young stars, while others are old red giants or even neutron stars at the very end of their lives. The observations, however, do not tell us stellar ages, and only through theory do we estimate the age of such diverse stellar types. In other words, we use scientific theory to calculate the changes stars undergo, and we determine from that theory what stars will look like when we perform certain observations. Thus, for example, we believe that a red giant is an old star that has undergone a specific series of changes in its lifetime.

Sometimes theory predicts certain phenomena long before a discovery is made observationally, as in the case of black holes. In the 1940s Einstein's theory of general relativity was used to predict the existence of completely collapsed, massive objects. Only in the 1970s, after considerable discussion about how such an object might be observed, did scientists first think that they had indeed discovered a black hole in space.

On other occasions astronomers have observed strange things and challenged the theorists to explain them. An example of this is the observational discovery of pulsars in 1967. Theorists had to figure out what sort of astronomical object would give off regular bursts of radio emission.

When modeling stars, astronomers have to take into account stellar sizes, luminosities, temperatures, masses, ages, and chemical composition, to name a few important characteristics. Some of these items, particularly mass and chemical composition, must be predetermined by the scientist doing the calculations, and the theoretical analysis then yields values of luminosity and temperature at different times in the model star's lifetime.

The complete marriage of astronomical observation and physical theory has provided scientists with the reasonably complete picture of stellar evolution to which the rest of this book is dedicated.

Protostars

There is little queston that stars are born out of the interstellar medium, particularly in the regions dominated by dark dust clouds. In the neighborhood of young stars, the remnant of this nebulosity is often found as a reflection nebula or even an HII region.

The large, dark nebulae that form lanes and rifts against the Milky Way and nearby emission nebulae can fragment into smaller volumes of dust, on the order of one parsec in diameter. Sometimes these appear as dark spots against nebulae, as seen in Figure 4.5. These relatively dense regions are called globules, or Bok globules, after Bart Bok, who extensively studied these objects. Perhaps globules are the true precursors of stars because they are regions that have condensed into small, dense volumes from considerably larger, more tenuous, dark nebulae.

Only the densest regions of dark nebulae can contract into globules by their internal gravitational force. Each molecule, atom, and dust grain exerts an attractive gravitational force on every other, and if the density of the cloud is high enough, say about 1,000

4.1 The Infrared Astronomical Satellite, under construction at Fokker in the Netherlands.

particles per cubic centimeter, it is likely that the cloud will start to collapse due to its own gravity. This is about the density of the thickest clouds we observe.

There has to be some mechanism that builds up the density of dark nebulae and actually starts clouds collapsing. Some intriguing theories explain the triggering of gravitational collapse, which we will examine later as we explore the past, present, and future of star formation in the galaxy.

In the meantime, regions of high density collapse to form globules. Although globules may appear as silhouettes against visible radiation from emission nebulae, they will begin to emit their own radiation during their gravitational collapse. As a globule contracts, it releases energy in the form of radio and infrared radiation, since about half of the energy released as it collapses goes into heating the cloud. Much of this heat is caused by friction from collisions between atomic particles.

As the collapse continues more heat is generated, and as the star shines more brightly the pressure from the outflowing radiation actually blows away some of the nearby gas and dust. Then we have a better view of the processes taking place.

As a cloud contracts under gravity, it begins to slowly rotate. The nebula develops angular momentum as it spins. The conservation laws state that in any physical system, energy and momentum are conserved; that is, they cannot be created or destroyed. Angular momentum in a rotating cloud, therefore, must be conserved as the nebula contracts. As the nebula grows smaller, its rate of rotation increases. This is analogous to spinning figure skaters. As skaters pull in their arms, they spin faster. So too does a collapsing cloud speed up as it collapses.

The slow rotation of the initial cloud eventually increases as a star forms to yield the rotation rate of an average star. For example, the sun rotates once in about 28 days, but the cloud from which the sun collapsed may have originally rotated with a period of thousands of years.

Late in the life of many stars, they contract further to a white dwarf about the size of the earth, or possibly even to a highly compressed neutron star a few

4.2 Left: *An infrared photograph of the Philadelphia area. Even some buildings can be individually identified. The red regions indicate vegetation, while white areas are hot and dark sections of the photograph are cool.*

4.3 Below: *The Multiple Mirror Telescope, atop Mount Hopkins in Arizona, consists of six large telescope mirrors and has been used for infrared observations of outer space.*

4.4 Left: *The Infrared Telescope Facility on Mauna Kea, Hawaii. This particular site, at about 13,000 feet above sea level, has proven valuable for infrared astronomy due to the exceptionally low water vapor content of the air.*

4.5 Below: *The Eagle Nebula in the constellation Serpens exhibits several dark globules in front of the HII region. These may someday be stars themselves.*

miles in diameter. As described by the conservation of angular momentum, such smaller stellar objects rotate much faster than normal stars. Some neutron stars spin as rapidly as three times per second.

The collapse of the dust cloud is essentially a gravitational free fall, its speed depending on the mass of the contracting cloud. The more massive the cloud, the faster the matter falls. The entire phase of gravitational collapse from dust cloud to a glowing protostar can be measured in hundreds of thousands of years, depending on the original mass of the globule.

The internal temperature of a globule may originally be less than 50° K, but after heating up while undergoing gravitational collapse, the interior may heat to 150,000° K.

The interior of the forming star collapses more rapidly than the outer portions, and the high pressure caused by increasing density and temperature becomes strong enough to prevent further collapse of the core. We call this state of balance *hydrostatic equilibrium*, and eventually the outer layers also fall into the star as it radiates into space the energy derived from the continued gravitational collapse. At this point we may refer to the glowing globule as a protostar.

Such a protostar is considerably brighter than the star it will eventually form because the diameter of the protostar is much larger than the stellar diameter to which it will contract. For example, a star that will become similar to our sun will shine some 300 times brighter at this point, according to theory.

The change of the protostar through time can be graphically illustrated on a Hertzsprung-Russell diagram, as shown in Figure 4.6. Here three stars, one as massive as the sun, one 10 times as massive as the sun, and one only one-tenth as massive, are plotted according to absolute magnitude and temperature. The values along the paths indicate the length of time in years that is required for each star to reach that phase of collapse. The early stages occur very rapidly, but as the star ages the changes occur more slowly.

Notice that in each case the star dims in magnitude as it contracts. This is strictly due to the decreasing surface area of the star. The temperature remains approximately the same at this point because the outer layers where the radiation we see comes from do not heat up at first.

The center portion of the protostar is considerably hotter than the outer layers, so heat flows out by convection. As over a heated radiator, hot gas rises into cooler regions. This outflow of energy is necessary for the star to be stable, and the convective flow ensures that the temperature is just right at every point so that the star neither collapses completely nor explodes. A protostar, then, is in thermal balance because of what is called *convective equilibrium*.

As energy is carried out of the protostar from the hot center, the pressure and temperature in the core

4.6 The Hertzsprung-Russell diagram for three stars in formation. As they collapse, the stars move to the left as they heat up, although their luminosity does not appreciably change.

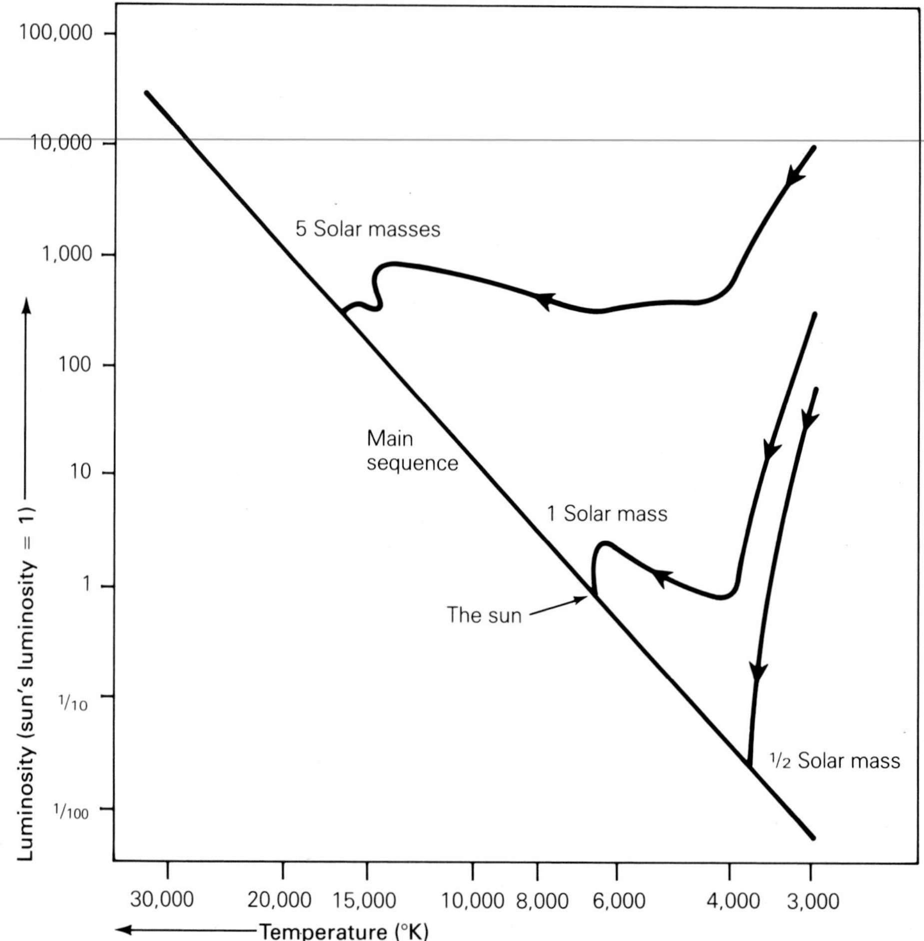

fall, and the great weight of the outer layers compresses the center to even greater density. The continual contraction of the star keeps energy flowing outward and of course leads to even higher temperatures and pressures in the stellar interior than existed before convective equilibrium was achieved.

At high temperatures and pressures, however, blobs of hot gas do not rise very efficiently from the inside, so convection cannot contribute substantially to the outflow of energy once the star's core reaches several hundred thousand degrees. The protostar requires another mechanism to take energy away from the center. It uses radiation.

When radiation becomes the dominant carrier of energy outward from the interior of a protostar, we say that *radiative equilibrium* has been achieved. Eventually most of the protostar's layers are in radiative equilibrium, and as the protostar continues to collapse, interior temperatures reach millions of degrees.

On H-R diagram, the continual contraction is seen throughout the drop in luminosity. When radiative equilibrium is achieved, however, the outer layers start to heat up and the observed temperature of the protostar increases. This is seen in the evolution to the left of the H-R diagram. Temperature and spectral type increase to the left. The slight increase in intensity is caused by the outer layers radiating more energy as they heat up.

A Star Is Born

When the contracting cloud of gas and dust has become dense enough and hot enough for radiative equilibrium to provide the energy outflow, the final event in star formation is at hand. When the temperature of the core is about 4 million° K, hydrogen nuclei are moving so rapidly that, when they collide, they stick together. We call this process *nuclear fusion*. The fusion of elements in stars will be discussed thoroughly in Chapter 5, but the important point for the evolution of protostars is that once fusion occurs, the star no longer needs gravitational energy to maintain the high internal temperatures. Fusion supplies the star's energy needs, and contraction stops. The star has reached the main sequence on the H-R diagram, and here it will stay most of its life.

Our understanding of the early stages of stellar evolution just discussed is the result of many years of mathematical and physical analyses of a simple question: What happens if a large cloud of gas collapses? So complex are the processes going on that scientists use large computers to do the calculations for them. The person who first calculated the evolutionary paths of newborn stars was Chushiro Hayashi in the 1960s, and the paths plotted on the H-R diagram are called Hayashi tracks. Additional work was done in 1969 by Richard B. Larson.

The fact that all newborn stars end up on the main sequence defines the main sequence for us. It is the relationship between luminosity and spectral type for hydrogen-burning stars. As we shall see in later chapters, not until stars have exhausted their hydrogen do they evolve away from the main sequence. Also, the most massive stars are the brightest and the hottest. This agrees with the mass-luminosity relationship described in Chapter 1. More massive stars are bigger, so they shine more brightly than less massive stars.

From theory, we also derive the duration of the early phases of stellar evolution as well as the temperatures and luminosities reached during this period. A star like the sun, of one solar mass, takes about 30 million years to reach the main sequence. A star 10 times as massive as the sun requires only 300,000 years to begin hydrogen burning, and a star one tenth as massive takes more than a billion years to evolve. The more massive a star is, the faster it evolves throughout its life.

Stellar Nurseries

The Hayashi tracks and the general outline of stellar birth are derived from theory, but observations support much of the computations. Of course we are unable to observe an individual protostar through its evolution, but astronomers have discovered many examples of each phase of evolution. HII regions throughout the galaxy (Figures 4.7 and 4.8, for example) fluoresce because of young main-sequence stars. Other regions of space contain infrared objects that are imbedded in globules and dust clouds. These are protostars, and elsewhere, large, cold dust clouds have yet to begin to collapse. Let us look at one specific region of our galaxy, where fortunately for scientists all of the early stages of stellar evolution are taking place: the Orion Nebula.

A Case Study: The Great Nebula in Orion

One of the most interesting nebulae in the entire galaxy is the Orion Nebula (Figure 4.9), which lies only 500 parsecs from our sun. Its visibility and proximity have made it one of the most studied objects in the heavens since its telescopic identification in 1611.

In visible light, the Orion Nebula is a spectacular cloud of glowing gas. It is an HII region that derives its energy from a small cluster of four young stars within it. The stars, called the Trapezium, are hot and emit plenty of ultraviolet radiation that ionizes the surrounding hydrogen gas. These stars are only about 100,000 years old. Figure 4.10 shows the Trapezium stars vividly.

In the radio section of the electromagnetic spectrum, observations reveal a limited region of space that contains a molecular cloud. The molecular cloud is on the far side of the emission nebular from us, but radio waves pass through the HII regions and we can detect them. Most of the molecular cloud has a density of about 1,000 particles per cubic centimeter, but the contours represent increasing density inward, so the center of the molecular cloud may even have a density of a million particles per cubic centimeter. This is so dense that gravitational collapse may begin to form new stars. Although there is not much dust observed in the region, the dust grains are dense enough to

4.7 Opposite page left: *The Lagoon Nebula glows because of the bright star located to the right of the dark dust lane. Several infrared sources have been detected here, pointing toward star formation.*

4.8 *The Omega Nebula in Sagittarius* (opposite page below left)

4.9 *The Great Nebula* (above right) *in Orion is a stellar nursery where four young stars are exciting the glowing HII region.*

4.10 *The Trapezium is the group of four stars at the heart of the Orion Nebula.*

protect the molecules from destructive ultraviolet radiation. It seems, in fact, that most of the dust of the original dark cloud that formed in this region was blown away by "stellar winds," which are the continuous outflow of atomic particles from the surface layers of a star. The sun has such a wind, and hot young stars blow up a storm that clears the region of dust.

The Orion Nebula is particularly interesting when observed in infrared radiation. One of the brightest infrared regions in the sky coincides with the densest part of the molecular cloud. It is called the Becklin-Neugebauer object, after the two astronomers who identified it. For several years, the B-N object was considered a protostar about to turn to nuclear fusion for energy, but in 1978 it was determined that the object is already a star, although a very young one, in the hydrogen-burning stage. The B-N object appears bright in the infrared because its light is reddened by the dense, dark nebula around it. Other objects nearby are also strong emitters of infrared light; they are probably protostars forming from the same nebula that fragmented and collapsed.

The Orion Nebula shows a diversity of objects in different phases of stellar evolution in one nursery. Much more research will be done on this region, including infrared studies from the Infrared Astronomical Satellite. The resolution of this telescope revealed many small regions where stars are being born.

Remnants of the Nebula

Not all of the material in an interstellar nebula collapses to form a star. Often, some of the material is still visible reflecting light from a young star. This is called a reflection nebula. Eventually, the radiation and outflowing gas from a star blow the remnant of the nebula away into space.

Planetary systems may also form from the material that does not go into building stars. Fragmenting and collapsing into even smaller regions, planets and other solar system debris can condense from a stellar nebula. Indirect observations of a couple of stars may suggest the presence of planets, and recently the Infrared Astronomy Satellite discovered an interesting region around the bright summer star Vega. IRAS recorded the existence of warm material extending some 7 billion miles from the star. This matter may consist of a few planets or a large cloud of dust that may someday form a solar system.

The Youngest Stars

When nuclear reactions take over as the primary energy source in a star's core, there is a slight period of adjustment as thermal and hydrostatic equilibrium restabilize. This causes the dip in the Hayashi tracks of Figure 4.8 just before the star reaches the main sequence. Although not yet stable, these objects *are* stars that are burning nuclear fuel in their centers. Observationally, they sometimes act rather strangely, changing brightness and spectral type as they settle onto the main sequence. These young stars can be considered variable stars, some of which have been described already in Chapter 2.

For example, T Tauri stars are observed in stellar associations, as one would expect of stars born of the same interstellar cloud. T Tauri stars are known to emit in the infrared, which suggests reddening by the dark cloud from which the star formed.

In the next chapter, we will look at stars that have settled down upon reaching the main sequence on an H-R diagram. The Pleiades (Figure 2.7) are very young, main-sequence stars. The sun is older than the Pleiades, and other main-sequence stars are even older than the sun, but they all have one thing in common—they burn hydrogen in their cores.

4.11 The Omega Nebula, also known as M8, is a prime example of a region where hot young stars have recently formed and where protostars are buried in an HII region.

5: STARS IN THE PRIME OF LIFE

Anatomy of a Star

Astronomers basically divide a star into two parts, its interior and its atmosphere. The interior of a star consists of the central core and overlying layers, where energy is transported outward. The stellar atmosphere consists of the visible top layers of a star and of the region that extends into space and consists of tenuous gas visible only with certain special techniques.

Stars become stable once they satisfy the conditions of hydrostatic equilibrium. The collapse of the protostar is completely halted once the nuclear fires ignite in the stellar core. This occurs when the outer layers are held up by the outflow of energy and by the pressure of the gas. This balance between gravity pulling inward and pressure pushing out keeps a star on the main sequence.

The Stellar Atmosphere

For the most part, the atmosphere of a star is simply defined as the region that we can see, whether in ultraviolet, visible, X-ray, radio, or infrared light. Figure 5.2 is a cutaway illustration of the outer layers of an average star on the main sequence. The stellar atmosphere is divided into three major sections: the *photosphere,* the *chromosphere,* and the *corona.*

The photosphere is the region of a star that emits the light we see on a clear night. The word *photosphere* is derived from the Greek word for light, *photos.* The photosphere is the coolest region of a star, since the temperature decreases from the stellar core to this visible layer. In Chapter 1, we mentioned that the color of a star is related to the temperature of the layers that emit the light we see. These layers are the photosphere, and the cooler the photosphere, the redder the spectral distribution of the star; conversely, the hotter the photosphere, the bluer the star appears in the night sky. We must remember that we see *only* the outer layers of a star—there is no way to observe a stellar interior directly. Stellar photospheres have a graduated temperature. The center of a star exists at millions of degrees, but the photosphere can get as low as 4,000° K. The temperature decreases to this value and then begins to increase into the outermost layers.

For the most part, the photosphere of a star emits a

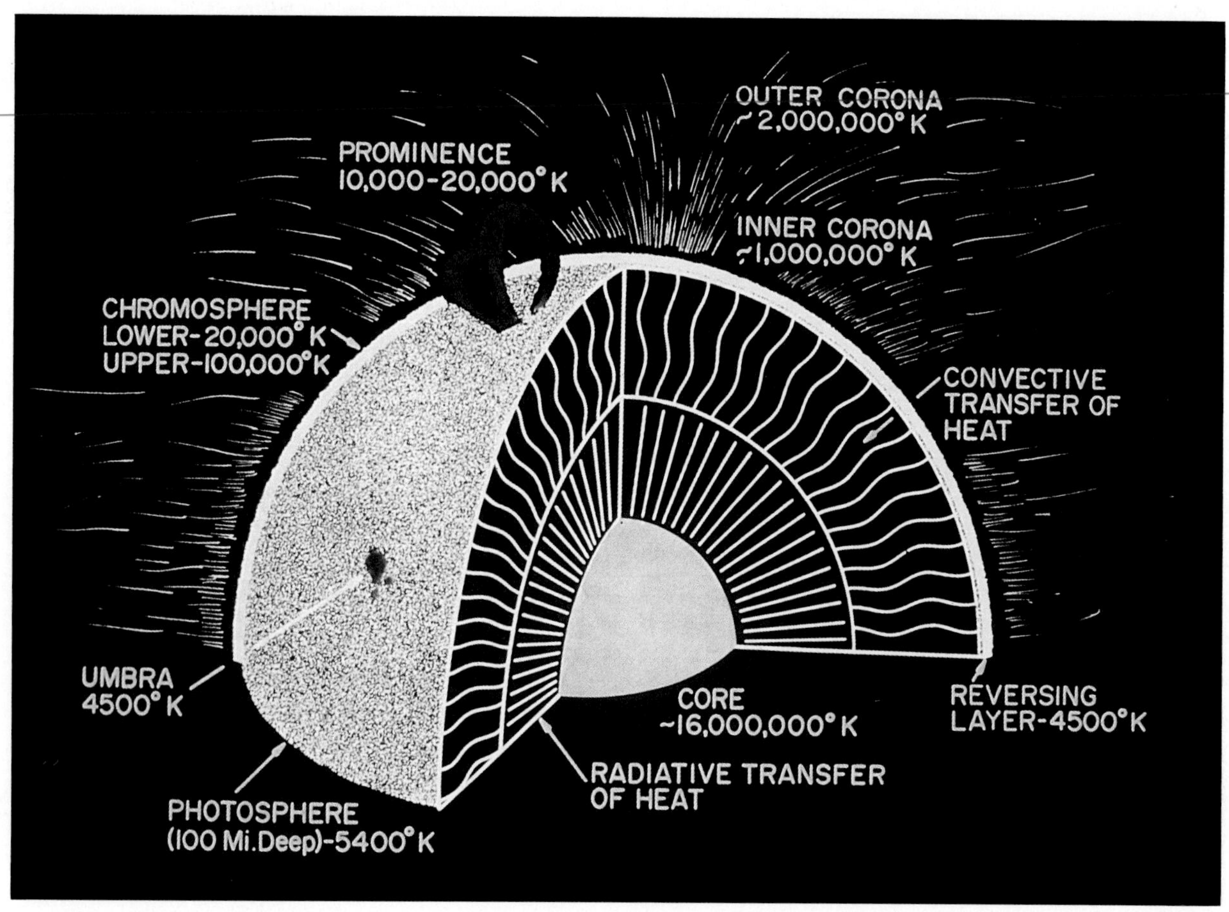

5.1 A stellar interior and atmosphere are informally defined by the hidden inner layers and the visible outer layers.

continuous spectrum, but the temperature of the photosphere begins to rise near the outer edge and the density continues to decrease, so absorption lines form both in the coolest regions and in the overlying chromosphere. We see these absorption lines in all stellar spectra. The formation of spectral lines is primarily due to the changing temperature throughout the emitting layers of gas. Cooler layers of gas absorb radiation passing through them, and these layers of cooler absorbing material have been called historically the reversing layers.

The temperature of the region that emits the continuous spectrum varies from star to star depending on its mass during formation, but some cool stars have photospheres with a temperature as low as 4,000° K, while others may only get as low as 50,000° K.

Because the detailed characteristics of the temperature and density gradients in a stellar photosphere are responsible for the formation of spectral lines, a careful analysis of absorption lines can yield information about the structure of the star. As discussed in Chapter 1, spectral lines are fingerprints of the specific chemical elements that form them. Thus, astronomers identify the source of lines in a stellar spectrum and recognize what elements are present. This information helps to determine the temperature changes in the photosphere, because atoms can absorb radiation only if the temperatures are appropriate to the makeup of each individual element. This is why stars can be classified according to spectral type, which has a direct correlation to stellar temperature.

The detailed shape of a spectral line also yields valuable information about the physical conditions in each layer of the photosphere. Although all absorption lines are dark, some are darker than others, and some are broad and some are narrow. This sort of information tells us just how many atoms are absorbing radiation, so in addition to the temperature and chemical abundances in a star, we can learn how many atoms are in the star's atmosphere. The more atoms that are

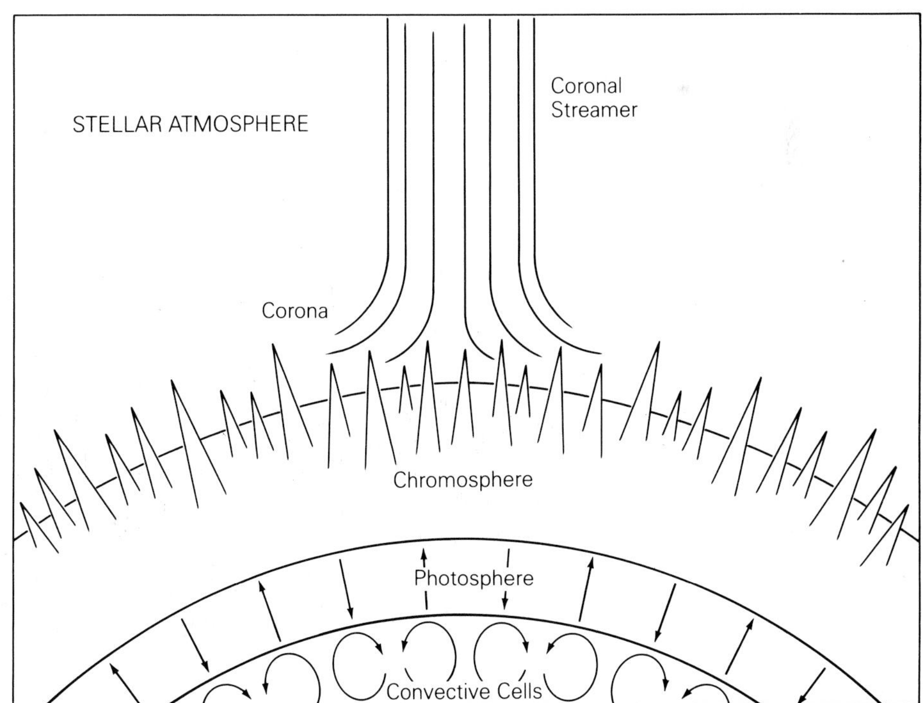

5.2 *The photosphere, chromosphere, and corona are schematically displayed in this cross-section of a stellar atmosphere.*

5.3 Opposite page: *All of the light from the individual stars in this photograph and the combined light of stars in the distant galaxy are visible because light from their photospheres escapes and travels through space.*

absorbing radiation, the darker the spectral line will be. In this way we can get a feeling for the density of a star's outer layers.

Other factors affect the way a stellar spectrum appears, including magnetic fields, pressure, and other overlying layers of gas. To account for all the possible processes going on, astronomers have developed a rigorous mathematical framework to calculate what the spectra we are observing should look like. This field is called *radiative transfer*. The problems are extremely complex and require large computers to handle the atomic data and physical characteristics of the star being modeled. A spectrum that has been computed can be readily compared to an observed spectrum. When a reasonable match between the two is made, astronomers get some insight from the model about the real nature of a stellar atmosphere.

Stellar Chromospheres and Coronae

The temperature of a star's outer layers increases above the photosphere into a region called the chromosphere. The chromosphere (*chromos* is Greek for color) of a star is a thin region in between the cool photosphere and the very hot corona. A chromosphere is not detectable with the naked eye because it is a very narrow region of the star that does not emit much light. Spectroscopic analysis of hydrogen absorption lines in a star's spectrum is the only clue we have that stellar chromospheres exist. (We can see the chromosphere of the sun with special filters and during solar eclipses, but as we shall see in Chapter 6, the sun is unique because we can see details on the surface.)

Not every star has a chromosphere; only cool stars of spectral types G, K, and M seem to have one at all. The chromosphere of our sun appears as a brilliant red sliver at the solar edge just before it is covered up during a solar eclipse. It is hydrogen that is emitting very strongly in red light. In Chapter 6 we will more closely examine the solar chromosphere and the rest of the sun's atmosphere.

The corona of a star is a tenuous, usually invisible layer extending from the top of the chromosphere millions of miles into space. A corona consists of dust and gas, much of which has escaped from the star's chromosphere. These particles include electrons and the nuclei of atoms and are streaming into space at thou-

5.4 *The color of stars depends on the temperature of the photosphere that is emitting the radiation.*

sands of miles per hour. This stellar wind of atomic particles blows away the dust and gas left over from the star's early formation.

Coronae are very hot, and scientists have proposed that shock waves formed in the atmosphere below move into the corona and dissipate their energy as they encounter regions of low density. This energy then goes into heating the corona to several million degrees Kelvin.

There are no real boundaries between the different sections of a stellar atmosphere. The terms *photosphere*, *chromosphere*, and *corona* generally locate certain regions of a stellar atmosphere, but in all stars the temperature drops to a minimum value in the photosphere, begins to rise and reaches a maximum in the corona. Figure 5.5 graphs the temperature distribution for two stars, one a hot star of spectral type B and the other a cool star like the sun, type G.

Although most of the energy in the outer layers escapes into space in the form of radiation, there is turbulence in stellar atmospheres that is caused by the convection of heat outward from the inside. As heat works its way out from a star's center, some regions of the atmosphere will get hotter than others. This causes a bubbling at the surface reminiscent of a pot of boiling soup. We see this clearly on the sun, and scientists assume that convection gives the surface of a star a mottled, turbulent appearance.

The Stellar Interior

We can divide the interior of a star into three basic regions. They are the *convective zone*, the *radiative zone*, and the *core*.

As we move into a star from its photosphere, we first encounter a region of great turbulence where energy is being transported outward by convection. Hot cells of gas are rising into cooler regions and depositing their heat at the base of the photosphere. Meanwhile, cool globs of gas fall inward, where they are reheated and rise again cyclically. Figure 5.7 illustrates the continual turbulence of the convective zone. In cool stars convection is the primary process by which energy is carried from the stellar core to the layers we see.

Beneath the convective zone is a very dense, hot region of a star where energy is transported in the form of radiation. Convection does not work well in

5.5 Below left: *The temperature as a function of height in two stellar atmospheres. The minimum temperatures reached in the photospheres are different by a factor of 10.*

5.6 Below right: *A schematic cross-section of a stellar interior labeling the core, the radiative zone, and the convective zone. Energy slowly works its way out to the stellar atmosphere, as it is transported by radiative processes and then convection.*

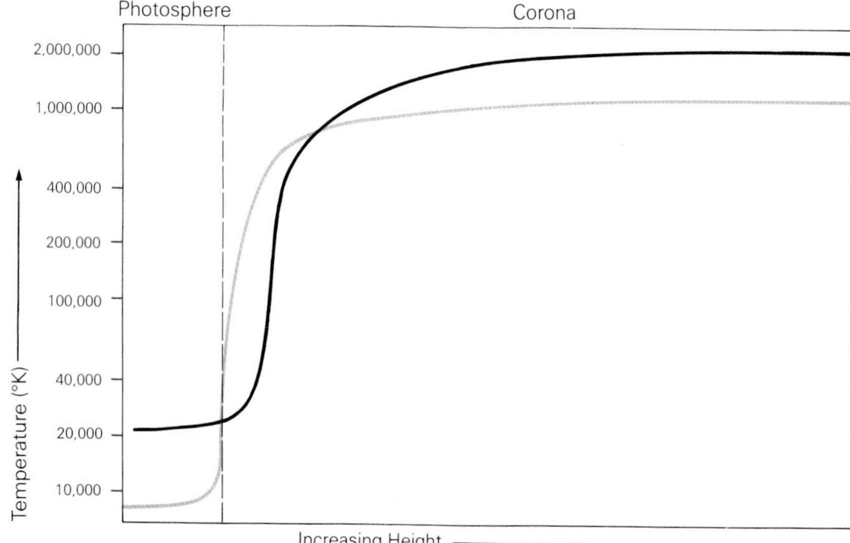

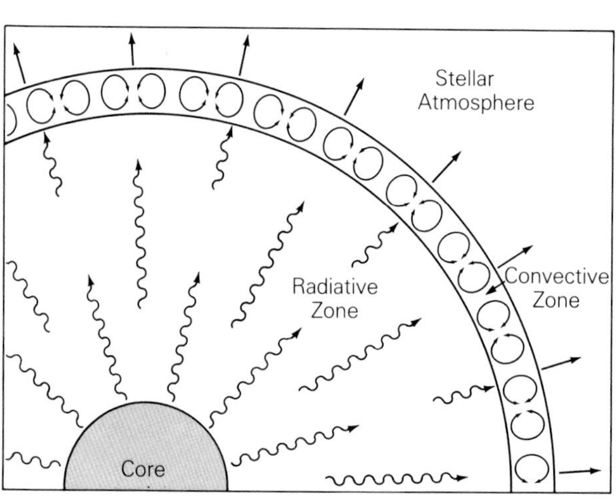

this region because of the high density and fairly constant temperature, so the best way that energy can work its way out is in the form of radiation that is continuously emitted and absorbed and then reemitted throughout this radiative zone.

The size of the convective zone and the radiative zone depends on the mass of the star—some very massive giant stars have a very narrow convective region. Energy, then, is transported in supermassive stars primarily by radiative processes.

The stellar core is where the energy that heats the star is generated. For decades in the early part of this century, scientists believed that the heat of a star was derived directly from the conversion of the energy of contraction into thermal energy. In other words, stars were thought to reach hydrostatic equilibrium only by continuing to gradually contract to heat their interiors. Stars could shine for only a few million years at most by this process, however, and we know the sun is older than even a few billion years since we have found rocks on earth at least 2 billion years old.

Some other source of energy must be supplying stars with heat for billions of years at a time. In the 1930s, Hans Bethe suggested that series of nuclear reactions are perhaps occurring in the hot, dense regions of an interior. Einstein had formulated his famous equation $E = mc^2$ several years before. E is energy, m is mass, and c is the speed of light; the equation relates energy to mass. The fact that during nuclear reactions a small amount of mass is converted into a large amount of energy, following $E = mc^2$, helped solve the question of where stars get the energy to shine. Before we examine the specific nuclear reactions occurring in stars, we should first take a look at atoms and the notation scientists use in describing them.

Atoms

An atom consists of a central nucleus with electrons rapidly orbiting it. Most of an atom is empty space because the nucleus and electrons are very small. Most of the mass of an atom is contained in the nucleus.

The nucleus of an atom is made up of constituent particles. Recent research in atomic physics has uncovered many new ones. For our discussion here, we need worry only about neutrons and protons, and not *their* building blocks. Table 5 lists the basic physical properties of electrons, protons, and neutrons. For an atom to be electrically neutral, it must contain an equal number of negatively charged electrons and positively

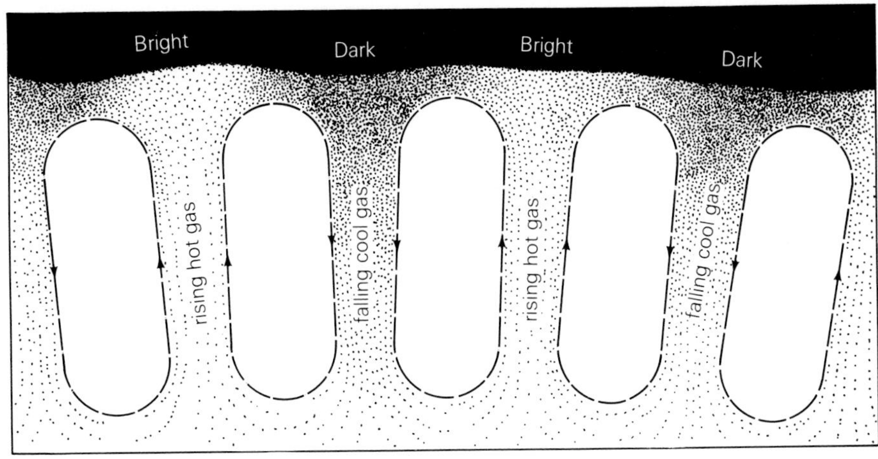

5.7 The convective zone transports energy outward by large-scale motions of volumes of gas that rise and fall like currents in the stellar interior.

charged protons. Electrons are bound to the nucleus by electric forces, but the neutrons and protons are held together in the nucleus by what physicists call the strong force. When enough energy is supplied to a neutral atom, either by collision with another particle or in the form of radiation, an electron can be torn away from the nucleus. The remaining atom, which now has one less electron to balance the positive charge of protons, ends up with a net positive charge. It is called an ion. The stellar core is so hot that all of the electrons are stripped away, and only nuclei with positive charges remain.

Hydrogen nuclei consist of one proton only. It is possible for neutrons to become bound to the proton, creating a slightly heavier version of the same element, which is called an isotope. When one neutron is bound to the nucleus with the proton, the atom is called deuterium; if two neutrons are in the nucleus, the isotope is called tritium. Scientists use the following notation to represent atoms and their isotopes: a subscript before the alphabetic symbol for the element indicates the number of protons in the nucleus, and the superscript after the symbol is the total number of particles in the nucleus. For example, normal hydrogen is written $_1H^1$, while deuterium is written $_1H^2$ because its added neutron increases the total number of particles in the nucleus from one to two.

A normal helium nucleus has two protons and two neutrons, so its notation is $_2He^4$. Much rarer is the isotope $_2He^3$, which is a helium nucleus with only one neutron. Note that the difference between hydrogen and helium is really the number of protons, since neutrons can be added or subtracted to form isotopes of the same element. The addition of protons, however, changes the atom completely to another element.

With this notation, physicists can describe all elements and their isotopes. The symbol for normal carbon is $_6C^{12}$, with six protons and six neutrons, and we might write normal plutonium as $_{94}Pu^{188}$. We are now prepared to discuss the nuclear reactions that lead to energy production in stars.

Stellar Energy Cycles

The great temperatures and densities in the center of stars are high enough for nuclear fusion to take place. The primary fusion process in stars is the fusing of hydrogen atoms into helium with the release of some energy. Stars have so much hydrogen that this process can fuel them for all of their lives on the main sequence. In general, the cores of stars fuse four hydrogen atoms into one helium atom. The mass of the resulting helium atom is slightly less than the total mass of the four hydrogen atoms that made it, and this

Table 5
Masses of Atomic Particles

Proton	$m_p = 1.6726 \times 10^{-24}$ grams
Electron	$m_e = 9.1096 \times 10^{-28}$ grams
Neutron	$m_n = 1.6749 \times 10^{-24}$ grams
Hydrogen atom	$m_H = 1.6735 \times 10^{-24}$ grams

5.8 *An artist's conception of an atom, with its nucleus being orbited by electrons.*

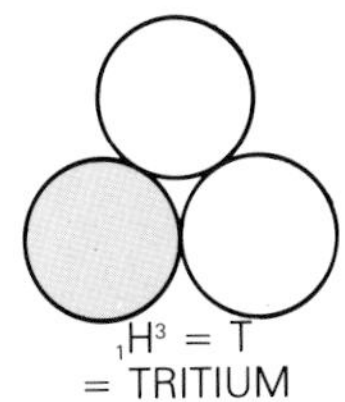

5.9 *Model atoms of hydrogen and its two isotopes, deuterium and tritium. The only difference among these atoms is the number of neutrons in the nucleus. The subscript in each case is the number 1, which indicates the number of protons. The superscript is the total number of protons and neutrons.*

"missing" mass has been transformed into energy according to Einstein's equation $E = mc^2$. Although the missing mass is a very small number, the speed of light squared (c^2) is enormous, so the energy from fusion reactions is sufficient to give a star all the power it requires for millions or even billions of years.

Three major chains of reactions occur in the center of stars. The dominance of each depends on the temperature at the core of individual stars. Let us look at stars with relatively cool centers, say less than 15 million° K, such as the sun.

The Proton-Proton Cycle

If the central temperature of a star is less than about 15 million° K, the simplest nuclear fusion reactions occur, which convert hydrogen into helium. Scientists call this the proton-proton reaction, often referred to as a cycle because some hydrogen atoms that are used in the chain are returned to the stellar interior at the end of the reaction to be reused later.

Figure 5.10 shows the proton-proton reaction in schematic form using the notation atomic physicists have developed. The first phase of this reaction requires two hydrogen nuclei (protons) to fuse, forming a deuterium nucleus, a neutrino (written as γ), and a positron (a particle that is similar to an electron in every way except that it has a positive charge). Neutrinos are essentially massless bits of energy that were first suggested theoretically and later experimentally discovered. They travel at the speed of light and have a very low probability of interacting with matter. The positron will not last long, for once it collides with its opposite particle, an electron, they annihilate each other and emit gamma radiation.

Once the deuterium nuclei are formed by two of the proton reactions, a deuterium nucleus fuses with another proton to form an isotope of helium. Energy is released as high-energy photons of light, and the last stage requires the two helium isotopes to fuse to produce normal helium ($_2He^4$) and two protons, which can complete the cycle by starting the reaction again.

Six hydrogen atoms were put into the cycle: two emerged, as did the nucleus of ordinary helium. As mentioned earlier, the net mass of four hydrogen nuclei is slightly greater than the mass of the helium nucleus,

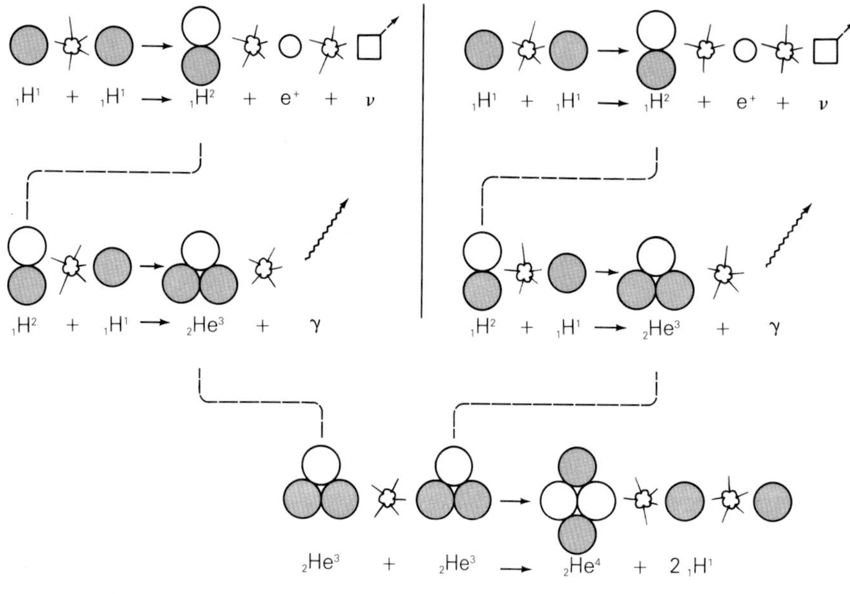

5.10 A diagram of the proton-proton cycle. The symbols are as follows: $_1H^1$ is a proton (hydrogen nucleus), $_1H^2$ is a deuterium nucleus, $_2He^3$ is a helium isotope, and $_2He^4$ is an ordinary helium nucleus. The wiggly arrows indicate the emission of radiation; the γ stands for neutrino, the e+ is a positron.

so this small fraction of mass is converted to energy along the way. The helium nucleus will remain in the stellar core until the hydrogen is used up in nuclear reactions.

The Carbon Cycle

A more complex chain of nuclear reactions is the dominant energy source in stars with central temperature ranging from 15 million° K to about 100 million° K. As in the proton-proton cycle, the carbon cycle has the net result of turning four hydrogen nuclei into a helium nucleus, but this time several nuclei of other elements are involved.

Figure 5.11 shows the schematic of the carbon cycle, which begins with the fusion of a proton with a carbon nucleus. Radiation and neutrinos are released at various stages, as well as ordinary nuclei and isotopes of carbon, nitrogen, and oxygen. At the end, helium is the result, as it was in the proton-proton chain, but this time a carbon nucleus is left that will be used in the beginning of the next chain of carbon-cycle reactions. This cycle could also begin at the intermediate stages with nitrogen or oxygen, so the entire cycle has been called the carbon-nitrogen-oxygen cycle.

The Triple Alpha Process

Figure 5.12 displays the triple alpha process, which is the dominant energy-generating process in stars with central temperatures higher than 100 million° K. The nucleus of a helium atom is called an alpha particle, and three helium nuclei go into making a normal carbon nucleus. First, two alpha particles fuse to make a nucleus of beryllium, then the third alpha particle combines with the beryllium to make a carbon nucleus.

These three basic nuclear fusion cycles play a role in the life of a star even though they come into play at different temperatures. How can one star have so many different temperatures in the core? Because stars change. We will examine what happens to stars at the

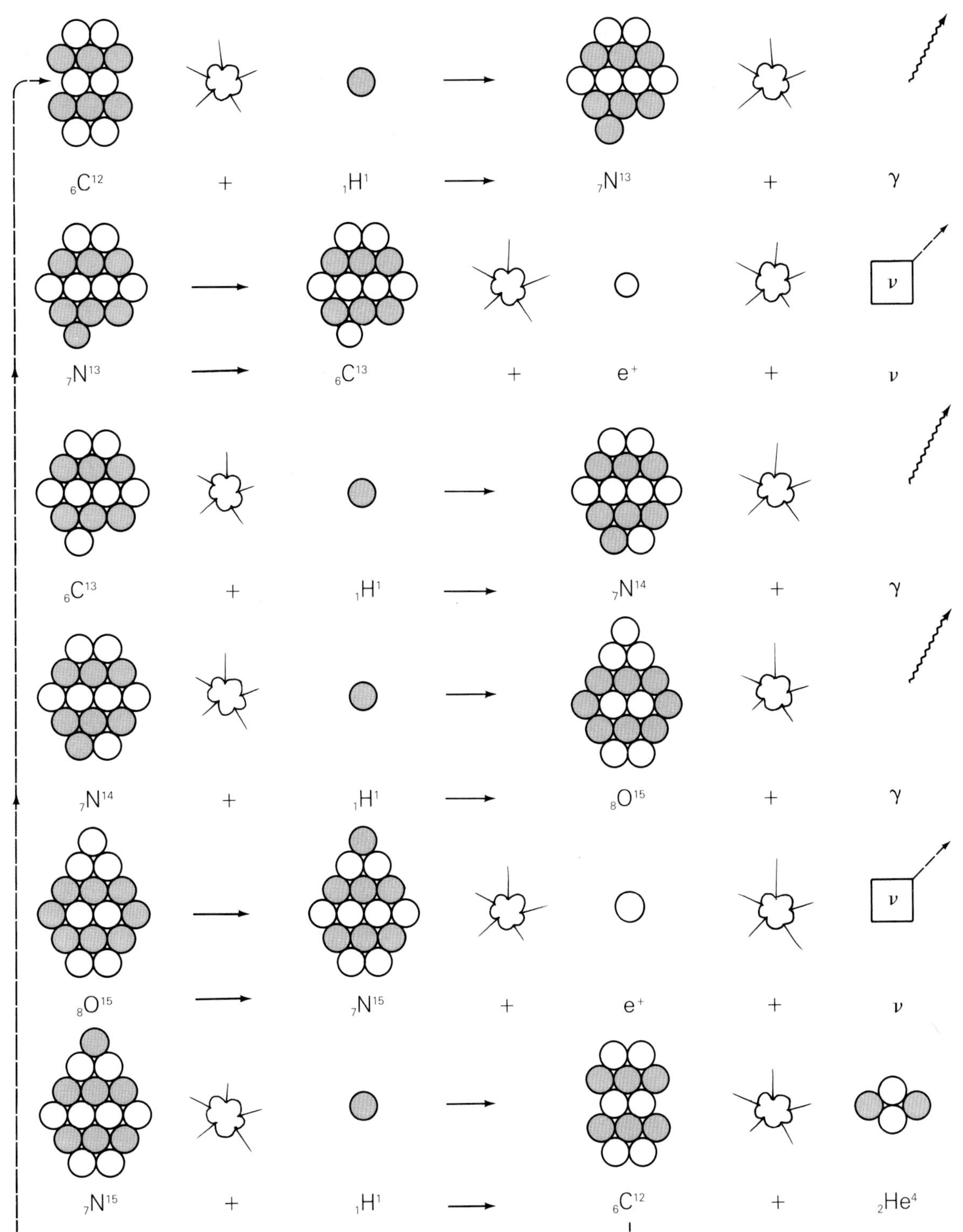

5.11 The carbon cycle. Oxygen and nitrogen are also used in this reaction. As with the proton-proton cycle, helium is the end product.

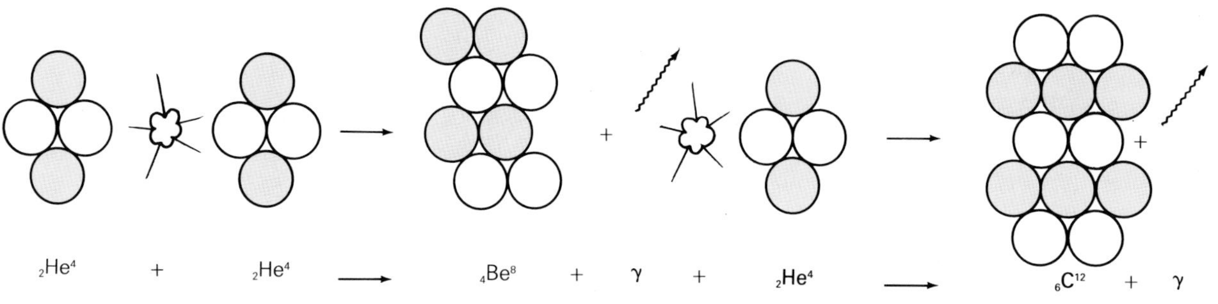

5.12 The triple alpha process, with carbon as its product, uses helium nuclei in the fusion process.

end of their lives in Chapters 7, 8, and 9, but for now we must realize that the temperature in a star changes as its hydrogen fuel expires. As the core becomes hotter due to the star's gravity, the helium that has accumulated is converted into carbon by the triple alpha process.

As more and more carbon forms, it becomes likely that a carbon nucleus will fuse with a helium nucleus to form an oxygen nucleus. Again, much energy is carried off from this reaction in the form of gamma radiation.

Such fusion reactions continue to form new elements, so new types of reactions take place. For example, a collision between two oxygen atoms may form isotopes of silicon or phosphorus with the release of neutrinos or protons. Carbon and oxygen can fuse to form silicon, and of course the carbon-nitrogen-oxygen cycle uses oxygen during its reactions.

The proton-proton chain and the carbon cycle both have the same result, the conversion of hydrogen into helium with the release of energy. The proton-proton reaction probably was the primary energy source for stars in the young universe, because the big bang produced hydrogen and some helium but none of the heavier elements. We will see in later chapters that stars that have formed heavier elements in nuclear reactions often eject these atoms in explosions at the end of their lives. Thus, the interstellar medium is now full of heavier elements, which someday will collapse to form new stars. The sun is such a second-generation star, and we can see heavy elements, such as oxygen, carbon, calcium, and iron, in its spectrum. When astronomers learned that carbon could be created during a star's explosive end, they realized that the carbon cycle can be a primary energy source provided the star has a very hot core and is made from dust and gas that has been enriched with carbon by dying stars.

Figure 5.13 compares the energy production of the proton-proton cycle with that of the carbon cycle. The two cycles produce equivalent amounts of energy at about 16 million° K, but at lower or higher temperatures, one cycle dominates.

The formation of heavy atoms in stars takes place in stages, with the end product of each cycle of nuclear reaction building up as an ash of the nuclear fires. For example, helium is accumulating in the core of the sun, and the actual hydrogen burning takes place in the thin shell around the core. Successive stages of a star's energy production build up layers of atomic ash, and these reactions continue until iron is formed and fills the core, as seen in Figure 5.15. This is only true, however, for the most massive stars that begin their lives with very high central temperatures. The sun will never convert carbon into oxygen because it is not massive enough.

Once the core of a star is pure iron, the internal temperature of the evolving star may be as high as 5 billion° K. The formation of iron is the last stage of nucleosynthesis that gives off energy to heat the star. After the core is iron and no more energy is being supplied to the star, it will continue to shine because of gravitational collapse. The outer layers are entirely supported by the pressure of the gas. Massive stars can continually form new elements heavier than iron by a process called *neutron capture*.

Neutrons become abundant in a stellar interior after helium burning has created carbon and other metals. The density of a stellar interior is so high that free neutrons are crushed into iron atoms, building successively heavier elements. This addition of neutrons alters the type of atomic species existing in a stellar core. Nucleosynthesis by neutron capture does not release energy to support the star's continued stability, and as we shall see in Chapter 8, massive stars die explosive deaths when the energy sources are snuffed out.

5.14 Hydrogen is turned into helium, which fills the stellar core of a main-sequence star.

Abundances of the Elements

Much of the theory of stellar nucleosynthesis centers on the observed abundances of the chemical elements. Hydrogen makes up about 92 percent of all the atoms

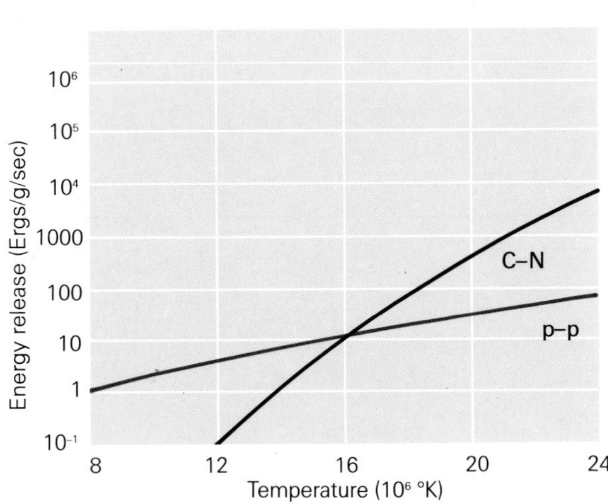

5.13 A graph of the energy produced by the proton-proton cycle and the carbon cycle.

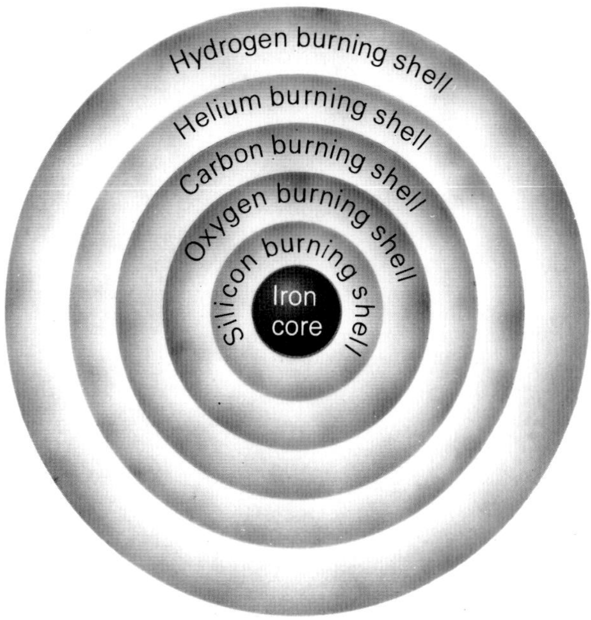

5.15 Once iron fills the core, any fusion process that releases energy to the star is extinguished.

and about 76 percent of all the mass of the universe. Helium accounts for about 7 percent of the atoms and about 23 percent of the mass. All of the other elements account for about 1 percent of the mass of the universe. Cosmic abundances are determined in a variety of ways, including an analysis of spectral lines in solar and stellar spectra and the measurements of abundances in the earth and in meteorites. Lithium, boron, and beryllium lie well below the abundances of atoms with slightly more protons in the nucleus because those three atoms are very unstable at the high temperatures of a stellar interior. On the other hand, iron is very stable and withstands temperatures of a few billion degrees Kelvin, so its cosmic abundance is higher than that of other atoms. The heaviest atoms, illustrated to the right of iron, have very low abundances because they are formed in the last stages of a massive star's life, so there is not much time to build up a large quantity of each element.

There are abundance anomalies in space that relate to specific stars and other astronomical objects, such as novae and some types of stars. One nova in particular possesses a high concentration of neon, and some stars have excess carbon, helium, iron, silicon, or manganese. For the most part, the chemical composition of these objects is probably due to the pressure and temperature of the star, which favored production of one or more of these elements. In addition, as discussed in Chapter 2, Population I and Population II stars have different abundances of elements heavier than helium, because Population I stars were formed from the interstellar medium that already had been enriched with heavy atoms from older exploding Population II stars.

The Mass of a Star and Its Life Expectancy

The most massive clouds of interstellar gas collapse, form protostars, and begin hydrogen fusion at the most rapid rate, taking only millions of years to reach the main sequence. Low-mass stars take billions of years to become stable stars in the prime of life. The mass of a star also determines how long a star will stay on the main sequence. Once again, the more mass a star has, the more rapid its evolution. A massive star has higher central temperatures and pressures than a low-mass star, and even though a massive star has more fuel to burn, it does so very quickly.

A star as massive as the sun burns hydrogen and thus stays on the main sequence for about 10 billion years. A star that is 15 times as massive as the sun may use up its hydrogen fuel in only 10 million years. In all cases stars spend most of their lives on the main sequence, where the proton-proton reaction or the carbon cycle is operating. Once the hydrogen fuel is exhausted, the prime of life comes to an end, and the star begins its final stages by moving off the main sequence. The final stage of stellar evolution will be discussed in Chapters 7, 8, and 9.

5.16 The majority of stars live most of their lives on the main sequence, so it follows that most of the stars we see are middle-aged stars in the prime of life. This is true in our own Milky Way and in other galaxies such as this nearby irregular galaxy called the Small Magellanic Cloud.

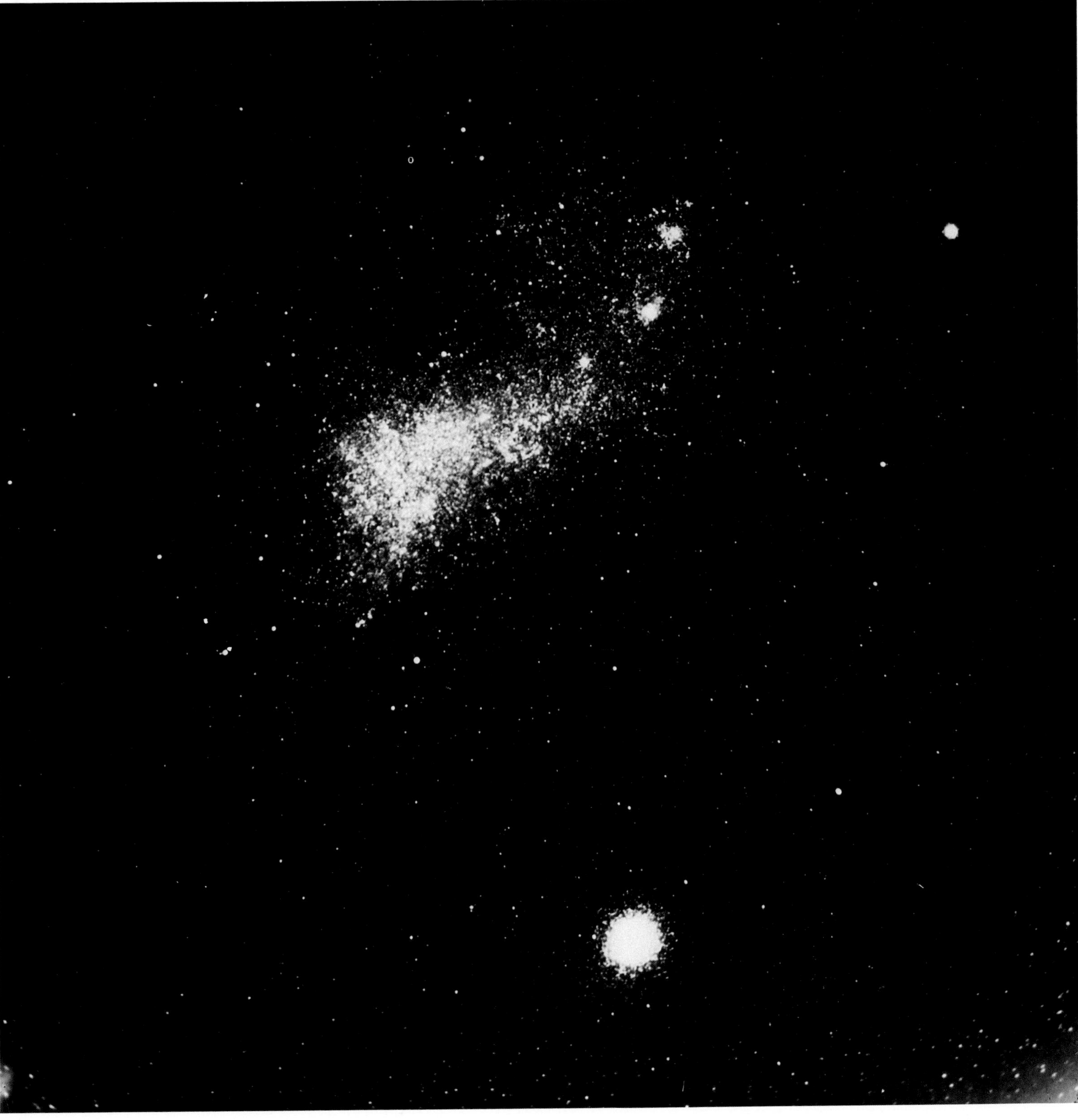

6: THE SUN: AN AVERAGE STAR

Anatomy of the Sun

There is nothing unusual about our sun, except perhaps that one planet in its solar system supports life (of course, that may not be a unique situation either). The sun is typical of the other 10^{11} (100,000,000,000) main-sequence stars in our galaxy and of the approximately 10^{20} normal stars in the known universe. The sun is of average temperature, about 6,000° K at the surface, and of average size, almost 1.5 million kilometers in diameter.

Although the sun is normal, average, and, if seen from a great distance, indistinct from the glow of its many stellar neighbors, scientists around the world continue their careful study of this nearest star. There is much to learn about, from nuclear fires at the sun's interior to the interaction of gas and magnetic fields. In short, the sun is important because it is the only star whose surface we can directly observe. All of the other stars are so far away that they appear merely as points of light in the sky even through telescopes, although the new technique of speckle interferometry is revealing some large surface features on nearby giant stars.

The sun is only about 150 million kilometers away (93 million miles). At this distance it takes up about one-half degree in the sky. This is large enough so that we can see individual surface features with telescopes and special techniques. Only on the sun can we also record the spectrum of individual surface features, because the light from other stars is a mixture of everything emitting radiation, and there is no way to separate the different parts of stars spectroscopically.

Thus, to scientists, the sun is unique because it can be observed spatially and spectroscopically over short intervals of time. We can see the sun change. For these reasons the sun is the most studied astronomical object, apart from the earth and moon.

Table 6 lists the basic solar data, including such items as its luminosity, mass, and age. Figure 6.1 schematically illustrates the structure of the sun. The temperatures and densities of the different layers are included, as are their approximate thicknesses. Notice that the sun has all of the components in the interior and atmosphere that we described in general terms in Chapter 5. We know much of the specific data for the sun, however, so this chapter is devoted to an examination of our observational and theoretical explorations of it.

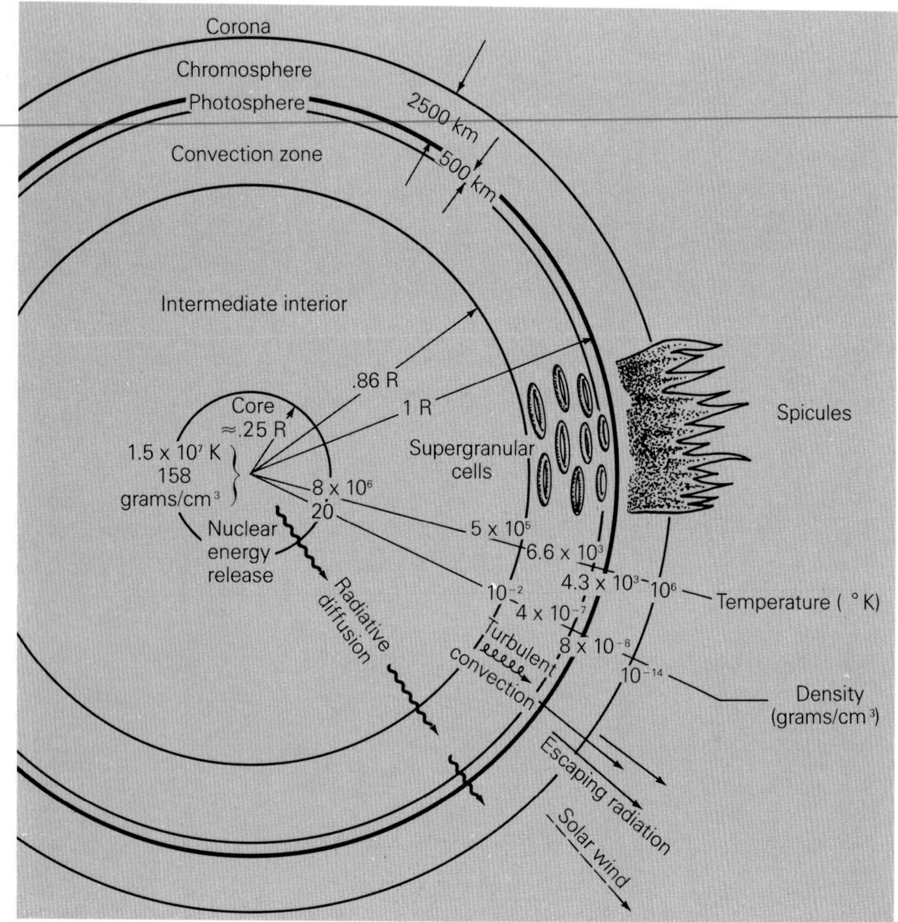

6.1 A schematic cross-section of the sun, detailing temperatures, densities, and dimensions of the different parts of our nearest star.

The Solar Interior

As you can see in Figure 6.1, the photosphere, that region of the sun that we see in white light every day, is not very thick. Its density is high enough, however, that we cannot see beneath it to the convective zone or below. Most of our understanding of the interior comes from the standard theory of stellar evolution, and up until a decade ago, solar physicists thought that their understanding of the sun's interior was complete. With the central temperature of the sun at about 15 million° K, 2 percent of its energy is generated by the carbon-nitrogen-oxygen cycle and 98 percent by the proton-proton cycle. The sun arrived at the main sequence some 5 billion years ago, and in another 5 billion years it will become a red giant.

Unfortunately, the entire foundation of the theory of stellar interiors is in jeopardy. This theoretical crisis arose as we developed a new way to "see" into the sun, by observing neutrinos. Nuclear reactions in stars release neutrinos, which are massless bits of energy that travel at the speed of light. Although it takes millions of years for radiant energy to work its way out from the center of a star and eventually radiate into space, neutrinos have a very low probability of interacting with matter, so they escape from the sun's center as soon as they are created. Neutrino detection is a very important tool for studying the solar interior because the qualities of neutrinos are determined by the characteristics of what is going on in the core, where nuclear reactions take place. Not only is the radiation from the photosphere characteristic only of the outer cool layers where it is emitted, but the energy takes so long to get out from the center that the nature of the light we see bears no relationship to how the energy was released millions of years in the past.

Where Have All the Neutrinos Gone?

Once neutrinos are formed, they escape immediately and reach earth in about nine minutes, traveling at the speed of light.

In the 1970s astronomers needed some way to measure the number of neutrinos reaching the earth. If the observed amount of neutrinos equaled the flux predicted by theory, scientists would have been able to

Table 6
The Sun As a Star

Mass: $M_\odot = 1.991 \times 10^{33}$ grams
Radius: $R_\odot = 6.966 \times 10^{10}$ centimeters
Spectral type: G2
Luminosity: $L_\odot = 3.86 \times 10^{33}$ ergs/second
Absolute magnitude: M = 4.8
Effective surface temperature: T = 5,800° K
Age: 4.7 billion years
Distance from the earth: 1.496×10^{13} centimeters (about 93 million miles)

verify that their understanding of nuclear burning was correct. Unfortunately, when astronomers measured the neutrino flux, they were very disappointed. They did not find as many neutrinos as were predicted by their theories.

The first problem in neutrino astronomy is the development of a detector that captures the elusive particle. Clearly, if neutrinos can leave the sun without interacting with any atoms along the way, it is very difficult to imagine capturing them on earth. So small is the chance of a neutrino reacting with other particles that if a neutrino travels through an ocean of water 100 parsecs thick it has only a fifty-fifty chance of interacting with a proton. About 65 billion neutrinos from the sun pass through a square centimeter on the earth every second. Even though there is a very slight chance of one reacting with matter on earth, so many neutrinos are coming all the time that we ought to have a few detectable events.

Raymond Davis of the Brookhaven National Laboratory built a neutrino detector one mile beneath the surface of the earth in a gold mine in South Dakota. Davis put over 600 gallons of dry-cleaning fluid, tetrachlorethylene, in a huge tank. A few of the approximately 10^{23} neturinos that reach the tank each week will interact with an atom of chlorine. Chlorine is an element consisting of 20 neutrons and 17 protons, but when the energy from a neutrino interacts with the chlorine atom, it becomes an atom of argon, containing 19 neutrons and 18 protons.

Every once in a while, Davis and his collaborators remove the new argon atoms by bubbling helium gas through the tank. These argon atoms are not stable, however, and as they decay they release electrons, which can be counted electronically. The more electrons released, the greater the number of neutrinos that have altered chlorine atoms. The theory of energy generation in the sun's core predicts that enough neutrinos reach the tank to produce 5.6×10^{-36} neturino captures per chlorine atom each second. The results from Davis's experiment are four to five times lower than this predicted value.

Where are the neutrinos? No one knows for certain what is wrong, but several scientists have proposed ideas to explain the case of the missing neutrinos. One possible explanation suggests that we do not understand neutrinos very well. They may interact with matter less efficiently than we think. Scientists have carefully examined the nuclear reactions that produce neutrinos, so it is unlikely that our theory is wrong. Billions of neutrinos are produced in nuclear reactors, and our theories account for them rather well.

It seems, then, that something is lacking in our understanding of the sun's interior. The most interesting proposition is that the sun is a variable star and that on occasion the nuclear fires turn off, so no neutrinos are emitted. Since it takes several million years for the radiation energy to work its way out from the center, the core could have turned off long ago, although we are just now seeing the diffusion of the energy from the solar interior. The architect of this notion is William Fowler, one of the scientists who has led the way into the realm of stellar nucleosynthesis. A specific mechanism involving the mixing of helium in the core has been suggested as a possible way that the core would expand and cool, shutting off the reactions that lead to neutrinos. The solar luminosity would decrease by about 10 percent later on, however, which has been suggested as a possible cause of ice ages.

Scientists have studied the history of the earth's temperature and believe that the sun has not altered its radiation output by more than about 3 percent during the past million years, and there have been ice ages in the meantime. Global weather patterns are one of the most difficult things to model mathematically, so we should not automatically discount that the sun may be a variable star simply on the basis of climate theory. There is much to learn about our weather and its relationship to the sun, and we still do not know where all the neutrinos have gone.

Is the Sun Round?

In the last decade another method has been devised to probe the hidden reaches of the sun's core. Robert

Dicke of Princeton University set out to observe whether or not the sun is slightly flattened at the poles and bulging at the equator. We call this lack of roundness *oblateness*. Even the earth is slightly oblate due to its daily rotation on its axis, but Dicke predicted that the radius of the sun's equator may be 30 kilometers greater than the radius at the pole. He suggested that if such oblateness existed, it could be explained by a central core that is rotating 20 times faster than the atmospheric layers. If the core were spinning very rapidly, the central temperature and pressure would be considerably lower and could account for the lack of neutrinos.

We still have the neutrino problem on hand, however, because a special telescope built in the mid-1970s by H. Hill and R. T. Stebbins has yielded results indicating that *no* oblateness exists, and that the sun's core is not rapidly rotating.

Solar observations with this same telescope have revealed that periodic brightenings at the sun's edge occur every 52 minutes, as well as other oscillations occurring even more frequently. These regular brightenings are probably caused by radial pulsations or pressure waves coming from the sun's interior. The variations of temperature and density throughout the sun have an effect on the period of these pulsations, so careful study will tell us much of the internal structure of the sun. This analysis is similar to seismology on the earth. After an earthquake, geologists can measure the oscillations of this planet and probe the structure of the earth's interior.

Scientists have measured gravity oscillations as well, and this solar seismology may eventually help in determining the true nature of the sun's interior and understanding the nuclear reactions that give us light and warmth as they power the sun.

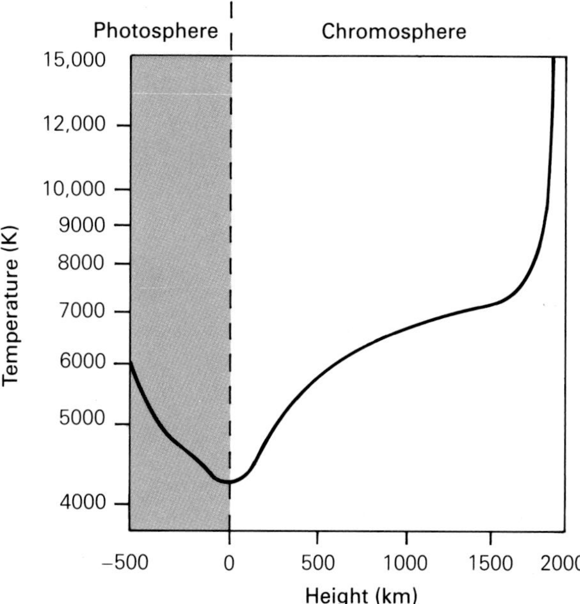

6.2 A graph of the sun's temperature at various heights through the solar atmosphere. The temperature continues to rise to over 2 million° K in the corona.

The Outer Layers of the Sun

Unlike the hidden solar interior, which we must probe with indirect methods such as neutrino capture, the solar atmosphere is there for us to see. It emits light in all ranges of the electromagnetic spectrum and in the past 10 years has undergone the most extensive scrutiny of any object beyond the moon.

Most of the impetus in solar research has occurred because of satellite technology. In the early 1970s, astronomers began to launch telescopes above the ozone layer to study the ultraviolet and X-ray radiations from the sun. Earthbound observatories have studied radio emissions and visual light from the sun for decades, but the ability to see the sun in the more energetic portions of the spectrum has enabled scientists to put much of the entire picture of the sun's outer layers together.

In previous chapters we explored how atoms emit light. One of the crucial factors that determine the distribution of energy in the spectrum is the temperature. Some atoms emit light from hot regions, while others emit light from cooler regions. By identifying the atoms present in a region of the sun by recognizing their spectral lines, we can learn about the temperature variations in the solar atmosphere. We combine observations with theory to make a complete picture. Figure 6.2 illustrates the change in temperature from the bottom of the photosphere through the solar corona. The minimum temperature reaches about 4,200° K, after which it rises into the chromosphere and corona. To observe certain regions of the solar atmosphere, we look at different spectral lines and different parts of the spectrum. For example, the photosphere emits the bright visible light we see. Some of the absorption lines are formed by the chromosphere, but most of them arise from the photosphere. The corona emits faintly some emission lines in the visible spectrum, but it is most readily seen in ultraviolet or X-ray radiation. Let us examine each part of the solar atmosphere in more detail, paying particular attention to the spectrum emitted by each region.

The Photosphere

The photosphere is the "light" sphere we see each day. It lies at the bottom of the solar atmosphere and is by definition the lowest level of the sun from which radiation escapes into space. Recall that energy is transported upward through a star by radiation that is continually absorbed and reemitted and by convection currents that rise and fall as does air over a radiator. None of this energy escapes the sun until it reaches the region of temperature and density where the light is not always absorbed and can leave.

It is no accident that we see visible light with our eyes. Because the layers of the photosphere are about 5,800° K, the radiation from the sun peaks in what we call the visible spectrum. The earth's atmosphere lets only certain portions of the spectrum pass through. They are the radio wavelengths and the visible light. Creatures on earth did not evolve big enough eyes to capture the long wavelengths of radio radiation, so the only radiant energy coming through the atmosphere that animals could sense was visible light. Had the earth's atmosphere absorbed visible light and passed infrared radiation instead, it is possible that our eyes would see the world in infrared. The sun is not as bright in infrared, so the world would look quite different.

The spectrum of the photosphere is a standard absorption spectrum. The continuous radiation is crossed with absorption lines from several chemical elements, ranging from hydrogen to iron, calcium, and sodium. The photosphere is too cool to excite helium atoms, so there are no spectral lines from helium in the photospheric spectrum.

In 1814 Josef von Fraunhofer labeled the darkest lines in the solar spectrum with the letters A, B, C, D, E, F, G, and H. Fraunhofer's original notation is seen in Figure 6.4. His C line is now known to be a strong absorption line; it comes from hydrogen and is called Hα. The D line of Fraunhofer turned out to be two very close absorption lines caused by sodium atoms. They are called today the sodium D lines. The H line is absorbed by ionized calcium (CaII), and farther in to the blue another CaII line has been labeled

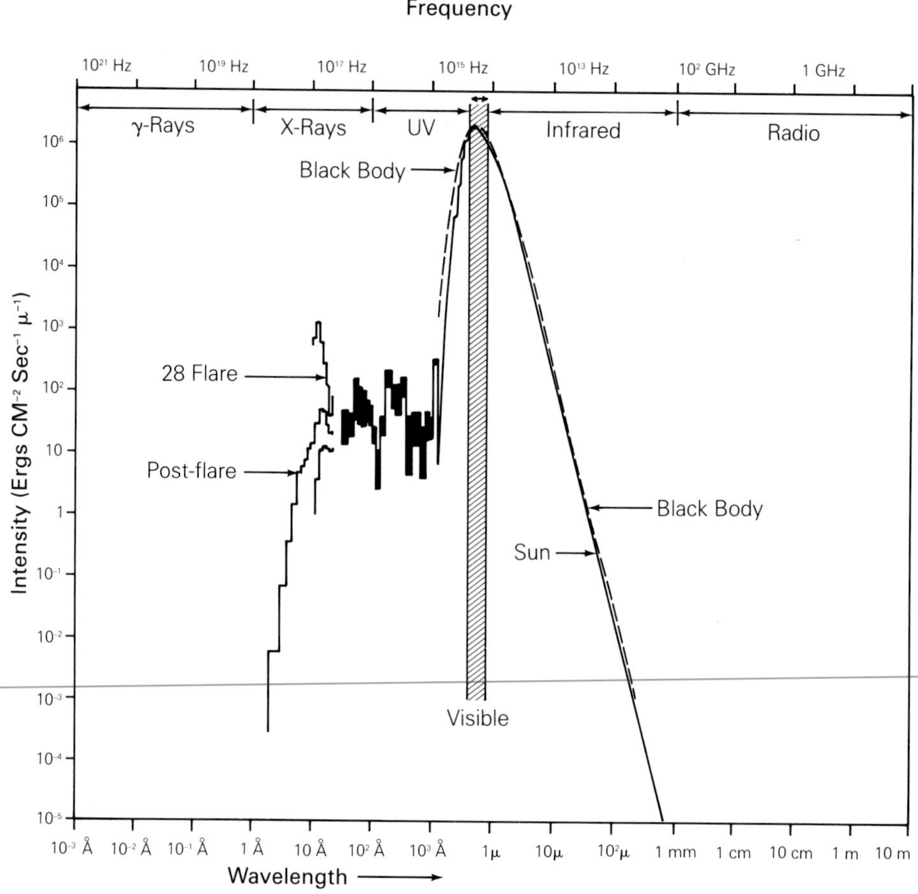

6.3 The energy distribution of the sun. Notice that the maximum intensity of solar radiation lies in the visible spectrum.

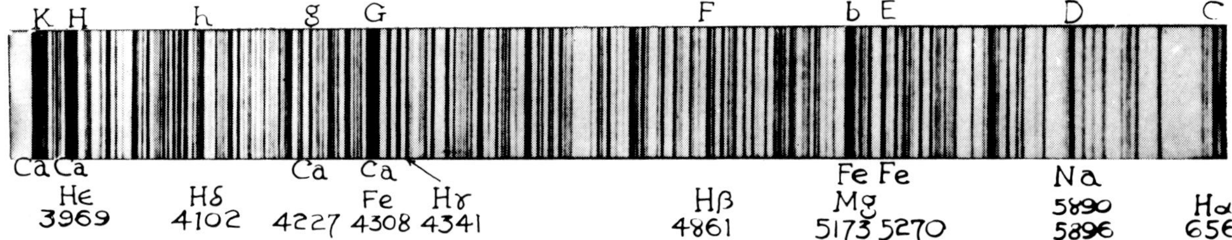

6.4 *A solar spectrum labeled both by the Fraunhofer system and with today's atomic notation.*

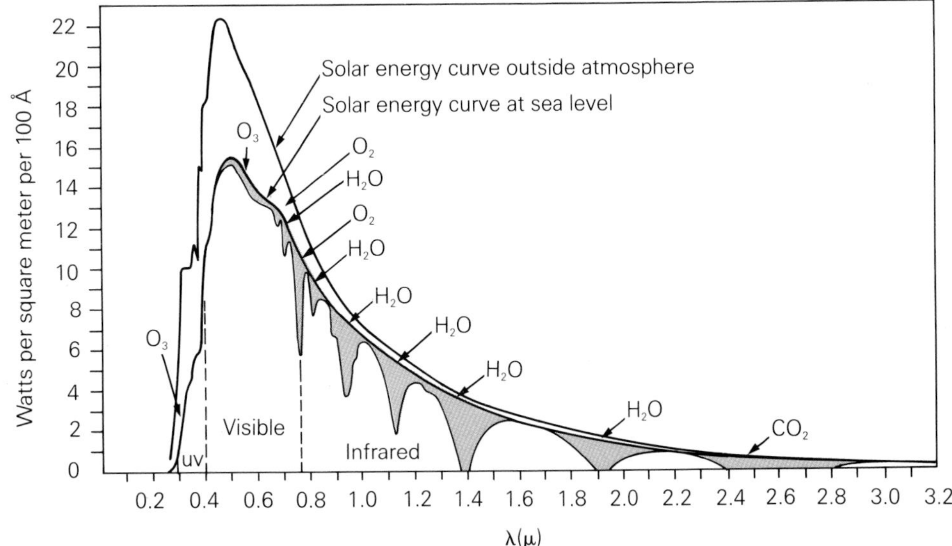

6.5 *The portion of the sun's spectrum as seen in visible light.*

the K line, for consistency with Fraunhofer's notation. The H and K lines are both the broadest and darkest lines in the solar spectrum. Figure 6.5 shows the complete spectrum of the sun in visible light. The earth's atmosphere absorbs much of the incoming radiation due mainly to ozone (O_3) in the ultraviolet and water vapor (H_2O) in the infrared region of the spectrum.

When observing the sun directly, astronomers face a major limitation on how much detail they can see on the solar surface. The earth's atmosphere is too turbulent to see anything smaller on the sun other than features about 700 kilometers across. The irony is that the turbulence is worse when the sun is in the sky because the earth's atmosphere and surface are heated, and convection is more severe than at night. The best seeing is found only at a few sites in the world, and astronomers have already set up solar observatories at those places.

In everyday white light, the sun is a large ball with a mottled surface. White light is all the frequencies of visible radiation together, with no filter or prism separating individual colors. Figure 6.7 is a photograph of the sun taken in white light. Notice the sunspot groups as well as areas of greater intensity where the temperature is slightly higher than in the neighboring areas.

A close-up of the solar surface would reveal the solar granulation. The granulation consists of rising and falling packets of gas that are transporting energy by convection from the center of the sun to the bottom of the photosphere. We can see the tops of the granules in white light. Special protective filters are available to amateur astronomers, permitting safe viewing of the sun in white light through small telescopes. Sunspots and other features of the photosphere are easily seen with such equipment.

Sunspots

One of the first astronomical phenomena ever seen through a telescope was the strange dark patches on the solar surface Galileo observed when he turned his small spyglass on the sun in 1610. At the time many people claimed that these flaws in the sun were either on the lens of the telescope or in Galileo's brain, and people were afraid to look through this new instrument lest they become like Galileo!

Sunspots, however, are normal manifestations of the complex magnetic fields in the sun. Other solar features we will discuss later in this chapter are also related to the magnetic structure of the sun, but sunspots, since they can be seen in white light, are the most visible and best-studied component of solar activity.

Sunspots are dark because they are cool, but do not let this fool you. The temperature of a sunspot is about 4,000° K, so it is cool only in contrast to the 5,800° K photosphere nearby. Sometimes a single spot appears on the sun, but often the sunspot region is complex, as in Figure 6.9. Notice the dark central region, the *umbra* (Latin for shadow), and the lighter boundary, called the *penumbra*. Sunspots are cooler than the normal photosphere because magnetic fields under the surface are preventing the normal outflow of energy to that region. Magnetic fields can constrain hot, ionized gases, and although scientists on earth have not yet been able to contain hot gases in laboratories, we see it happening all the time in the sun's atmosphere.

The magnetic field of the sun is complex, and its cyclic change over a period of about 22 years is reflected in the number of sunspots appearing on the solar surface at any one time. The formation of sunspots is not very well understood. The most widely

6.6 Big Bear Solar Observatory stands in the middle of a lake because studies have shown that the earth's atmosphere is calmer above bodies of water than above land.

6.7 The sun as seen in everyday white light.

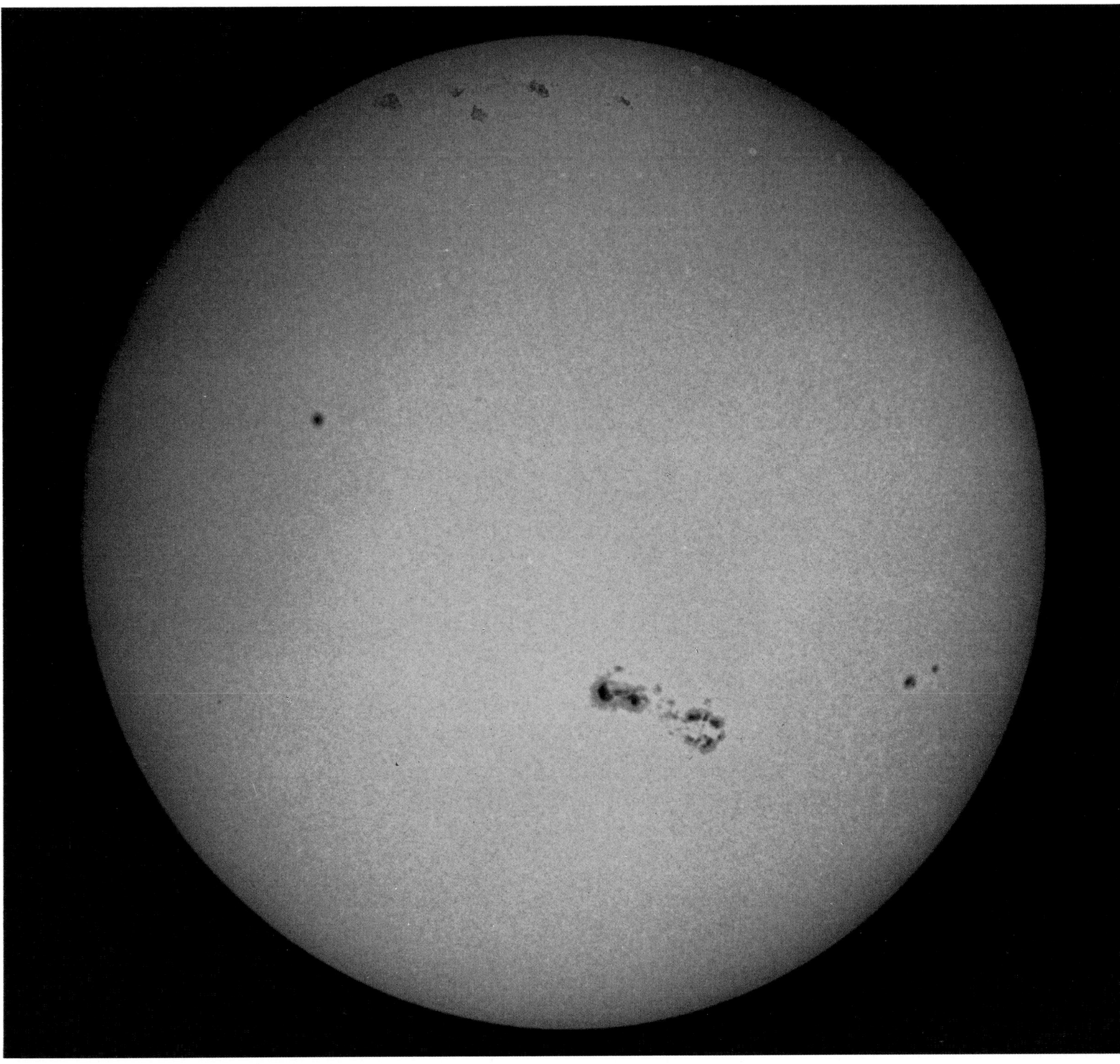

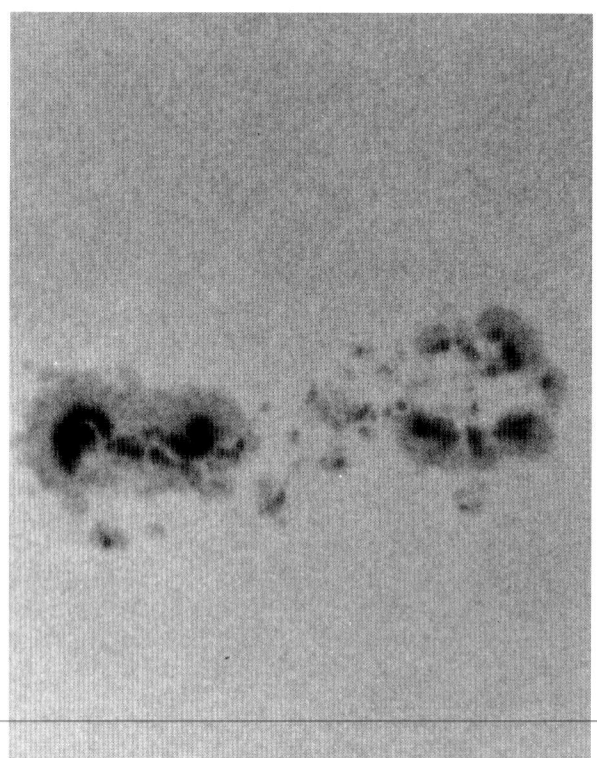

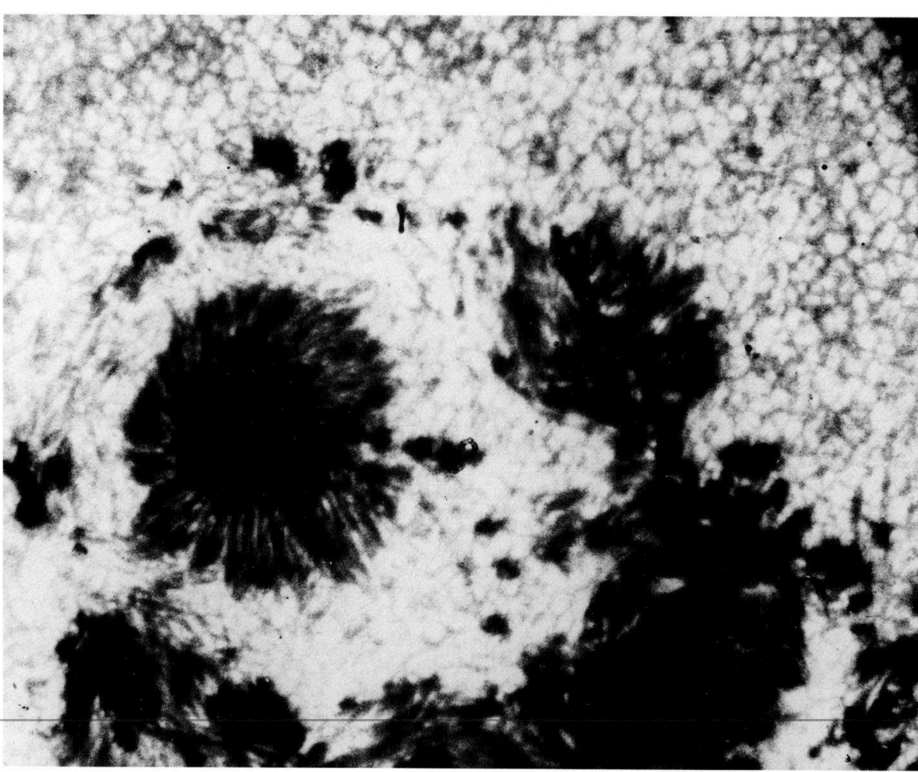

6.8 Above left: *A sunspot is a region of magnetic activity in the sun's photosphere. The darkest part of the spot is called the* umbra *(Latin for shadow), and the lighter boundary region of the sunspot is called the* penumbra.

6.9 Above right: *A sunspot group can be a complex manifestation of the sun's magnetic field.*

accepted theory to date was proposed in 1961 by Horace W. Babcock of the Hale Observatories in California. The Babcock model contends that tubular magnetic fields lie just under the photosphere, running from north to south. As the sun rotates, the equator goes around in about 25 days, while higher latitudes rotate more slowly. This is called differential rotation, and it forces the magnetic fields to wind up around the sun. From time to time, a magnetic tube pops through the surface. At the area where the tube emerges, a sunspot forms. Most sunspots appear in pairs of opposite magnetic polarity—one is north polarity and the other is south.

The Babcock model accounts for these observations, as well as the fact that sunspot activity varies in a cycle of 11 years. The number of sunspots increases from a minimum to a maximum in about 5.5 years and then decreases back to a minimum in the following 5.5 years. The 11-year sunspot cycle is represented in Figure 6.11 as far back as continuous records have been kept. The Babcock model of sunspot formation accounts for the cyclic variation in sunspot numbers because as the magnetic fields wrap up with time, more and more sunspots form as magnetic fields loop out of the surface. After 11 years the fields are very tightly wrapped, and the sun's poles change their polarity. The south pole becomes magnetically north and vice versa. Eleven years later, the sun's polarity returns to its original configuration, so the sunspot cycle lasts about 22 years.

The combination of the magnetic fields and the rotation of the sun produces a solar dynamo, analogous to electric power plants on earth, where turbines are turned by steam or water power to make electricity. Sunspots are the most obvious manifestation of the solar dynamo only because they have been observed for almost 400 years. Other active regions of the sun reside in the outermost layers of the atmosphere.

The Chromosphere

Lying above the photosphere, but invisible in daily white light observations of the sun, lies a hot layer called the chromosphere. The chromosphere is visible just before the moon completely blocks the sun during a solar eclipse. Figure 6.13 shows the thin sliver of chromosphere peeking out from behind the moon's edge. It is red because hydrogen atoms are emitting a bright spectral line of that color. The chromosphere emits no spectrum of continuous color and only emits emission lines of several elements; we can observe the chromosphere by using filters that pass only the specific wavelengths of those emission lines. The most popular line is the strong red line of hydrogen, called Hα. A filter that passes only Hα was used to take the photograph in Figure 6.14, making the complex network of the solar chromosphere immediately visible. The swirling patterns of thin filamentary structure are caused by the interaction of magnetic fields and hot gas. The fingers of gas radiating from the sun are called spicules; they have been compared to blades of grass. They generally form the chromosphere itself and are about 700 kilometers in diameter and about 7,000 kilometers tall.

The material in the chromosphere is hotter than the photosphere, about 15,000° K, but its density is quite a bit lower. This explains why we can see through it in white light to the denser photosphere.

Solar Flares

Hα photographs also show many active solar features. One of the most important events on the sun is a solar flare. Solar flares are tremendous explosions near sunspots that emit intense radiation and eject energetic atomic particles into space. Figure 6.16 shows an eruptive phase of a flare. There is a relatively rapid rise in intensity for so large an area. Flares are the largest explosions in the solar system, and because they have important effects on earth, scientists around the globe are trying to understand why they occur.

Temperatures in flares may reach 5 million° K. Although they are very bright in Hα light, they emit most of their energy in ultraviolet and X rays. A major thrust of solar satellite studies has been the observation of flares in these portions of the spectrum. Figure 6.17 shows a flare in the light of oxygen that has lost five of its electrons in the hot gas. The material surges outward from the bright flare and reaches thousands of miles into space.

Since flares erupt in the vicinity of sunspots, the energy that does not reach the photosphere probably is somehow stored in the strong magnetic field. It builds up to such a point that it ruptures the magnetic field and is deposited rapidly in the overlying layers of the solar atmosphere. Not only do scientists wish to learn how this works, they also are trying to find clues that will tip them off as to when a flare is about to happen.

Solar Prominences

If a flare erupts at the edge of the sun, we can see with an Hα filter large blobs of gas being thrown out into space. These are called eruptive prominences or surges. They form in the chromosphere and shoot out into the solar corona. Most prominences, however, form from material in the corona and rain down slowly on the surface. Sometimes this rain takes the shape of loops or long hedgerows. Hedgerows are also called quiescent prominences because they can hang above the surface for several months supported by magnetic fields. When a prominence is viewed against the sun's disk, it appears dark in Hα radiation and is called a filament. These can be as long as 100,000 kilometers and take on aesthetic shapes, as do clouds or smoke in our own atmosphere.

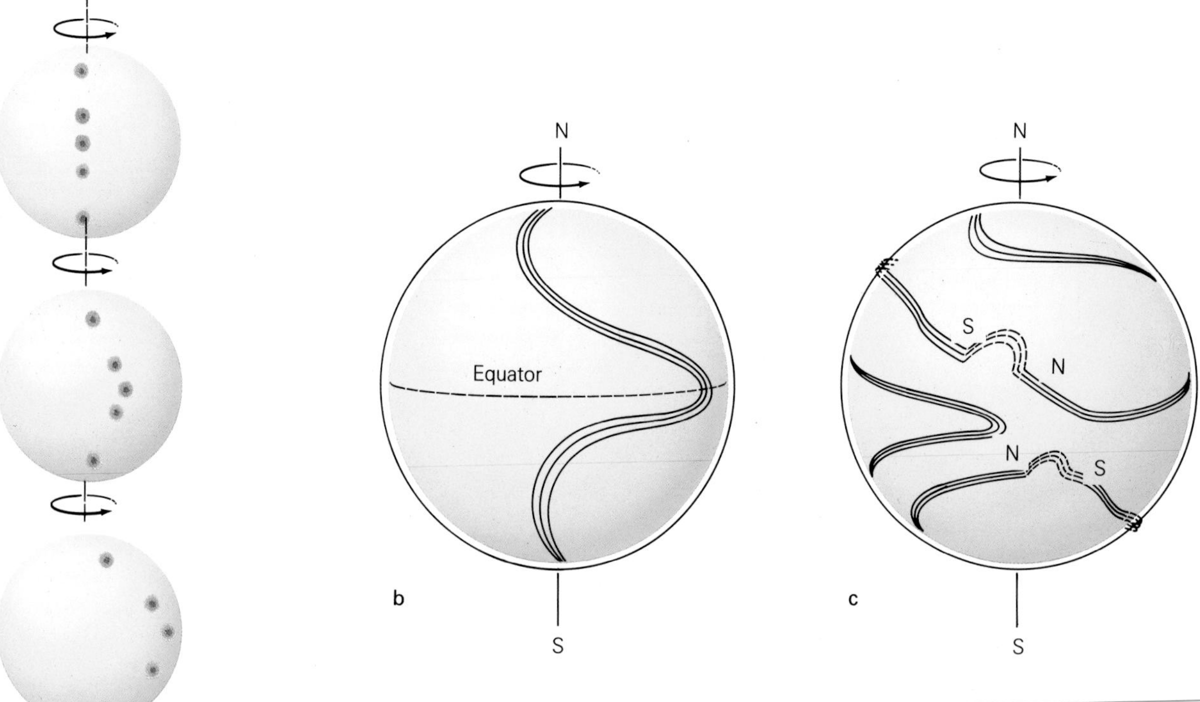

6.10 a,b,c The Babcock model of sunspot formation describes the eventual wrapping around of magnetic fields due to the sun's differential rotation and magnetic field. The sequence (a) *shows that the equator rotates more rapidly than the polar regions, making the magnetic field wrap up* (b)*. Magnetic tubes pop out of the surface* (c)*, and sunspots form where these tubes enter the photosphere.*

6.12 Below: *The surface of the sun as seen in the light of singly ionized calcium shows the large-scale granular structure as well as a dark sunspot. The bright areas are called* plages *(French for beach) and occur because of the magnetic field in the region.*

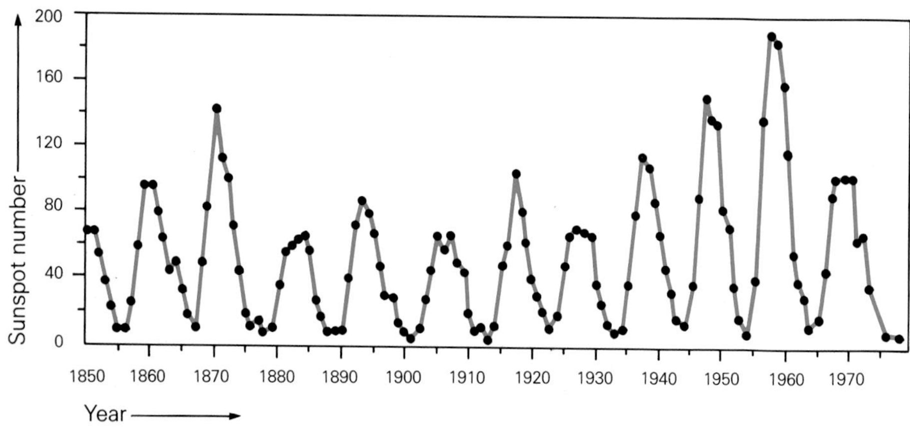

6.11 The yearly sunspot count for more than 100 years shows the periodic rise and fall of sunspot numbers.

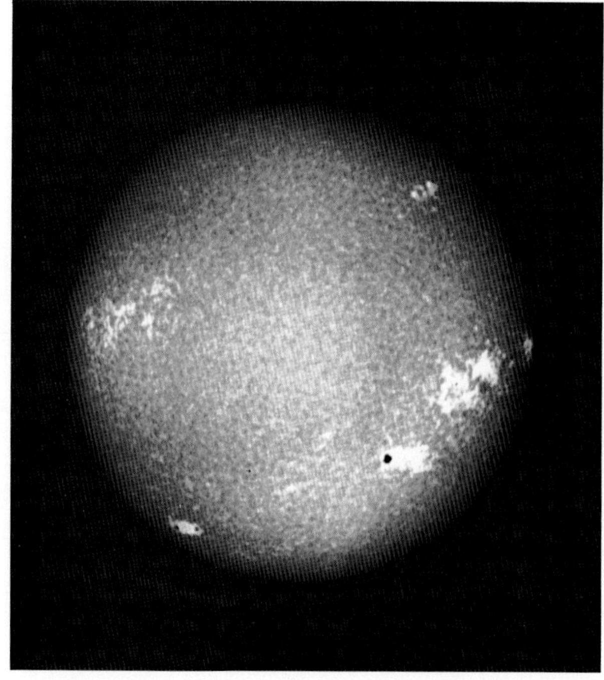

6.13 Right: *The red chromosphere shines brightly just before the moon totally obscures the sun during the 1972 solar eclipse.*

6.14 Below: *A photograph taken in the red light of hydrogen with an Hα filter shows the turbulent nature of the chromosphere.*

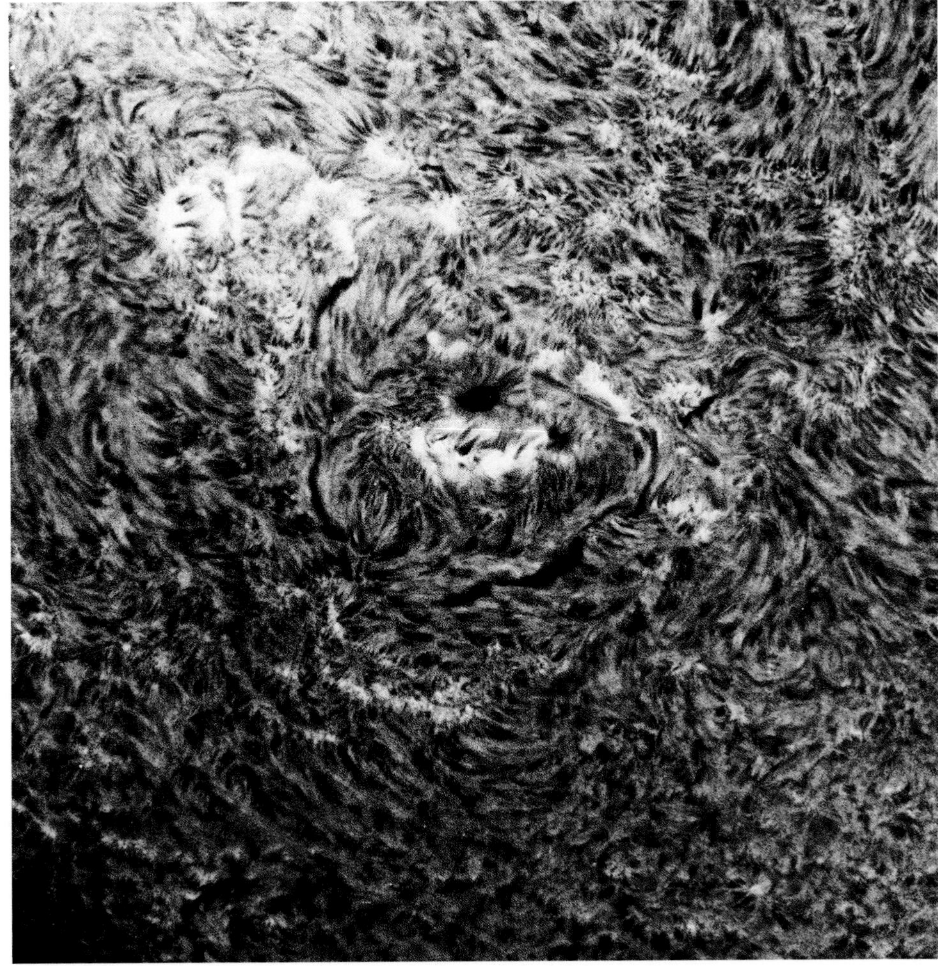

The Solar Corona

From the top of the chromosphere, reaching far past the earth, is the solar corona, a tenuous hot halo of pearly white light that is most visible during solar eclipses, when the moon completely covers the sun. Figure 6.19 shows the corona during an eclipse, but earthbound photographs such as this hide the true nature of the corona.

For several years, astronomers have known that the corona is about 2 million° K, but some million times less dense than the chromosphere. Figure 6.1 shows the temperature and density of the various regions of the sun. In the last decade, photographs from space have revealed that the corona is probably a conglomeration of large loops of gas that for the most part join separate regions of the sun's surface. Figure 6.20 is an X-ray image of the sun. The photosphere and chromosphere are too cool to emit X rays; only the corona and solar flares are hot enough. Notice the intense loops that are probably associated with flares and the more diffuse large loops that reach thousands of kilometers around the sun.

The dark line that runs from north to south is called a coronal hole. There is a corona there, but it is about three times less dense than the normal corona. Coronal holes appear to be cooler regions, perhaps with a temperature of only about 1 million° K instead of the almost 2 million° K in the bright average corona. In addition to occasional coronal holes that appear on the solar disk, the north and south poles of the sun always have coronal holes associated with them.

Coronal holes seem to be regions of the sun's outer atmosphere where magnetic tubes do not loop back onto the surface. Instead, the magnetic fields open into space, and high-speed atomic particles escape into space, forming a wind that blows past the earth and into the depths of the solar system. This solar wind is responsible for driving back the tails of comets as they orbit the sun. No matter where the comet is in its orbit

(Figure 6.21), its diffuse tail of vaporized gas points away from the sun as the solar wind blows it outward.

The Sun–Earth Relationship

The solar wind is a prime example of a solar phenomenon that affects the earth. The earth's atmosphere is constantly bathed by the streaming particles from the sun, and one of the effects of the solar wind is to reshape the earth's magnetic field. The earth has north and south magnetic poles, but, unlike a simple bar magnet, the terrestrial magnetic field is distorted because the particles in the solar wind push the field lines back into space.

Aurorae borealis (or northern lights) is caused by atomic particles from the solar wind that become trapped in the earth's magnetic field and cause atmospheric atoms to glow. Aurorae are most often seen during periods of high solar activity, including flares, which expel great numbers of particles in the solar wind.

Aurorae are beautiful patterns of color in the sky. Other effects of the solar wind are less pleasing, however. Short-wave radio transmission can be disturbed, and power lines are often plagued with excess voltages when charged particles from solar flares reach the earth. Above the earth's atmosphere, which absorbs the high-energy end of the electromagnetic spectrum, X rays and ultraviolet radiation from flares, in addition to these high-speed particles, would present a lethal shower to unwary astronauts in space.

Of course the sun supplies the earth with the light and heat necessary for life. The sun drives our weather machine and ocean currents. The earth is located in the middle of the region around the sun where temperatures are suitable for the sustenance of life, and the chemical and physical evolution of this planet have made it possible for life to develop.

The solar activity cycle seems to affect the earth's climate in ways that are still poorly understood by

6.15 At the sun's edge, the chromosphere appears to be made of spicules, long jets of gas that rise above the photosphere like blades of grass.

astronomers and meteorologists. We have already suggested that the sun is a variable star because of its magnetic field and the solar dynamo and that the cycle of sunspots is only one manifestation of solar activity. Between 1650 and 1710, far fewer sunspots appeared than even at the normal sunspot minimum periods every 11 years. During this time the earth suffered what has since been called a mini-ice age, when the average temperature throughout Europe dipped several degrees below the normal value. Perhaps more severe variations in the energy output of the sun led to the real ice ages. A decrease of several percent in the luminosity of the sun is all that is required to sink the world into an extended winter.

The Solar Constant

Although the sun is apparently a modestly varying star, astronomers have a term that makes one think that the sun's output does not change. The *solar constant* is the total amount of energy from the sun that hits a square centimeter each second just outside the earth's atmosphere. We measure it there because the molecules in the air absorb various wavelengths of the sun's radiation, so only a small amount of energy reaches the surface of the planet.

The solar constant is equal to about 2 calories per

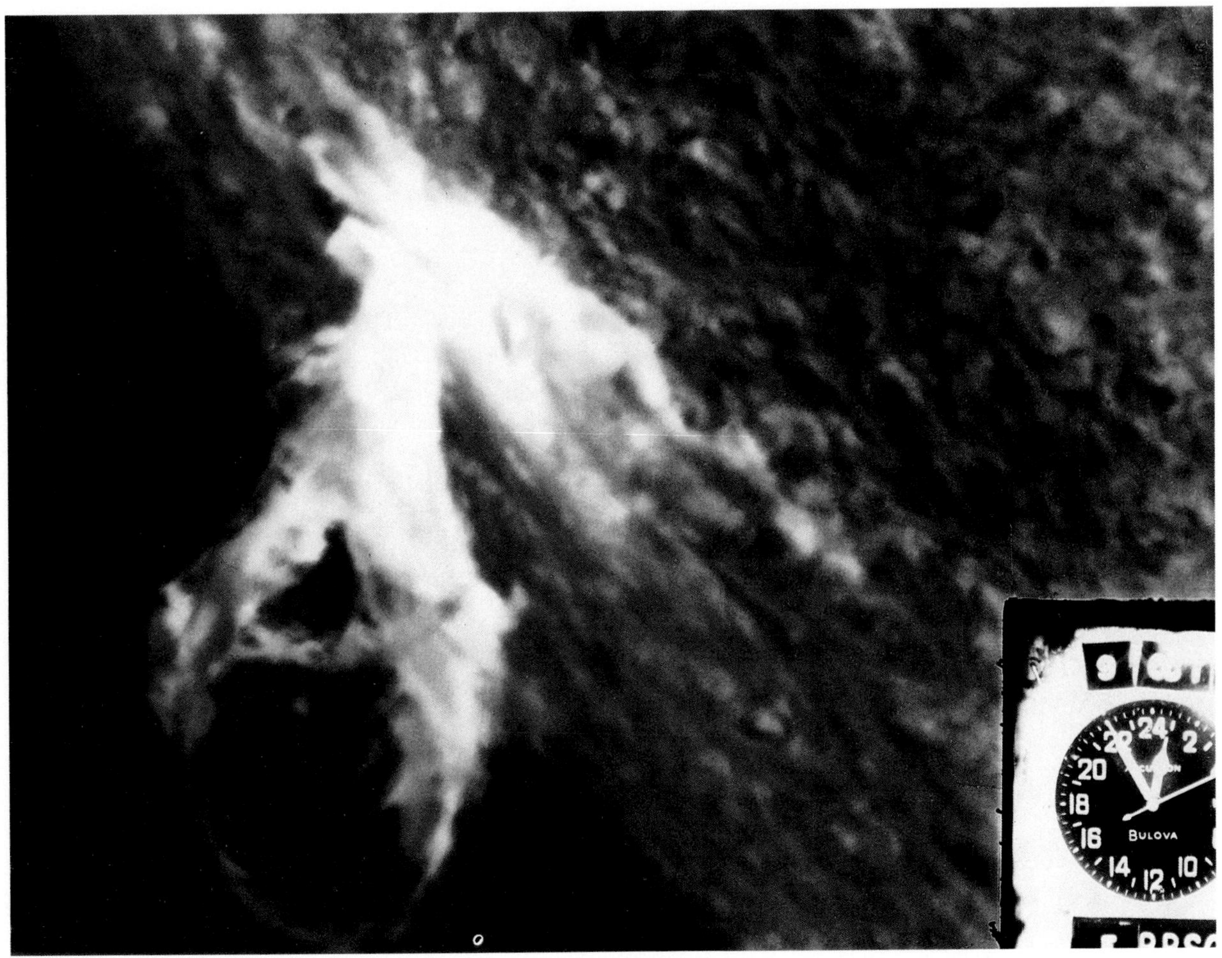

6.16 A solar flare photographed with an Hα filter. The brightening here occurs over about one-half hour, but the flare took several hours to die down.

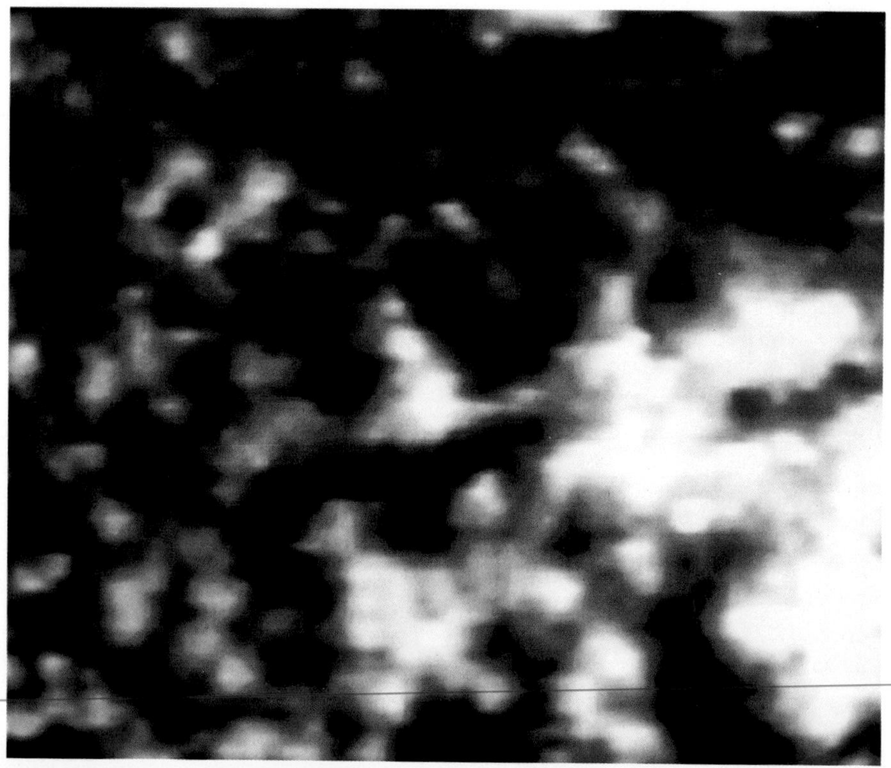

6.17 Left: *A solar flare in the light of O VI (oxygen that has lost five of its electrons). The gas we see in this photograph must be 600,000° K.*

6.18a Below left: *A surge forming from a solar flare reaches thousands of kilometers into space.*

6.18b Below center: *A large prominence in Hα light stretches thousands of kilometers along the sun's limb and delineates the local magnetic field.*

6.18c Below right: *A quiescent prominence, photographed in the ultraviolet light of hydrogen and artificially colored by computer, is seen bending around the sun's edge. Above the limb the prominence appears bright, but against the solar disk it is dark and is called a filament.*

6.19 Opposite page: *The solar corona at eclipse, 1983. The bright bead of light at the edge of the moon is actually the last bit of the solar photosphere streaming through a lunar valley before totality begins. This is called the diamond ring effect.*

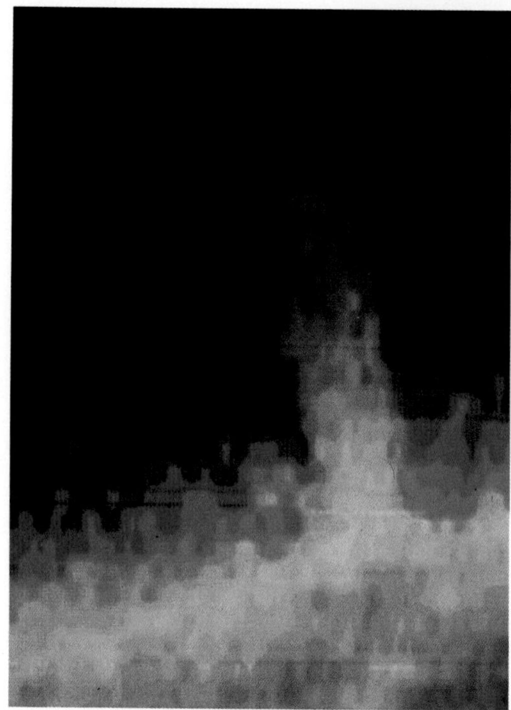

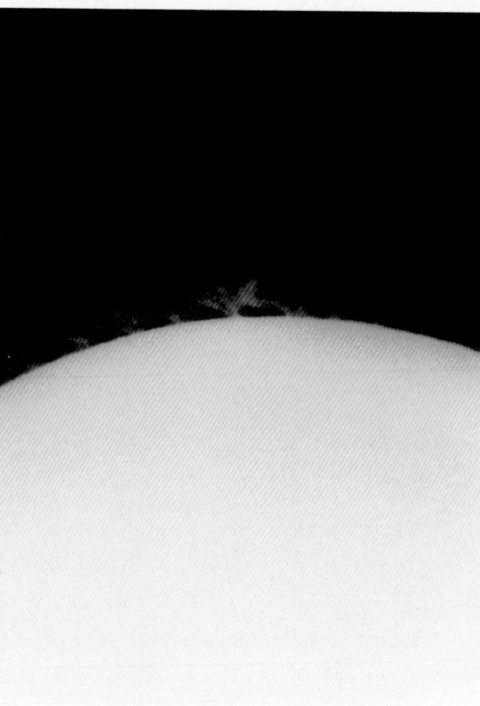

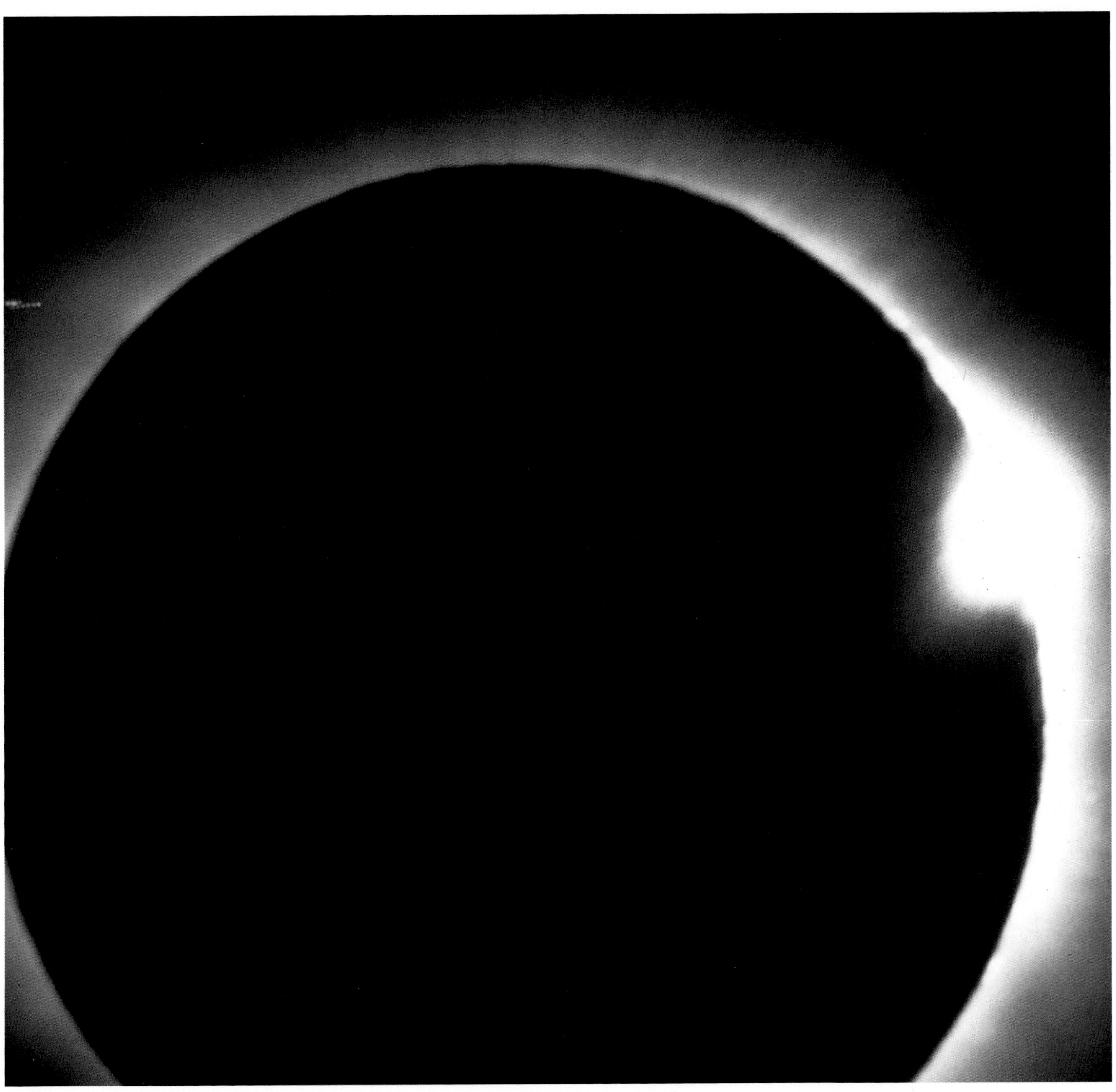

centimeter per minute, which is equivalent to the amount of heat needed to raise the temperature of 1 gram of water about 2 degrees. This value has been measured to an accuracy of about 1.5 percent, but astronomers want better accuracy so they can observe any small long- or short-term variations in the solar constant. Fluctuations in the solar constant would have profound effects on our climate and on the earth's atmosphere. Of course, the solar constant is not much of a constant if its value changes with time.

After the sun uses up its hydrogen fuel in some 5 billion years, the value of the solar constant will continually rise as the sun evolves into a red giant star. The next chapter will explore the major changes that the sun and similar stars will undergo as they reach the end of their lives.

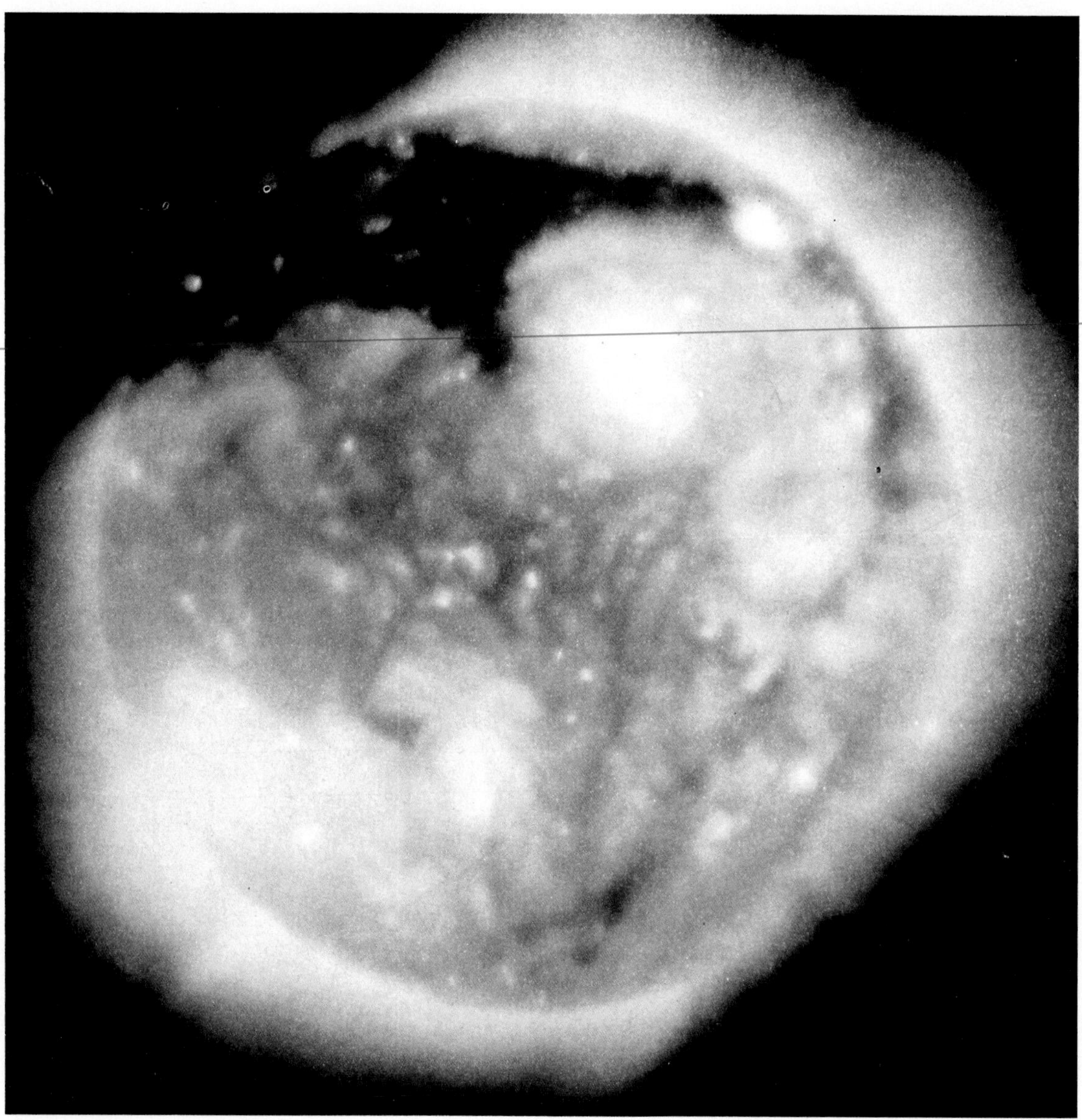

6.20 An X-ray image of the sun showing the million-degree-Kelvin corona and its complex loop structure. The coronal hole is a region where no coronal material is emitting X rays. This photograph was taken from Skylab in 1973.

6.21 Artist's conception of a comet orbiting the sun.

7: THE DEATH OF STARS LIKE OUR SUN

The Beginning of the End

In 5 billion years, the sun will undergo changes that will signal that our nearest star has reached the final stages of its lifetime. If the earth is still here that far into the future, and if life still resides on this tiny foothold in the cosmos, the changes the sun will make will be catastrophic. All of the planets in the inner solar system, including the earth, probably will be destroyed as the sun grows into a huge red giant star. Yet from a cosmic perspective, the end of the sun will be an insignificant event in the great expanse of space we call the universe.

Stars approximately as massive as the sun begin to show their age when the core of the stellar interior is made of pure helium. Depending on the mass and temperature of the core, this helium was produced by the fusion of hydrogen nuclei, following either the proton-proton cycle or the carbon cycle.

The helium core is surrounded by a shell where hydrogen fusion is still active, but the core itself, once it is made only of helium, is supplying no energy to the star, because its temperature is not high enough to convert helium into carbon via the triple alpha process. With no energy being generated in the core, it begins to shrink under its own gravity. As with the core in a protostar, the gravitational collapse heats up the gas in the center.

The star now has a markedly different structure than it did while in the prime of life. No longer is hydrogen burning in the core, but rather it is rapidly fusing to make helium in a shell around the core, which is heated by the gravitational collapse within it. The core itself is not in balance between gravity pulling inward and the energy flowing outward because there is no source of energy in the core. The core is collapsing slowly.

The core grows hotter and raises the temperature of the hydrogen-burning shell to such a degree that more energy is produced by nuclear reactions than was produced during the main-sequence life of the star. With more energy being produced, more energy is flowing outward, so the outer layers of the star expand while the inner core continues to collapse.

Although the star is producing more energy than ever before, it does not shine more brightly at first because the radiation emitted in the hydrogen-burning region takes a long time to work its way out of the atmosphere. The star is expanding, however, and as the surface area becomes greater, the star's surface cools. At this point the star's luminosity is constant, but the star's spectral type changes to a cooler classification. If we plot the star on the Hertzsprung-Russell diagram, it leaves the main sequence to the right horizontally. Figure 7.2 is the H-R diagram for a star as

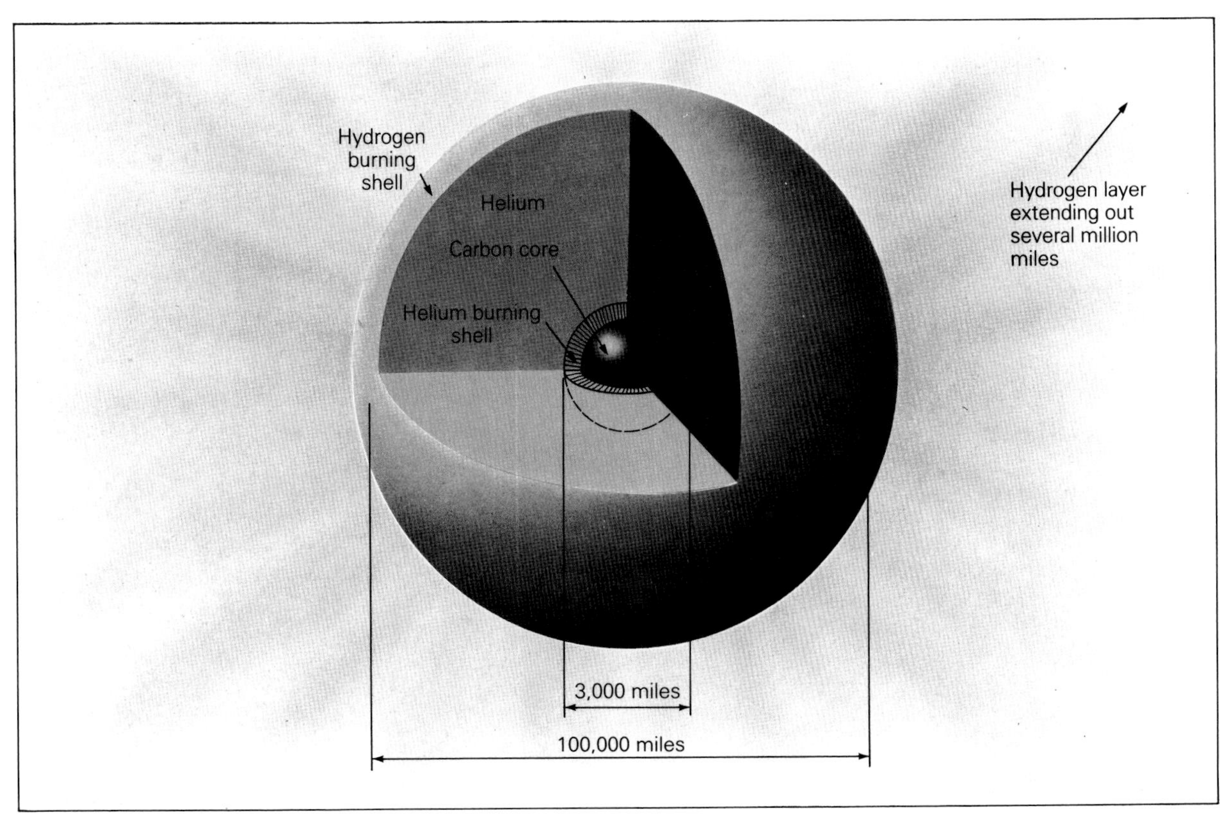

7.1 Helium is being made in a shell around the collapsing core, which eventually heats to the point where carbon is fused from helium nuclei.

massive as the sun from the time that its core is pure helium until it reaches the status of a red giant. The horizontal track is the period of constant luminosity as the star swells and the photosphere cools. The expanding star is seeking hydrostatic equilibrium, but with more outflowing energy to support the star its dimensions must be greater than they were while on the main sequence.

From the time the star of one solar mass left the main sequence and followed the constant-luminosity track, only about 1 billion years have passed. The final stages of stellar evolution, as with the birth of stars, proceed at a very rapid rate. As the star expands and cools, a convective zone develops that reaches deep into the star's interior and transports energy rapidly to the outer layers. At this point the star becomes considerably brighter, moving up into the red giant area on the H-R diagram. The luminosity of a star the mass of the sun may increase by some 500 times in only about 300 million years. Thus, from main sequence to red giant will take the sun only about 1.4 billion years.

7.2 A Hertzsprung-Russell diagram for a $1M_\odot$ (one solar mass) star from the point where the stellar core has become pure helium from the burning of hydrogen while on the main sequence. The star becomes a red giant in only a little over a billion years.

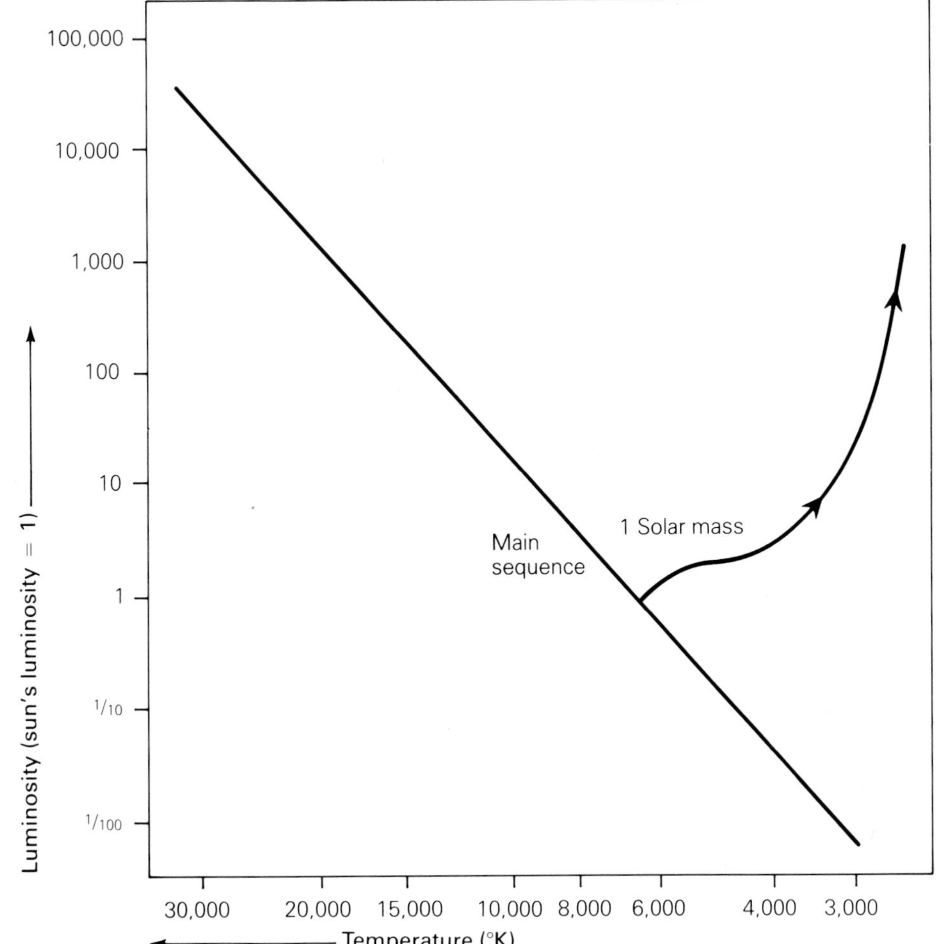

Red Giant Stars

It is instructive to compare a main-sequence star with a red giant. In its prime of life, the sun is about 1.4 million kilometers in diameter, but the red giant it will eventually become will be about 100 million kilometers across, and its atmosphere will reach close to the earth. The red giant's core will be more than twice the size of the earth. As its temperature reaches about 100 million° K the star will begin a completely new state in its life—the burning of helium.

One would think that once the core is hot enough to commence the fusion of helium as an energy source, the star should become brighter and bigger, but something is happening in the interior of a red giant that bears no resemblance to activity on the main sequence.

The atoms of the pure helium core are so densely packed that they cannot be packed any more tightly. The electrons have been stripped away from the nuclei because of the very high temperature, and nuclei and electrons alike are compressed into something so dense that it is comparable to metal. When metal is heated, it expands, but not as much as a gas would, so the core of a red giant does not expand very much even though its temperature increases considerably. With the core having many properties of a sphere of metal, the star reacts quite differently from the way it acted during hydrogen fusion. As helium nuclei are converted into carbon nuclei, the energy released in the nuclear reactions makes the core hotter. The triple alpha process goes faster and faster and the core gets hotter and hotter. Where once a controlled set of nuclear reactions released energy, there now exists a runaway fusion process—like a bomb. In only a few hours' time, the core becomes so hot that it explodes, an event we call the *helium flash*.

Figure 7.3 shows a cutaway drawing of a red giant's core after the helium flash. There is still a hydrogen-burning shell around the core, and the helium nuclei in the center core are being converted into carbon at a very rapid pace. Figure 7.4 is a continuation of the evolutionary path shown in Figure 7.2. The star drops from the red giant region because the temperature of the core and the hydrogen-burning shell drop rapidly after the explosion in the interior. The diameter of the red giant begins to shrink because less energy is flowing out now than before the helium flash. This period in a star's life lasts only a few thousand years, until the helium burning is capable of supporting the swollen outer layers that previously were collapsing. Once hydrostatic equilibrium is achieved, the star stops shrinking and begins to brighten. On the H-R diagram, this is the move to the left that brings the star very close to the main sequence.

Carbon and oxygen, however, fill the core of the star at this point, and helium is burning in a shell around it. The carbon-oxygen core collapses as did the helium core, the star is driven back toward the red giant region, and the star nears the end of its life. From this point on we cannot be certain of the details of stellar evolution, but we have a general idea of what transpires in the next several million years. The story described above holds true for stars up to about four times as massive as the sun. The core of a star approximately as massive as the sun will never begin burning carbon or oxygen that has built up in the core; the end lies in the story of white dwarf stars.

Planetary Nebulae

It is the fate of stars less massive than about $4M_\odot$ (4 solar masses) to have relatively slow, inconsequential deaths. The star's core is about 200 billion° K, but it has become solid carbon and oxygen and cannot produce nuclear reactions at so *cool* a temperature. The star returns to the red giant region with an increased diameter and cooler surface temperature.

The outer layers become so cool—about 3,500° K—that nuclei begin capturing electrons and forming complete atoms. As atoms recombine in the extended stellar atmosphere of a red giant star, they emit radiation that is captured by other atoms. This heats the gas up and causes it to expand outward, but this time the expansion continues and what started as a stellar atmosphere becomes an envelope surrounding the core. Eventually, the envelope expands to the point that it actually leaves the star's core completely and blows into interstellar space.

If we could observe the entire process, we would at first see little change in the star. We could measure the expansion of the outer layers of the star, but the total

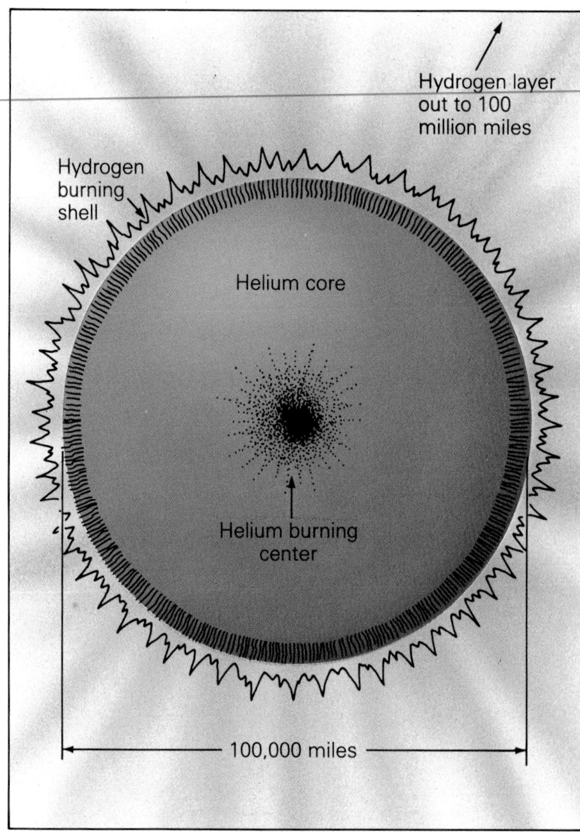

7.3 A cutaway of the core of a red giant star in which carbon is forming during helium burning. Hydrogen still fuses to form helium in a thin shell around the core.

luminosity would stay the same. After a while the envelope would have expanded far enough to become somewhat transparent, and we would see the exposed core.

We have seen objects that fit this description, which we call planetary nebulae because through small telescopes their disk shape made people think they looked like planets. Figures 7.8, 7.9, and 7.10 are examples of planetary nebulae that clearly show the expanding shell and a faint hot star in the center. Planetary nebulae are beautiful, often appearing greenish because of emission by oxygen atoms. Many planetaries look like rings, but this is a geometric effect that occurs because we look at them obliquely through the edges. Figure 7.5 shows the geometry of an expanding shell and why we see more gas when we look at the edge. Other planetary nebulae do appear to be spherical shells, such as those in Figures 7.6 and 7.7.

When we described some planetaries as glowing in green light, we alluded to a very important fact. Oxygen, which was made in the star during its lifetime, is being returned to the interstellar medium, where it will someday be part of another, younger star. We will see other processes that enrich the space between the stars, but the ejection of atmospheres by stars at the end of their lives is certainly one efficient way.

As the envelope blows off into space, the central core is left. In several photographs of planetary nebulae this tiny star is easily identifiable. Figure 7.12 is an H-R diagram that continues on from the red giant stage through the formation of a planetary nebula. The dotted line is what we presented previously, and the solid track, although not a theoretical certainty, represents the last stages of a $1M_{\odot}$ star. Now the final years of the star are displayed. As the outer layers heat up and

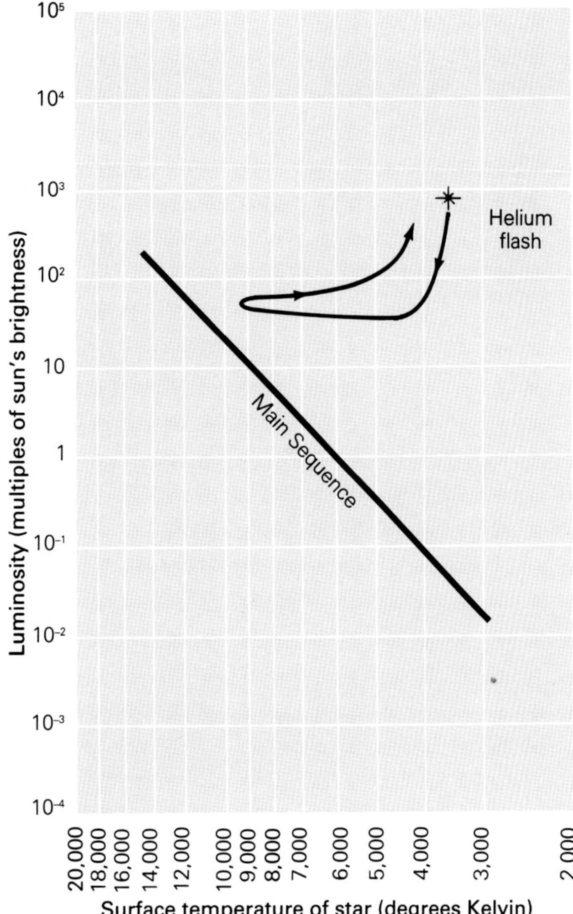

7.4 The evolutionary path of a $1M_{\odot}$ star once the helium flash has occurred. The luminosity and size of the star decrease rapidly until hydrostatic equilibrium is achieved.

Electron Degeneracy

In the 1920s some of the greatest minds in the world of physics began developing a new understanding of how atoms work. This part of physics has become known as quantum mechanics. It is based on the notion that energy exists in discrete packets called quanta.

One of the quantum mechanical properties of electrons was outlined by the distinguished scientist Wolfgang Pauli. He showed that there is a minimum volume into which a given number of electrons can be compressed. This state of maximum compression does not occur because the electrons have negative charges that repel each other, nor because the electrons might be touching. In fact, the electrons never touch in this complicated quantum mechanical process. This state of electron compression is called electron degeneracy. When a star collapses to the point at which degeneracy occurs, the electrons resist further compression and the stellar collapse can be halted.

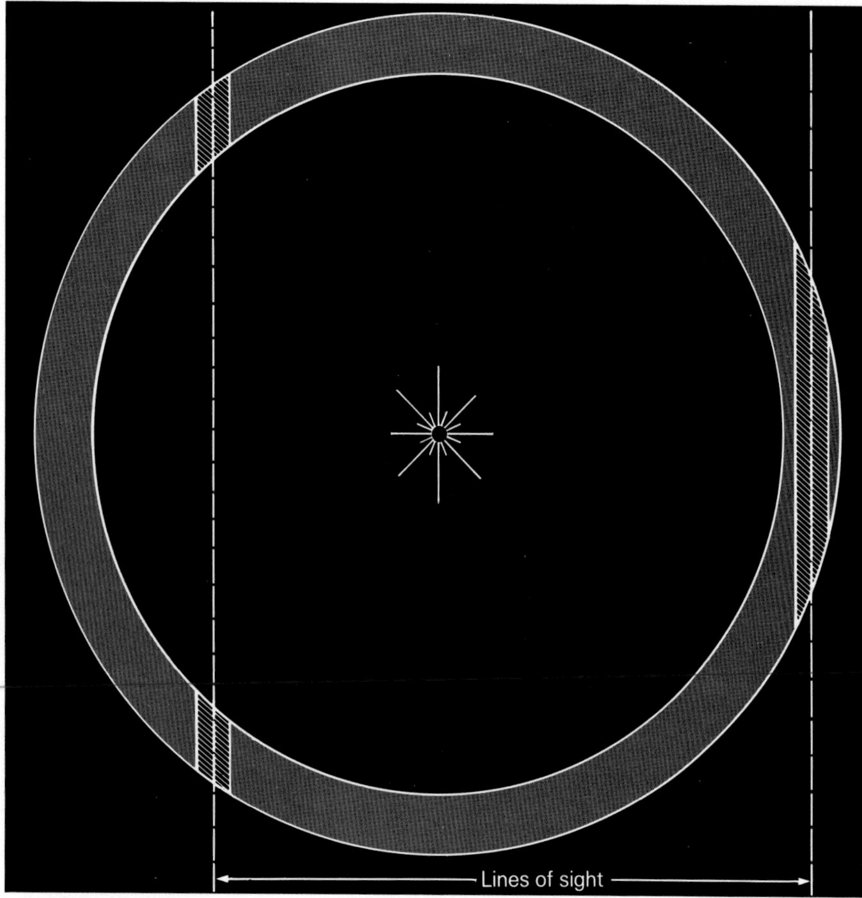

7.5 The geometry of an expanding shell (top view) *that illustrates why planetary nebulae often look like rings. The line of sight at the edge "sees" more gas and thus appears brighter than the view through the center of the nebula.*

expand due to radiative processes within the atmosphere, the star moves rapidly to the left of the diagram because of increased temperature, but its luminosity does not change very much. The rapid shift to the left occurs because we were first measuring the 3,500° K atmosphere, but as it dissipates, we suddenly observe the core of the star, which is about 50,000° K at its surface.

When the hot core is fully exposed, the star will be ringed by a planetary nebula like those in the photographs we have seen. A cutaway of the core might look like Figure 7.13. The hydrogen layers have been blown off to reveal the helium-burning shell surrounding a dense core of carbon and oxygen. The temperature of the core never reaches the 800 million° K required to ignite carbon, so this central remnant of the red giant star collapses slowly under its own weight. As it collapses it heats up, but before it can become hot enough to ignite carbon, the gas reaches that strange realm of incompressibility of the electrons and nuclei, just as it did before the helium flash. This state is called *electron degeneracy*. It is derived from quantum mechanics and is not intuitively obvious, but it does stop the contraction when the object is about 16,000 kilometers across and has a density of several tons per cubic inch. The star is called a white dwarf and is very hot, but it is faint because it is so small.

Figure 7.14 shows the relative sizes of the sun, the

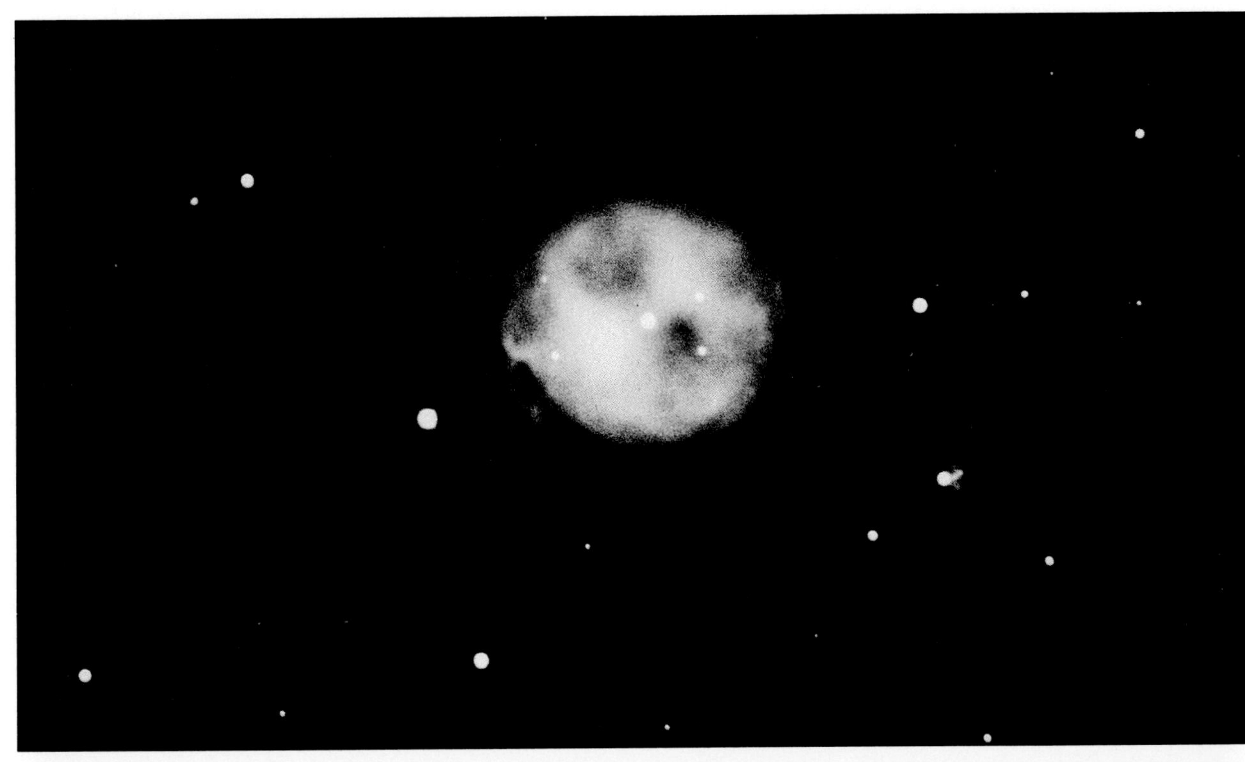

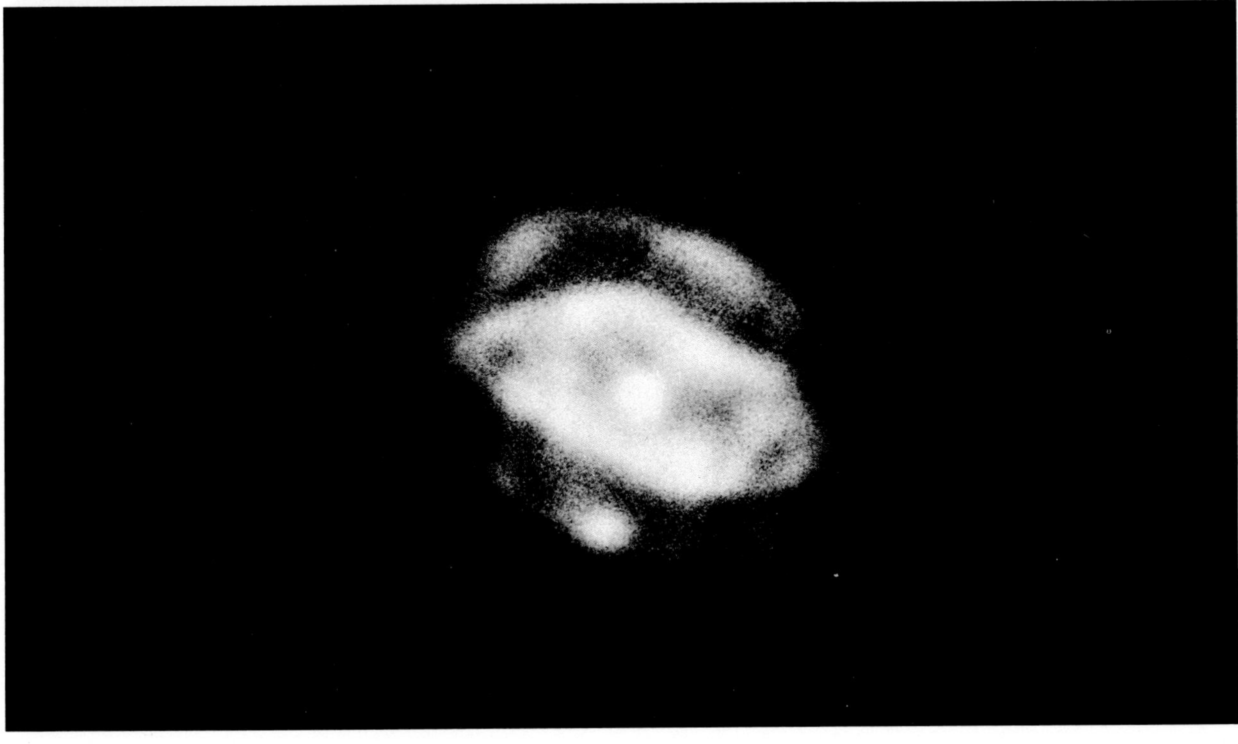

7.6, 7.7 *Planetary nebulae do not always look like rings. Sometimes more of the expanding cloud is visible, as in these two examples.*

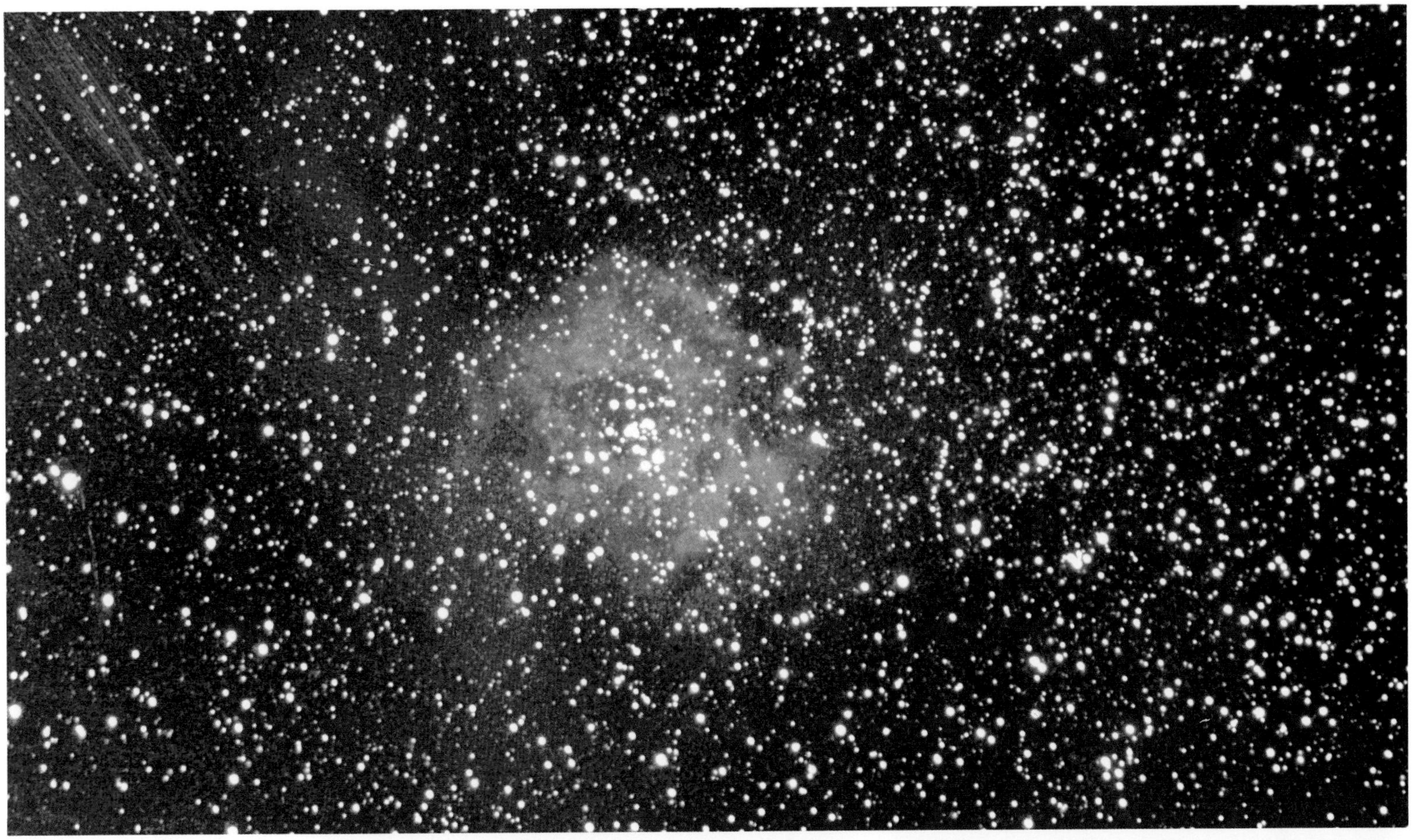

7.8, 7.9, 7.10 *Planetary nebulae appearing to the observer as a ring with a small white star at the center.*

7.11 Far right: *A low-magnification photograph of a planetary nebula with the disk shape that led people to think that they were planets.*

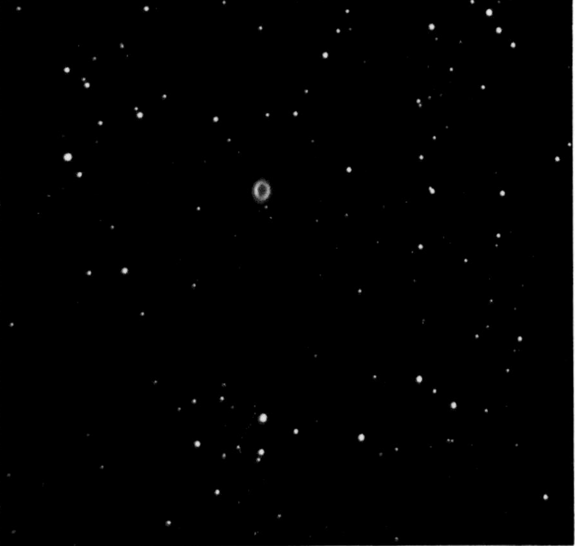

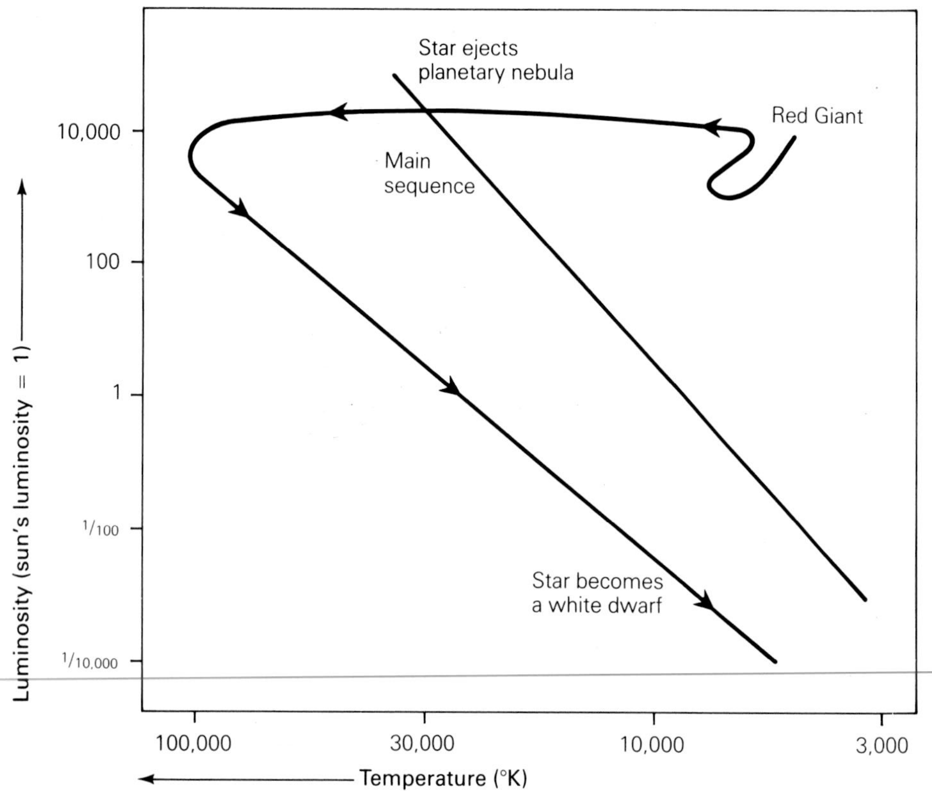

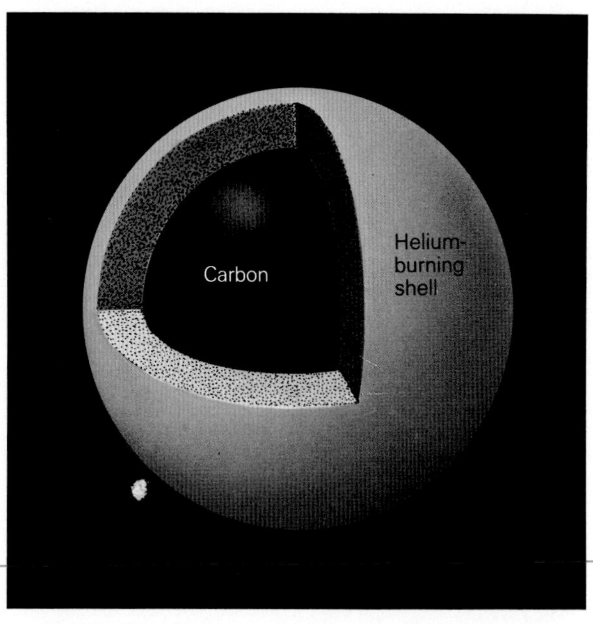

7.12 Left: *The H-R diagram of a $1M_\odot$ star as it goes from the red giant stage to ejection of the planetary nebula.*

7.13 Right: *A schematic of the remaining core of a star that has formed a planetary nebula. Helium is burning in a shell around a core of carbon and oxygen. The surface of the stellar remnant is about 50,000° K.*

earth, and a white dwarf. On the H-R diagram in Figure 7.12 the stellar core in the planetary nebula drops rapidly in luminosity and temperature as the white dwarf forms from the stellar remnant. White dwarfs have played an important role in the development of the theory of gravity. It is worth a brief digression to see the way scientists postulated white dwarfs and later observed them.

A Case Study: Sirius A and B

Much of the pioneering work on white dwarf stars was done by Subrahmanyan Chandrasekhar in the 1930s. While a student in England, he developed the theoretical framework that helped describe their properties. He relied on Einstein's theory of gravity, called the theory of general relativity, and on quantum mechanics, which determines the way atoms work. One of the important parts of Chandrasekhar's work included electron degeneracy, which he used to predict the maximum mass a white dwarf might have. He found that a white dwarf could be no more than $1.4M_\odot$, but even stars that are 3 and $4M_\odot$ can eject enough of their own body in planetary nebulae to meet this upper limit on the mass.

The theoretical notion that such highly condensed stars exist made sense out of a puzzle that had been plaguing astronomers for years. Sirius, which appears as the brightest star in the night sky, has a small companion star that can be photographed with special techniques. This tiny star exerts a great deal of gravitational pull on the far brighter, more massive Sirius. Scientists understood why only once they realized that a star that has become a white dwarf is small and hot, and has a very high gravitational attraction. Sirius B,

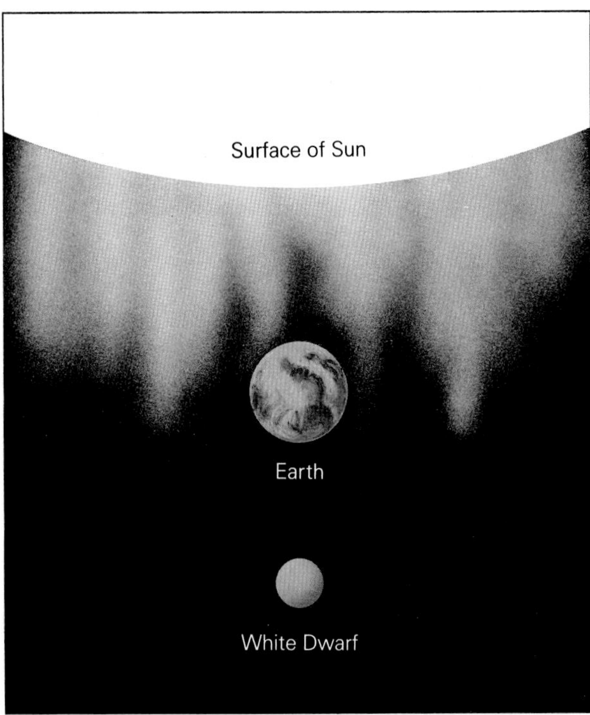

7.14 The relative sizes of the sun, the earth, and a white dwarf star.

as the companion is called, is a white dwarf.

Astronomers have located more than 500 white dwarf stars, which when plotted on an H-R diagram fall in the region of hot, faint stars at the lower left. The evolutionary track of a dying star of approximately the same mass as the sun leads down into this region of the diagram.

To Dying Embers

Central stars of planetary nebulae fall on the H-R diagram as hot, bright stars in the upper left region, but as we have seen they are on their way to a dark finale. As the remaining bit of star in a planetary nebula contracts once the core is solid carbon, it heats up, but not to a point where carbon is ignited. The star is on the way to a state of electron degeneracy and twilight existence as a white dwarf.

Once the star is a white dwarf, it simply cools off by emitting energy into space. As the temperature of a white dwarf declines, it emits less and less light, much as a dying ember fades in the fireplace once the fire has gone out. The final extinguishing of a star like the sun occurs when all of the heat is gone and a dark cinder remains in space. Naturally, it is not possible to observe a star that is not emitting any light; astronomers call these objects *black dwarfs*. The cooling of a white dwarf takes many billions of years, and it has even been suggested that the universe is not old enough for any black dwarfs to have yet formed.

The Death of the Sun

In about 5 billion years, our earth will end its last perfect day as the sun stumbles upon old age. If humankind still dominates the world, perhaps only humans will be able to recognize what is happening. The rest of the animal world will be as surprised as the dinosaurs were some 65 million years ago when they faced mass extinction unaware of the events that were taking place.

When we imagine the earth 5 billion years hence, we should not think of it as we know it now. Since its beginning 4.5 billion years ago, the earth has changed much, due primarily to geologic activity and the development of life. The earth formed, as did the other planets, asteroids, and comets, from material in the nebula that formed the sun. We see evidence all around us that heavy elements such as iron, nitrogen, oxygen, and uranium exist in the sun and planets, so the solar nebula was undoubtedly enriched by dying stars long before the solar system formed.

As the protoearth orbited the new sun, the liquid sphere was bubbling and beginning to harden. The heaviest matter sank to the core, and jets of gases such as water vapor and carbon dioxide escaped the surface.

These gases formed the earth's atmosphere. The precise characteristics of the atmosphere at that time are crucial to our exploration here, because from it came the atoms and molecules that shaped life. We will discuss this shortly.

As the molten surface hardened, solid islands of granite may have been the predecessors of the continents. These giant conglomerates of crystal spread outward and downward until they rested on a previously hardened crust. The earth was still very hot, and it was shrouded with a thick layer of clouds. As the earth cooled, the vapor in the atmosphere condensed into drops and fell to the earth as rain. The hot rocks boiled the rain into steam, which rose again into the sky. The rain, however, continued to fall and cool the rocks to the point where the water no longer turned to steam at contact, but rather ran down the mountains into the valleys, lay in pools, and emptied into large basins that we call the oceans. As the clouds thinned, the new continents and seas lay beneath the sun for the first time.

The generally accepted theory about the origin of life was published in 1924 by the distinguished Russian biochemist A. I. Oparin. Life's origin is the result of the long, slow evolution of matter from the big bang to successively more complex chemical structures.

So far in the earth's young life, there was no free oxygen in the gaseous envelope surrounding the earth.

7.15 Sirius A (the bright star) and its faint companion white dwarf (Sirius B). The spikes on the stars are caused by the method of photography and are not part of the stars themselves.

7.16 The Dumbbell Nebula is a planetary nebula that does not appear as a ring. The tiny white star at its center ejected its outer layers at the end of its life as a red giant.

This is one of the most important features during the years preceding the dawn of life. Solar radiation and lightning gave energy to the chemical reactions going on in the earth's atmosphere. This was crucial to the development of life, but ultraviolet radiation is also hazardous to life forms since it causes chemical reactions that lead to the destruction of cells. In the beginning, however, the world needed the ultraviolet radiation because it supplied vital energy for the synthesis of a great many chemical compounds. Life then formed in the oceans, where the water probably shielded the cells from radiation until plant life, through photosynthesis, had supplied oxygen to the atmosphere.

Oxygen is dangerously corrosive; only by complicated chemical means are life forms protected from oxidizing. Oxidation would cause severe problems for organic compounds that had not yet developed protective means. On the other hand, the free oxygen formed the ozone layer that protects life from solar radiation. Once shielded from the lethal bath of ultraviolet light that the sun emits, life could get a foothold on land, and the world changed forever as plants and animals proliferated and spread to the frigid regions of the poles and into the hottest desert.

There is no guarantee that the world in 5 billion years will look anything like it does now. But imagine, if you will, a tranquil scene far in the future. The land is green, and oceans gently lick the beaches of the world. A small group of the dominant animal species meanders at the water's edge. The yellow sun shines brilliantly through the clear sky.

The sun, however, is about to change. Its hydrogen core is used up, converted to a solid core of helium. The helium core contracts because there is no energy to support it from its own gravitational pull. As it collapses, it heats up and drives the temperature of the surrounding region higher until hydrogen fuses in a shell around the core. As this happens the sun begins to expand into a red giant star.

On earth, the sun appears to be getting bigger in the sky. The earth heats up as the sun gives off more energy than before, and the ice caps at the north and south pole melt. The oceans rise and cover the coastal regions, destroying thousands of seaside cities.

The earth gets hotter still, until the water on the surface boils away in great clouds of steam. The sun, now a large red ball in the sky, is almost invisible through the thick layers of clouds. The earth looks much like Venus.

The temperature continues to rise as the sun expands. The atmosphere boils away and the stars shine in the daytime next to the bloated sun. The sun's ultraviolet radiation destroys plant life, and animals die species by species. The herbivores are the first to go. Needing flesh to survive, the carnivores die out also.

Eventually, the earth turns molten as the rocks melt and the sun fills the cloudless sky. The outer layers of the red giant star reach the earth, vaporize it as if nothing were in their way, and expand toward Mars.

That is the end of the earth, but the sun lives on. Its outer atmosphere will begin to contract again and helium will ignite in the core. Eventually, with an interior of solid oxygen and carbon, the sun will expel its outer layers for good in a beautiful planetary nebula, and the sun will cool and grow dim. Somewhere, perhaps, an intelligent civilization will watch the elegant expression of one dying star we called sun.

7.17 The diffuse nebula 30 Doradus in the Large Magellanic Cloud is one of the few nebulae resolvable in galaxies other than our own Milky Way.

8: SUPERNOVAE

The Fate of Massive Stars

In the previous chapter, we explored the death of stars whose mass is approximately the same as that of our sun. What of more massive stars? How do they meet their end? Stars with masses greater than about $4M_\odot$ have explosive deaths, a fact realized only in the 1960s. Before that people thought that all stars would become white dwarfs, although some interesting notions about superdense stellar objects had surfaced in the 1930s and 1940s that were not taken seriously until the entire picture of stellar evolution was developed theoretically.

During most of their lives the only substantial difference between the evolution of massive stars and those such as the sun is the speed with which they evolve. Massive stars use up their hydrogen fuel faster than do less massive stars. Once the hydrogen is gone, stars with mass greater than about $4M_\odot$ become red giant stars, ignite a helium flash, and eventually form a core of solid carbon and oxygen. The carbon core is massive enough to collapse and raise the internal temperature to almost 600 million° K, which is the point at which carbon can fuse to produce oxygen, neon, and magnesium. Helium continues burning in a shell surrounding the carbon core, and around the helium is a layer of hydrogen that is fusing into helium.

The mass of a star again determines the next step in its evolution. If the mass is more than about $6M_\odot$, the core collapses and heats to 1 billion° K and the oxygen ignites. Figure 8.2 shows the eventual state of a massive star that has undergone successive ignition of the fusion process. After exhausting oxygen, the core burns silicon, which requires a temperature of at least 2 billion° K. At each stage the star's size and luminosity change; a star may become a red giant many times. Figure 8.3 is an H-R diagram of two massive stars that have evolved off the main sequence once the hydrogen in their cores has been depleted. The evolutionary tracks of the stars run horizontally, with slight steps up in brightness when each new element ignites in the core. As the stars expand and contract, their surface temperatures change (as the star expands, it cools; as

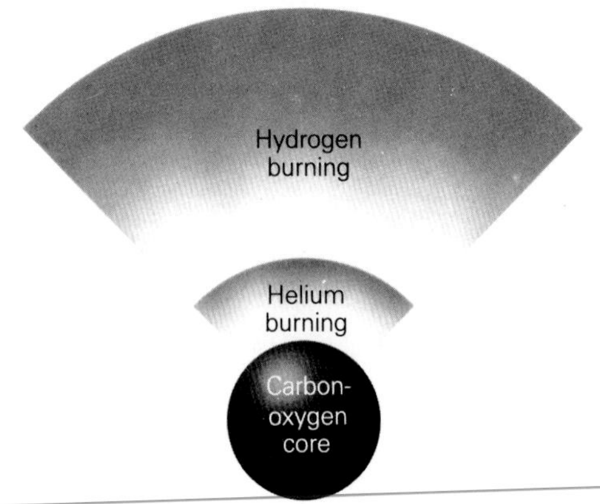

8.1 *The composite nuclear burning of hydrogen, helium, and carbon is illustrated in this schematic of a massive star.*

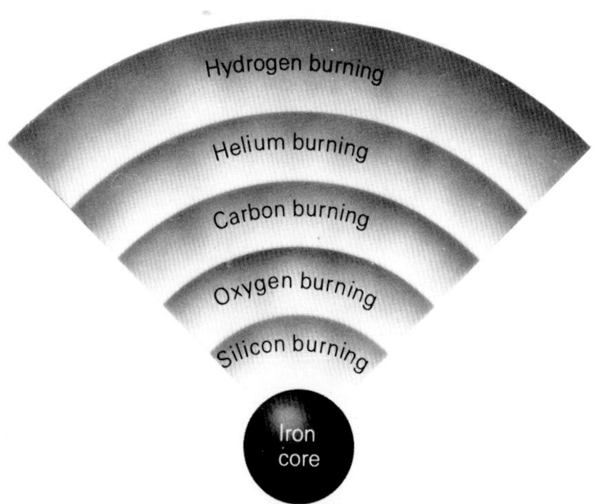

8.2 *The state of a massive star that has undergone several successive periods of nuclear burning. Layers are built upon layers, where different elements fuse into heavier nuclei.*

8.3 Below: *The H-R diagram of two massive stars after leaving the main sequence. Each ignition of a different nuclear fuel results in the stepped increase in luminosity and the left-to-right shifting of temperatures at the stellar surface.*

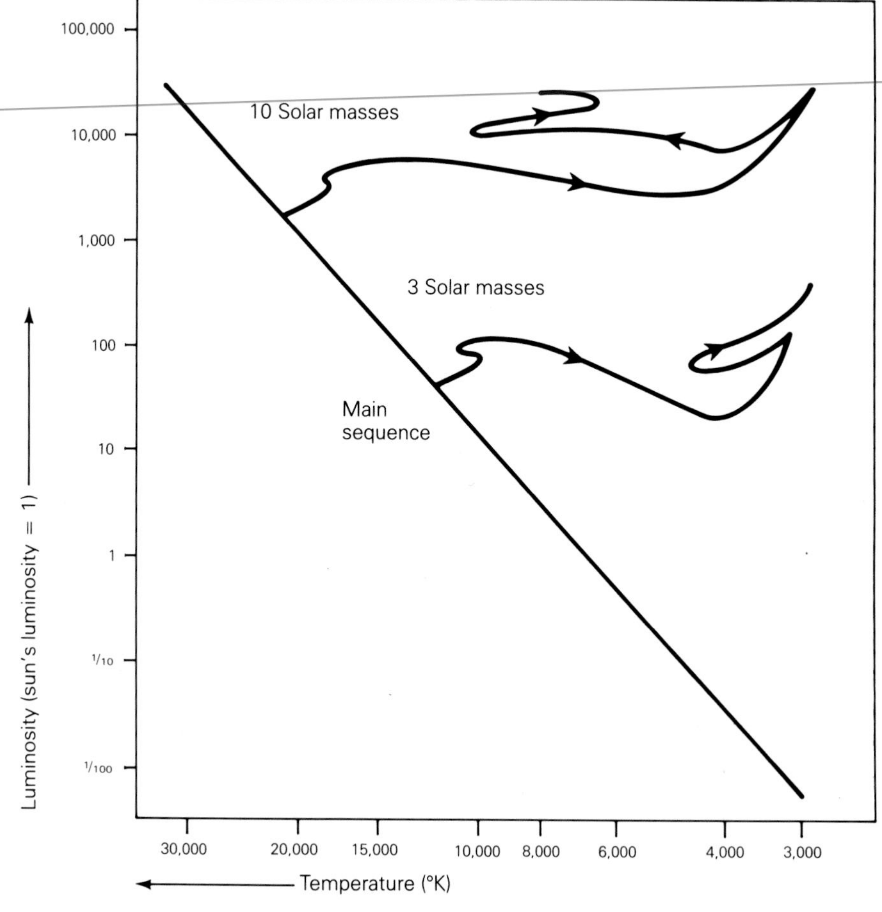

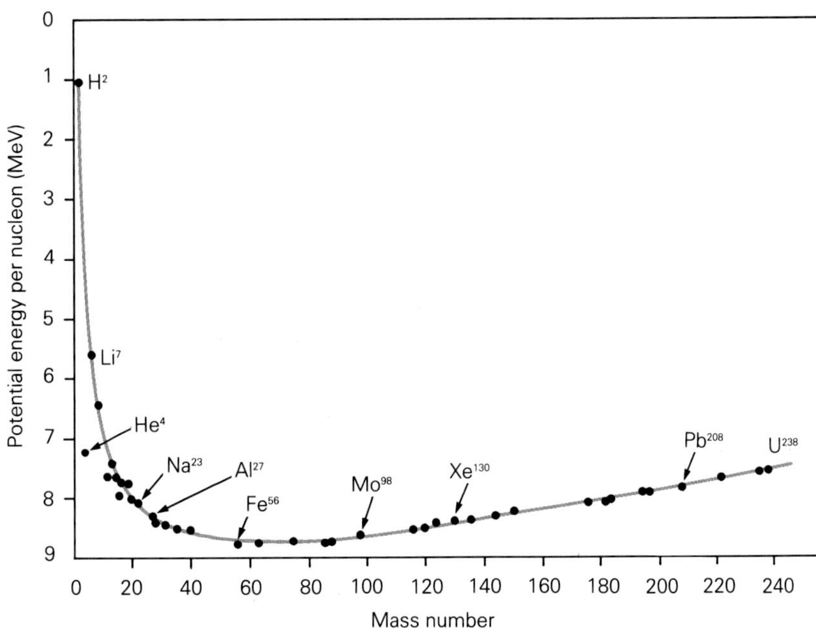

8.4 *Very massive stars can build all atoms up to iron (Fe). The nuclear reactions cease at the center once the core is pure iron. A graph of energy of different nuclei shows the unusual character of the iron nucleus, caused by its dense nature.*

it contracts, it heats up), accounting for the left-to-right shift on the H-R diagram. Eventually, the core of a very massive star is pure iron.

Iron is an unusual element in that it has a particularly dense nucleus that keeps it from fusing and releasing energy. In fact, iron tends to absorb energy, so when the star collapses the iron core absorbs the heat and will never ignite and release energy to keep the star supported. The nuclear fires have been extinguished.

What happens to massive stars when energy production in the core ceases? They explode in a cataclysmic moment of destruction.

Supernovae: Explosive Deaths of Massive Stars

Stars with a mass of between about $4M_\odot$ and $8M_\odot$ explode when the carbon ignites in the core. When a temperature of about 600 million° K is reached, carbon starts fusing into oxygen, but as with the helium flash in stars of $1M_\odot$ to $4M_\odot$, the carbon burns in a runaway reaction of increasing temperature and faster rates of nuclear fusion. In a sense the core detonates itself, and the incredible pressure built up by the exploding core throws practically all of the star into space. This explosive event is called a supernova.

Another kind of supernova occurs when iron builds up in the cores of stars with masses greater than about $8M_\odot$. Once the iron extinguishes the nuclear fires at a massive star's center, the pressure that supported the outer layers decreases and the star collapses in one of the most dramatic events in the cosmos. As the star collapses on itself, the density gets so high in the center that the nuclei are touching each other and the contraction halts. But like a tightly wound spring, the star rebounds with such tremendous energy that it explodes into space. So violent an event is this that it seems as if a new star suddenly glows with the brightness of a billion stars as its matter is heated and hurled into space.

During supernova explosions, nuclei capture free neutrons and in this way build many of the elements heavier than iron. The interstellar medium becomes enriched with matter that may someday play a role in the formation of the second-generation stars such as the sun and of rocky worlds such as the earth.

When a supernova explosion occurs, we observe that it increases very rapidly in luminosity and then decreases over a period of several months until the star fades from view. We have observed supernovae in distant galaxies that have shone with the brilliance of all the stars in the galaxy combined. Nearby supernovae might be seen in the daytime, although none has occurred in the solar neighborhood for several hundred years.

There is another type of supernova that is observed in close binary star systems, but the rapid brightening in emission is not caused by collapse and detonation of an old star. In a double star system in which one star has evolved to a compact state such as a white dwarf or neutron star, material is pulled from the normal star onto the surface of the collapsed one. The accreted

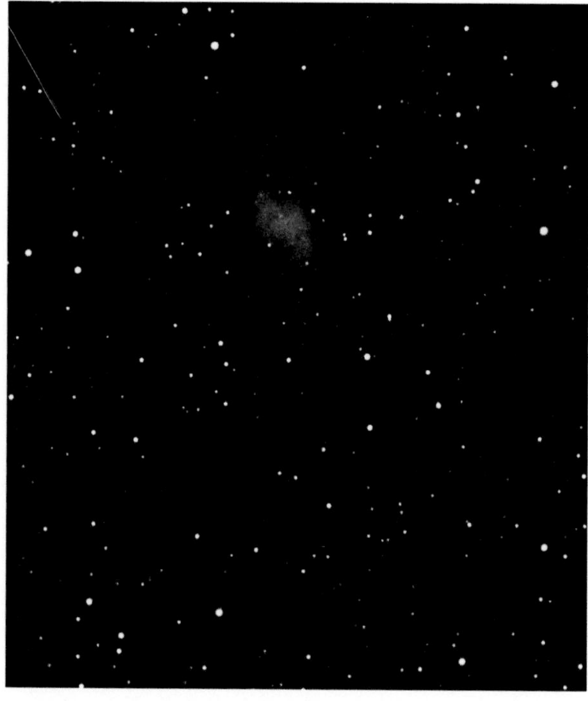

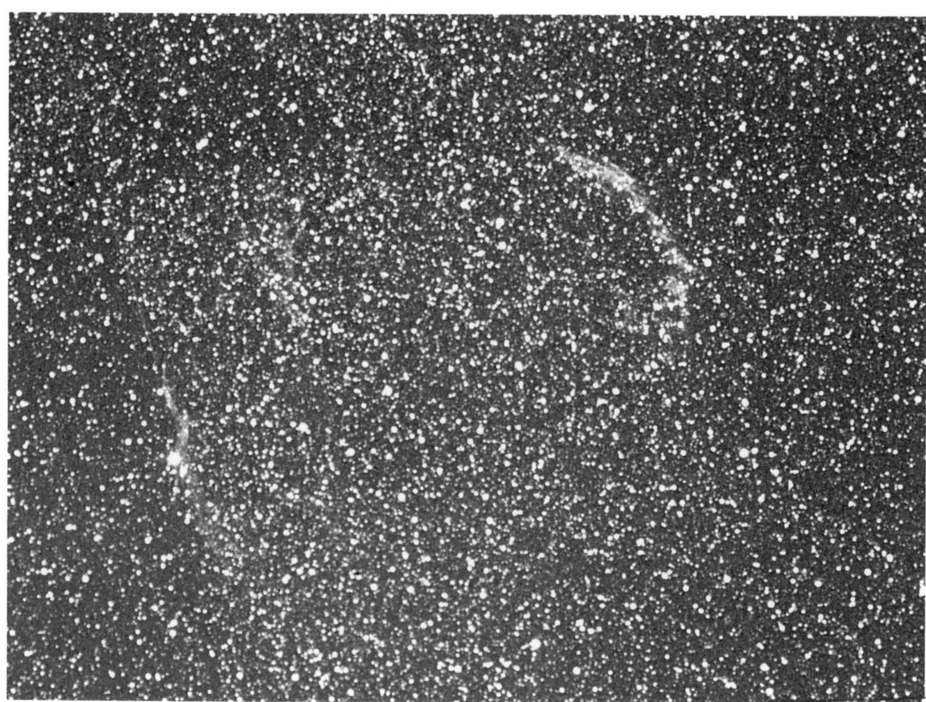

material can build up on the surface of the stellar remnant until it becomes unstable and explodes with great force. This family of supernovae is called type II.

The star system shines very brightly in a way similar to the normal type of supernova (type I supernova), although the light curves of the types differ in detail. It is also likely that novae operate on much the same principle as type II supernovae.

Supernova Remnants

As with planetary nebulae, a supernova ejects a great deal of matter into space that may be visible through telescopes. We call these clouds of gas supernova remnants: they are reminders of the explosive death of massive stars. Figures 8.5, 8.6, and 8.7 are three supernova remnants of different ages. The Cygnus loop is a very old remnant that has been expanding for millions of years, so that its filamentary structure is spread out across a large portion of the sky. A young supernova remnant is considerably more compact. This is the case with the remnant called Cassiopeia A (Figure 8.8). We know these clouds are expanding because we can measure the Doppler shifts of atoms as the gas rushes toward us from the explosion. In time all supernova remnants will expand and grow diffuse as the matter from the dead star spreads out through the interstellar medium. Supernova remnants are among the most exquisite and delicate nebulae in the universe. Their tenuous filamentary structure is often a clue of the cataclysmic end of a massive star.

8.5, 8.6, 8.7 Above left, right, and opposite page top: *Three supernova remnants that have expanded to different sizes because of their age difference. The oldest remnant has become considerably larger because it has had time to do so. It also becomes more diffuse as it spreads out across the interstellar medium.*

Guest Stars

People in many cultures have considered celestial events to be portents. During the Dark Ages in Europe, Asian and Oriental astronomy flourished as dynasties sought important astronomical signs, such as

8.8 Below right: *Cassiopeia A, a supernova remnant shown here in X-ray emission, is a relatively young nebula that is still very compact.*

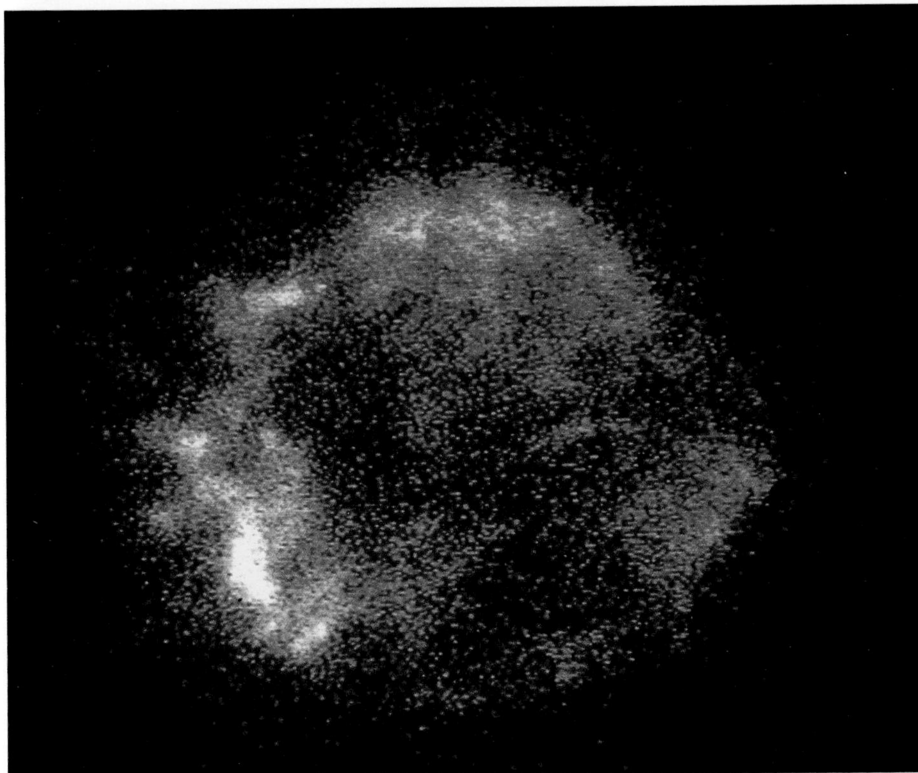

comets, novae, and supernovae, upon which to base decisions.

Although a few dozen supernova remnants have been observed to remind us of the explosive death of massive stars, only four supernovae themselves, "guest stars," have been recorded in human history. Only recently have these been connected to observable remnants.

In April A.D. 1006, a supernova occurred in the constellation Lupus, the hare. Scientists and historians have worked together to translate chronicles of Arabic and Chinese court astrologers, who observed this supernova shining brightly for more than a year before fading from view. It is very difficult to spot the gaseous remnant of the stellar blast, but in 1965 radio emissions were detected by astronomers from this location in the sky.

In A.D. 1054, Chinese astronomers again recorded a guest star, this time in the constellation Taurus. The Crab Nebula was later cataloged by Charles Messier in the 1770s, but not until the latter part of the 1920s was it suggested and essentially verified that the Crab

Nebula is the remnant of the 1054 supernova. Edwin Hubble, who is known for his measurement of the expansion of the universe, also suggested that, at its current rate of expansion, it formed about 900 years ago. Later studies by several scientists provided confirmation of Hubble's suggestion.

The great observational astronomer Tycho Brahe saw a supernova in 1572 and studied its brightness daily until it faded from view. He published a book about this new star in which he reported that it appeared brighter than any other fixed star in the sky and that on a clear day it could be seen at noon. Finally, in early 1574 it disappeared from view. In 1952 the gaseous remnant of Tycho's supernova was found first with radio waves and then with the 200-inch telescope on Mount Palomar.

Johannes Kepler, whom we remember because of his studies of planetary orbits, recorded a supernova in the year 1604. Not until 1941 did Walter Baade, at the Mount Wilson Observatory in California, find a nebula in the approximate location of Kepler's supernova. It has been more than 350 years since a supernova has been observed in our galaxy. Since astronomers expect one every hundred years or so, we are due for one soon.

Most recent supernovae have occurred in galaxies other than our own. Figure 8.11 shows an example of a supernova in a distant galaxy where the intensity of the exploding star was as great as that of the combined light of all the other stars in that galaxy

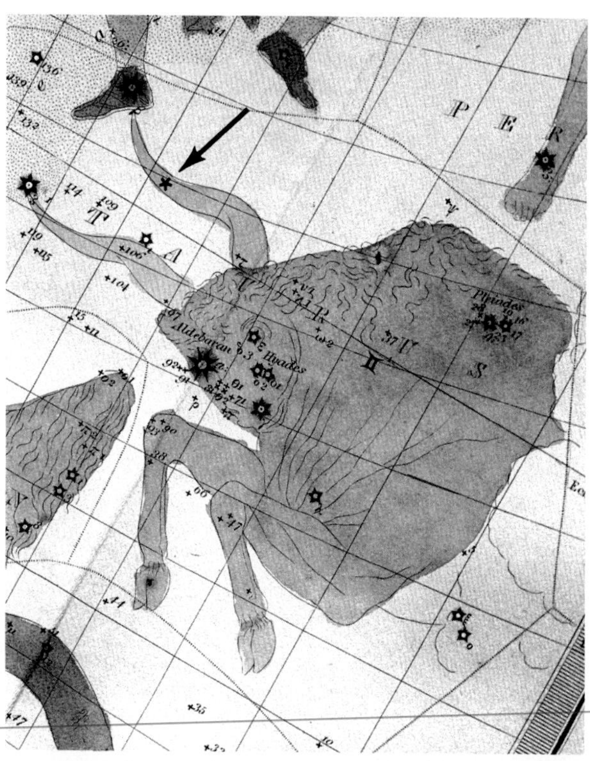

8.9 *The constellation Taurus and the location of the supernova of A.D. 1054.*

8.10 *Tycho Brahe, one of the greatest observational astronomers who ever lived.*

The Making of a Neutron Star

It is possible for all of a star to be destroyed during a supernova, but in some cases the star's core may remain at the center of the supernova remnant. The existence of a compact object was predicted by theory in 1933 by Fritz Zwicky and Walter Baade at the California Institute of Technology. They calculated that electrons and protons could be squeezed together in a star to form neutrons provided that temperatures and densities are high enough. These conditions exist at the center of massive stars once the final collapse begins. Much of the star's original mass is crushed into a ball only about 32 kilometers across, and this region of pure neutrons is left behind when the star explodes and throws its outer layers into the space between the stars. Astronomers called this theoretical object a *neutron star*.

8.11 A supernova in a distant galaxy outshines its stellar system, but it fades over a period of months and eventually disappears.

SUPERNOVA IN IC 4182

a

b

c

a) 1937 Aug.23. Exposure 20^m. Maximum brightness.
b) 1938 Nov.24. " 45^m. Faint.
c) 1942 Jan.19. " 85^m. Too faint to observe.

A neutron star exists because the gravitational collapse is halted by what is called degenerate neutron pressure. White dwarfs consist of approximately $1.4M_\odot$ compressed into a volume only slightly smaller than the earth but supported against gravity by electron degenerate pressure (that is, the state when electrons can be packed no more tightly together). Neutron stars are supported against gravity in an analogous fashion when neutrons are packed as closely as possible. In the case of neutron stars, however, between $1M_\odot$ and $3M_\odot$ are compressed into a ball only about 30 kilometers in diameter. A teaspoonful of a neutron star might weigh as much as 1 billion tons.

It seemed that there would be no way of observing a neutron star, and for decades the notion of finding one in space proved fruitless, until 1967.

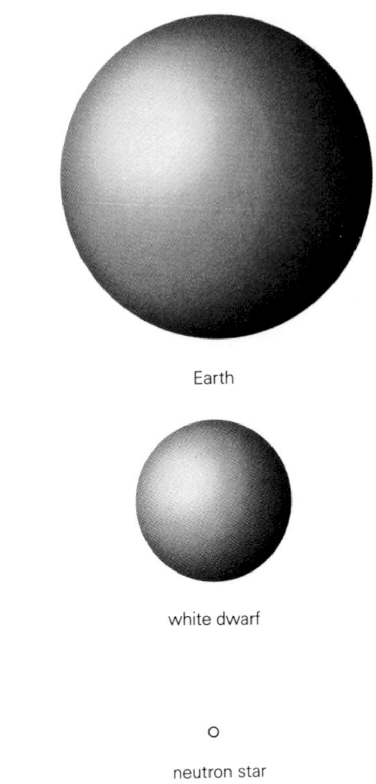

8.12 A size comparison of the earth, a white dwarf, and a neutron star.

Radio Astronomy and the Discovery of Pulsars

Beginning in 1931 with Karl Jansky's discovery of radio waves in outer space, astronomers began to build large radio telescopes around the world. They aided us in discovering the shape of our galaxy, protostars in formation, and a few interstellar molecules (most of the interstellar molecules have been observed since the late 1960s).

Most radio sources from space emit a constant flux of radiation, and just as with radios in our homes, there exists a low-level static in the signal from celestial sources. Astronomers have devised ways to average the signal over a period of time so that any rapid variations in intensity due to static will tend to cancel themselves and leave only the true signal. Although this averaging also removes any true rapid variations from the source, celestial objects were not expected to emit rapid fluctuations of radio waves, so scientists did not consider this a problem.

One reason that radio sources appear to fluctuate in "brightness" is that clouds of electrons in the solar wind pass between the earth and radio objects in the sky. To study the effect of the solar wind and thus learn more about it, Antony Hewish, an astronomer at Cambridge University in England, developed a large radio telescope that could specifically record rapid fluctuations in a radio signal.

In 1967 Jocelyn Bell was working on Hewish's project while she was still a graduate student and noticed extremely strong variations in the middle of the night, when solar wind effects should be smallest. Several weeks of observing these fluctuations made it clear that they were coming from a celestial source instead of from the solar wind. The pulses were being emitted every 1.3373 seconds. Figure 8.16 shows the radio pulses of this unusual object.

At first astronomers thought that the signal arose from a civilization out in space that was attempting to communicate with other beings. This radio source became known as LGM, for little green men. Shortly

8.13 Karl Jansky at a blackboard describing his discovery of celestial radio waves.

8.14 Great radio telescopes, such as this one at Bonn, West Germany, are used around the world to gather and record radio emissions of celestial objects. The diameter of this disk is 100 meters, more than a football field across.

8.15 A few of the radio dishes that make up the Very Large Array, located in New Mexico. Working in harmony, these radio telescopes can record emission from celestial sources with very high resolution.

after the discovery of LGM 1, Bell discovered three other pulsating sources with regular periods of 0.253 second, 1.1879 seconds, and 1.2738 seconds. For a while, these objects were called LGM 1, LGM 2, LGM 3, and LGM 4, but they were certainly not signals sent by extraterrestrial intelligence. Something special was going on in these four instances.

The objects became known as *pulsars,* and to date more than 300 have been discovered in our galaxy. Figure 8.17 shows the distribution of pulsars in the Milky Way Galaxy.

What mechanism is emitting regular bursts of radio emission? As we shall now see, the discovery of pulsars was one of the most important observations of the 1960s, because an understanding of these objects paved the way for great advancement in the theory of stellar evolution.

Not only was the regularity of the pulsars a puzzle,

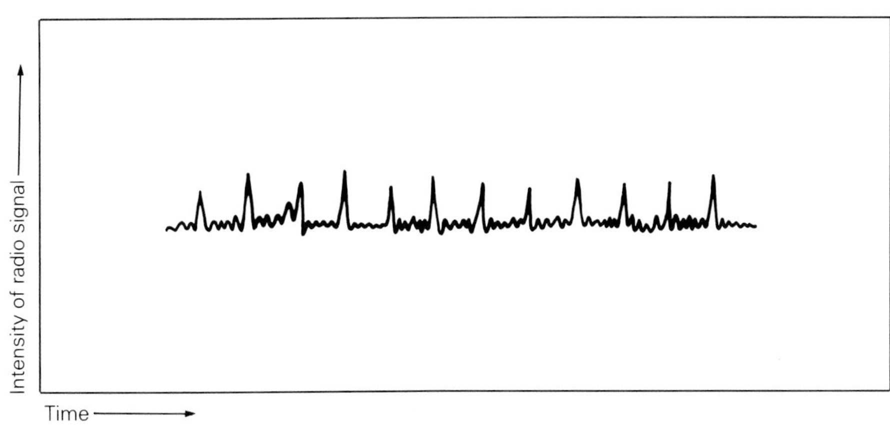

8.16 The radio emission of an unusual celestial source that emits regular pulses every 1.3373 seconds.

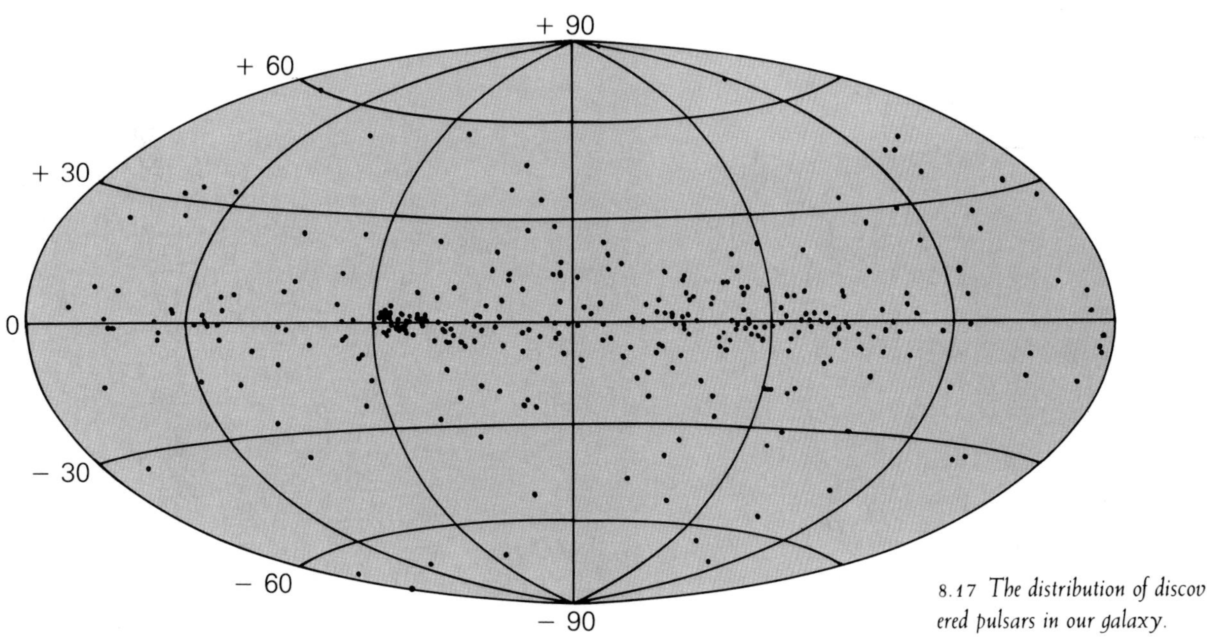

8.17 The distribution of discovered pulsars in our galaxy.

but theorists had to determine mechanisms for the output of energy in the beam of radiation. Scientists at first looked at pulsating stars on the main sequence, but stars are entirely too large to pulsate every second or less. White dwarfs and those theoretical entities called neutron stars were left as possibilities.

When scientists considered the pulsation problem, they came up with two reasonable ideas. First, an object could be changing size, and second, an object could be rotating rapidly while emitting a steady beam, as a lighthouse does. A white dwarf star can oscillate in size in about a minute, but that is too slow to explain pulsar emissions. On the other hand, neutron stars would oscillate in size too fast to account for the regular pulses we observe.

White dwarfs cannot rotate rapidly enough to behave like pulsars without being torn apart by the centripetal force of the outer layers, but neutron stars are considerably smaller and *could* spin fast enough without destroying themselves. Astronomers today generally accept the notion that pulsars are rapidly rotating neutron stars.

The Forces of Nature

Most physics textbooks refer to four fundamental forces of nature. They are the gravitational force, the electromagnetic force, and the two nuclear forces called the strong and weak interactions. It seems that we best understand the electromagnetic force. Not only do we have a good mathematical framework for describing electricity and magnetism, but we also think we understand what is going on.

The electromagnetic force is caused by the interaction of plus and minus charges on matter. For example, electrons are negatively charged and protons carry a positive charge. (Incidentally, there is nothing special about the terms *plus* and *minus* or *positive* and *negative*. These are man-made conventions. The point is that opposite charges attract and like charges repel each other.) Thus, electrons are held onto the nucleus.

We are not so certain how gravity works, although Einstein's general theory of relativity gives us the mathematical ability to understand its effects. All massive bodies distort space and time in their vicinity. This is often called "curving" space, and although the general theory accurately predicts gravitational interactions, it does not explain why mass tells space how to behave.

The strong interaction is a powerful force that operates only at close distances. It is the force that holds atomic nuclei together, and it must overcome the electromagnetic repulsion of protons. This is a force that is not yet well understood.

The other nuclear force is called the weak interaction. It determines radioactivity and the decay of nuclei. In the past decade, theorists have managed to relate the weak force to the electromagnetic force. The combination of the two forces is now called the electroweak interaction, since one general framework encompasses both forces. Another way of saying this is that the weak interaction and electromagnetism are two manifestations of a common physical process.

For the most of the twentieth century, it has been the goal of many physicists to link all of the four forces into one unified theory. The electroweak theory is a start, and it is one that was recently recognized as important when Steven Weinberg, Stanley Glashow, and Abdus Salam won the 1979 Nobel Prize in physics for their efforts in unification.

The Lighthouse Model

As a neutron star rotates, it sends out a beam of radiation that, in the case of those we have observed, flashes past the earth and is recorded as a radio pulse. Figure 8.18 illustrates a likely model for a pulsar.

Neutron stars have very strong magnetic fields associated with them that are left over from the original star. As a star contracts during its final phase before supernova detonation, the magnetic field is pulled in closer and closer, increasing its strength as the star shrinks. As in the diagram in Figure 8.18, it is very possible that the axis about which the star spins is not aligned with a neutron star's north and south poles. (The true location of magnetic north of the earth is some 1,400 kilometers away from the north pole.)

At the magnetic poles of a neutron star, all of the magnetic field lines come together. These are clearly avenues leading out from the surface where the lines of force do not curve and return to the opposite pole. Charged particles can escape from the neutron star at its magnetic poles, and as these particles are accelerated outward they emit light along narrow beams. An observer in the right position will see the beam of radiation sweep across his or her line of sight and register a pulse. Of course if we are not in line with the beam, we would never know that the pulsar existed.

Case Study: The Crab Nebula

One of the most famous supernova remnants of all lies in the constellation Taurus. It is the Crab Nebula. Within a period of months after the initial discovery of pulsars, a pulsar was discovered lodged in the middle of the Crab Nebula. This discovery was of great importance, because it confirmed the neutron star theory for many researchers. The Crab Nebula is a supernova remnant, so it is likely that the pulsar is a stellar

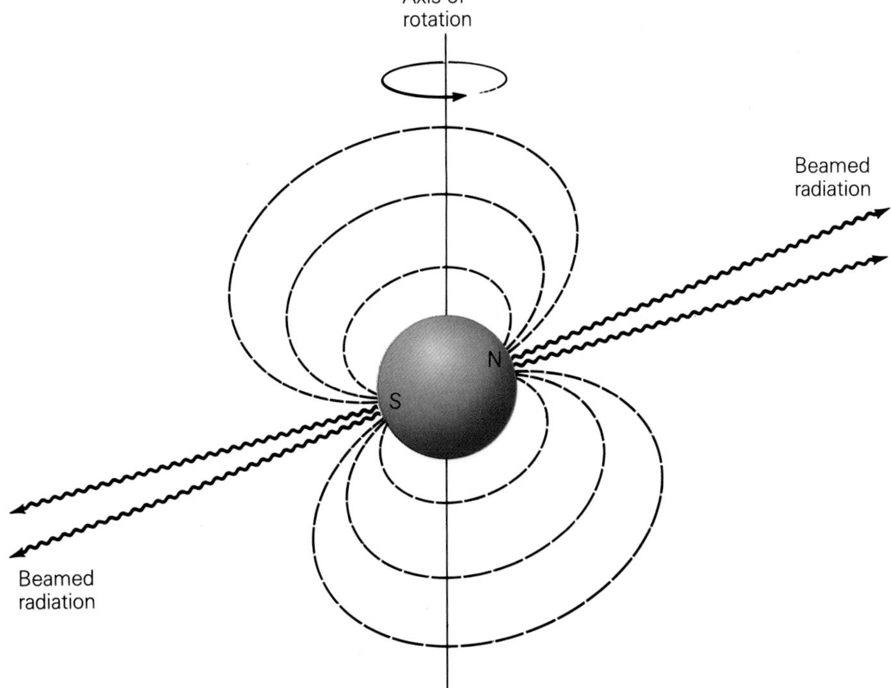

8.18 An artist's sketch of the most popular model for pulsar emissions illustrates the beacon that periodically sweeps past the earth as the pulsar spins on its axis.

corpse. The Crab pulsar is flashing about 30 times a second, so any theory involving white dwarf stars had to be ruled out. Only collapsed objects such as neutron stars can explain the observations.

Figure 8.20 shows the Crab Nebula and the location of the pulsar. After the radio discovery of the Crab pulsar, scientists tried to find optical pulses originating in the same location with special electronic equipment that will measure rapid optical pulses. The quest was successful—the Crab pulsar does emit visible radiation with the same pulse rate as it emits radio energy. It took a decade for astronomers to locate another optical pulsar.

The discovery of the pulsar at the center of the Crab Nebula also helped astronomers solve a problem that had plagued them for years. For more than 900 years after the supernova, the filaments in the Crab Nebula have glowed brightly in visible light as well as in ultraviolet and X rays. Where does the energy come from to power this glowing nebula?

8.19 A painting of one model of SS 433. Jets of matter are being ejected in two directions, and the blue and red Doppler shifts of the emitted radiation indicate that this star is both coming and going.

Although we have mentioned the regularity of pulsar flashes, after several years of observation it became clear that pulsars are really slowing down slightly. The reason is that they are losing energy. When astronomers measured the total energy output of the Crab Nebula, they found that it was equivalent to the amount of energy being lost by the Crab pulsar.

Figure 8.20 shows views of the Crab Nebula in blue light and red light. Notice the more prevalent filamentary structure in red light, where hydrogen atoms are emitting strongly in the spectral line of Hα. Doppler shifts both to the blue and to the red can be measured because the supernova remnant is expanding as the near side approaches us and the far side recedes. Measurements of the Doppler effect yield velocities of expansion of about 1,000 kilometers per second.

Case Study: SS 433

Perhaps one of the most fantastic celestial objects ever encountered by astronomers bears the impersonal label SS 433. In 1979, SS 433 was carefully studied and found to have Doppler shifts simultaneously to the red (moving away from us) and to the blue (moving toward us), corresponding to velocities in excess of 40,000 kilometers per second. This is about 15 percent of the speed of light.

After considerable analysis, scientists at the Dominion Astrophysical Observatory in Canada determined that SS 433 is an object that is orbiting around something else—that is, it is part of a binary system.

It seems that SS 433 is a collapsed object, perhaps a neutron star, that is pulling material in from its companion star. This matter forms an accretion disk around the neutron star, and from it atoms may be ejected at great velocities in opposite directions at the same time. This yields red and blue shifts and makes the stars appear to be coming and going at the same time! Figure 8.19 is an artist's rendition of SS 433. As with normal pulsars, the spin axis may not be aligned with the jets

8.20a *The Crab Nebula photographed in blue light.*

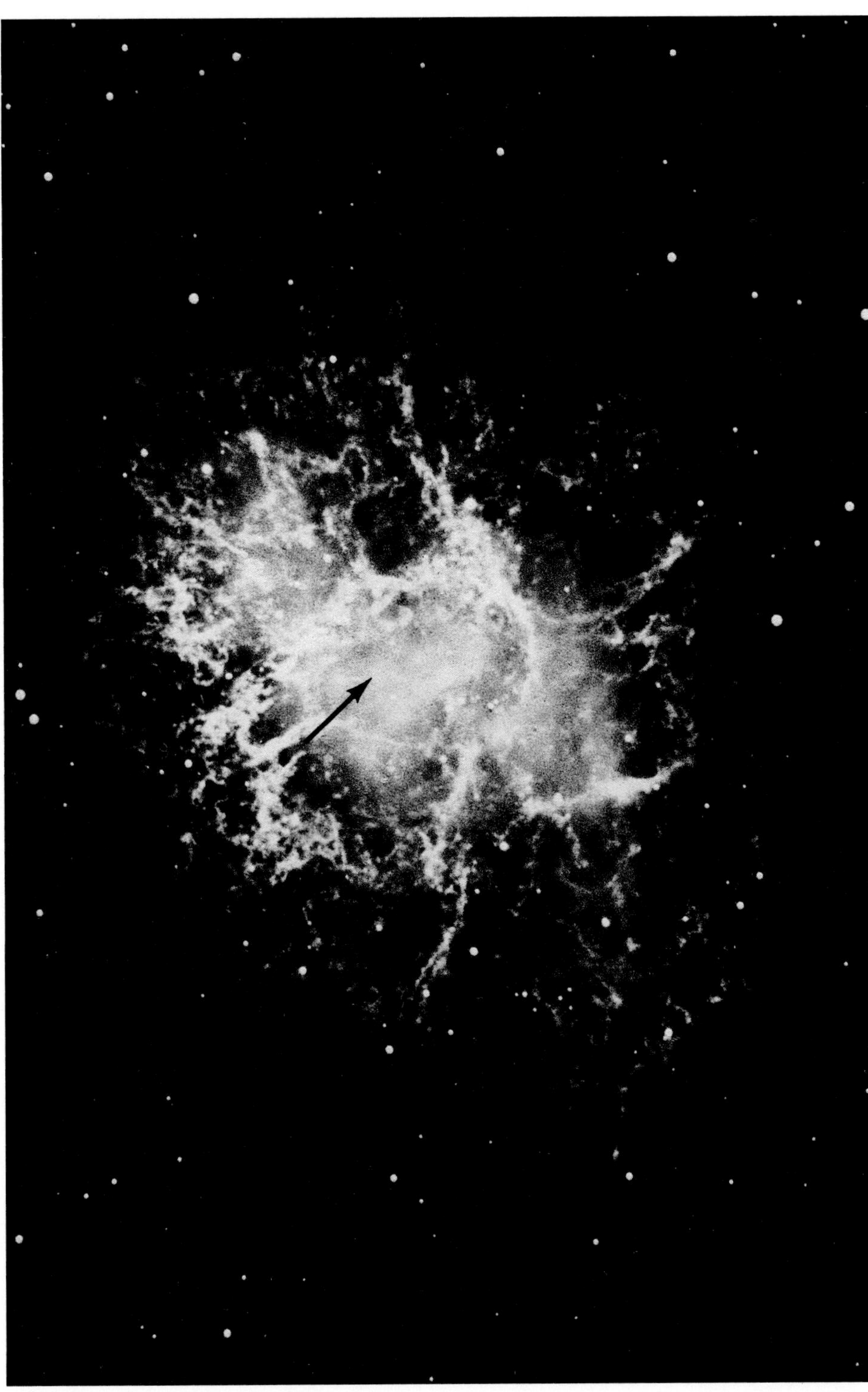

8.20b *The Crab Nebula photographed in red light.*

of ejected matter, and so we record changing Doppler shifts as the jets trace out cones, sometimes moving toward us and at other times moving away. SS 433 is one of the most exciting discoveries of modern astrophysics, and it is being studied by astronomers around the world.

Gravity Waves, Neutrinos, and Cosmic Rays

Although the spectrum of electromagnetic radiation is the primary source of information we gather from the cosmos, supernovae and other phenomena are responsible for other detectable forms of energy. We have already discussed neutrino generation in solar interiors, but the nuclear reactions that are present during the explosive phases of a supernova produce phenomenal numbers of neutrinos, which are emitted in all directions from the stellar explosion.

Cosmic rays are high-energy particles (not rays) that travel through space. Most cosmic rays are the nuclei of atoms and come from deep space. The source of these particles continues to be a controversial subject, but the high temperatures in supernovae strip atoms of their electrons and could accelerate the nuclei into space with tremendous force.

One of the most exciting and controversial topics in modern science is gravitational waves. Gravitational waves are predicted by Einstein's theory of relativity to be emitted by massive bodies that are undergoing acceleration. We should detect their presence by their effect on other massive bodies, but only extremely massive objects will emit gravitational waves of any measurable amplitude.

Joseph Weber of the University of Maryland built the first gravitational wave detector, which consisted of a precisely hung metal cylinder that should begin vibrating when a gravitational wave passes through it. Although Weber reported success in measuring gravitational waves, other scientists with different apparatus have not confirmed his findings. Nevertheless, theory predicts that the acceleration of a collapsing star of high mass should indeed produce gravitational waves that travel freely throughout the universe.

The Next Guest Star

We have mentioned that we are a few hundred years overdue for a nearby supernova, and sure enough, astronomers have a candidate picked out for the next stellar death. Figure 8.21 shows an emission nebula called the Eta Carinae Nebula, and the bright star Eta Carinae is indicated by the arrow. This star is currently a massive red giant nearing the end of its life. Astronomers predict it could begin collapsing and exploding in the very near future—anytime within about 2 million years. Of course, 2 million years is a very short time on a cosmic scale.

8.21 *The Eta Carinae Nebula is the location of the star named Eta Carinae, which as a red giant may be near the end of its life and may soon die in a supernova explosion.*

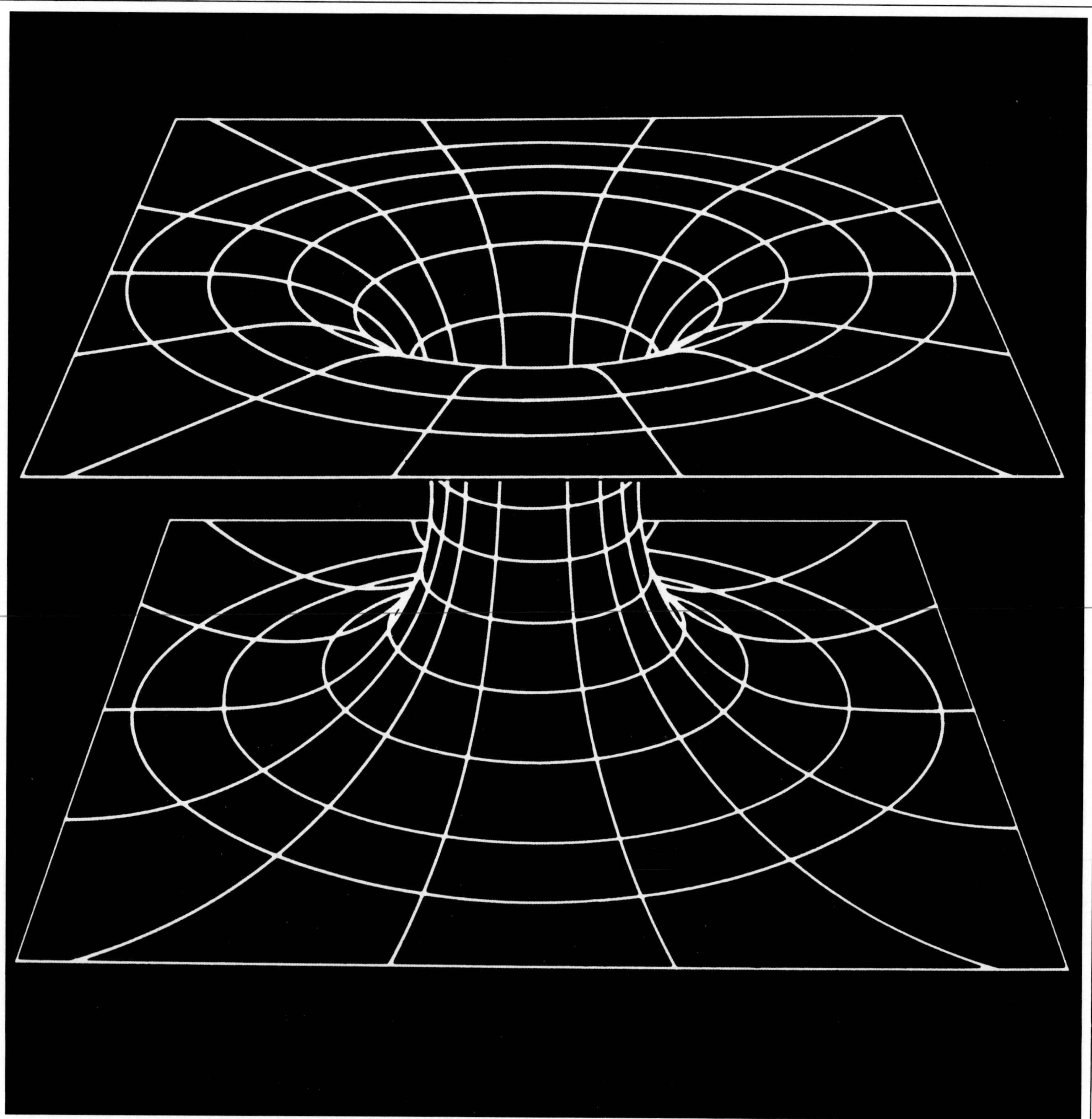

9: BLACK HOLES

Gravity and the Forces of Nature

In describing the life and death of stars, we have encountered in one way or another all four fundamental forces of nature. They are the electromagnetic force, the strong nuclear force, the weak nuclear force, and the gravitational force. The electromagnetic force is responsible for holding electrons of negative charge to positively charged nuclei. The release of energy in a lightning bolt, the operation of electric motors, and the fact that a balloon will stick to the ceiling if you rub it on a sweater are all commonplace examples of the electromagnetic force. The strong and weak nuclear forces operate in the close confines of atomic nuclei. Physicists have been working for years to discover if the four forces are actually different manifestations of one universal force. The weak nuclear force has been related to the electromagnetic force, so perhaps future advances will provide us with what has been named the unified field theory.

Our understanding of gravity has evolved and changed during the past four centuries. In the last half of the seventeenth century, one of the great thinkers of all time formulated a theory that revolutionized people's ideas about nature. Isaac Newton's contributions to science are awe-inspiring. His invention of the calculus permitted him to study mathematically the time-dependent motion of moving bodies. He studied light with a prism, breaking the light into its component colors. He built a small reflecting telescope to view the heavens, but his discovery of gravity and its properties is most important for our present discussion.

There are many stories, some true, some not so true, about the accidental way that some great discoveries were made. The famous myth about Galileo dropping two spheres of different mass from the Leaning Tower of Pisa, discovering that bodies fall at the same rate of acceleration, is not true. In Galileo's time no equipment was available to measure with the necessary precision the acceleration of the spheres when dropped, so he rolled them down an inclined plane.

On the other hand, the story of Newton witnessing an apple falling from a tree is most likely true. Countless people had observed apples falling to the ground: Newton was different from the rest. He had the ability of a genius to consider simple questions that have profound answers.

Newton saw an apple fall from a tree. The apple appeared to be attracted to the earth. Newton immediately began thinking about this attractive force of gravity. He had to consider such questions as What is the force? How far does it extend between two bodies? Newton reasoned that no matter how high the tree might be, the apple would still fall to the earth.

Slowly, by induction, Newton realized that the moon must also "fall" toward the earth much as the apple does. He realized that the moon never reaches the surface of the earth because the moon is in motion. The moon travels around the earth in an orbit because as it moves through space parallel to the earth's surface, it is continually falling toward the earth at the same time. One component of its motion is directly into the earth, and the other component is perpendicular to the first. Figure 9.2 illustrates how the moon "falls." If we turned off the gravity suddenly, the moon would continue out in a straight line into space. On the other hand, if we could somehow stop the moon's motion through space, it would immediately fall to earth. It is the combination of these two motions that makes a complete orbit.

These considerations led Newton to an even more fantastic idea. This was the concept of universal gravitation, that every body with a mass has a gravitational attraction to every other massive body. This is true for any microscopic particle, any star, or any galaxy, and thus is universal. Stars and galaxies are, of course, themselves held together by gravity, but they also behave gravitationally as if they were solid bodies. The total mass of all the atomic particles in a star add

9.1 Sir Isaac Newton (1642–1727).

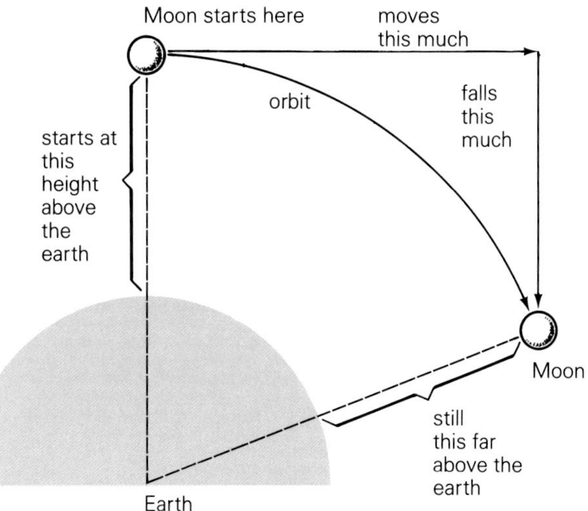

9.2 *We can think of the moon "falling" around the earth in a series of small steps, which are somewhat exaggerated in this diagram.*

together to give the star its mass. This is a fact that only Newton's understanding of gravity could uncover, and he was the first to create a mathematical framework within which to work.

Newton's law of gravitation is basically simple. It states that the gravitational force between two bodies is directly proportional to the product of their masses and inversely proportional to the square of the distance between their centers of mass. The reason that the distance is measured from the centers of mass is that gravity behaves as if all the mass of a body were located at the center.

The law of gravitation is one of many inverse square laws found in physics. We say, in the case of gravitation, that the force is inversely proportional to the square of the distance. In other words, if you increase the distance by a factor of 2, the force of gravity *decreases* by a factor of $4(2^2)$.

Newton used his calculus, his law of gravitation, and his laws of motion involving forces to verify Kepler's laws, which describe the properties of planetary orbits. This was one of his great triumphs.

The philosophical implications of Newton's concept of universal gravitation are as important as its applications. Practically all of his predecessors had considered the universe a great machine, operated by gears and wheels and chains. Newton showed that forces, not mechanical parts, are responsible for binding the solar system and other elements of the universe together. He had generalized physical laws first noticed on earth to explain the motions of the planets.

Gravity is the force of nature that has an effect over long distances. The electroweak (the combined weak and electromagnetic forces) and the strong interaction dominate only at very short distances, and their effect falls off very rapidly with increasing distance. Gravity is the weakest force of all, but its effect can be far reaching, particularly where large masses are involved.

Newton's law of gravitation is still applicable in most day-to-day situations, and astronomers of the 1700s and 1800s used it to predict with great accuracy the movements within the solar system. But in the early part of the twentieth century, a young German physicist began examining the foundations of Newtonian physics and classical dynamics and began a revolution in scientific thought that was even greater and further reaching than that begun by Newton more than 300 years before.

His name was Albert Einstein, and his departure from classical ways of thinking began with the notion that the laws of nature should be independent of our unique and limited perspective on the universe. If we can write down equations that do not reflect our own chauvinism, we might then call the laws truly universal.

What emerged from Einstein's careful considerations is called the general theory of relativity. It is a theory of gravity, but unlike Newton's theory, which treats gravity as an attractive force between massive bodies, the general theory of relativity describes gravity as a distortion of space and time by massive bodies. Figure 9.4 shows a schematic diagram of such distortion. The true distortion illustrated here takes place in four dimensions, called *space-time,* but the diagram is a three-dimensional rendition printed in the two dimensions of

9.3 *Albert Einstein (1879–1955).*

the flat paper. The greatest distortion is near the surface of the massive body. Farther from the object, the distortion is less, and very far away space appears normal (flat in the illustrations).

Several observational experiments were devised to test the general theory. These included observation of the orbit of the planet Mercury, the bending of starlight by massive bodies such as the sun, and the fact that wavelengths of light are lengthened (red-shifted) when emitted by a massive body. The latter test is called gravitational red shift and can even be measured by observing sunlight as it is shifted leaving the sun's gravity. Each of these three tests of Einstein's theory has confirmed, within observational limits, that the theory is correct.

Not long after Einstein published his theory in 1915, other scientists began working with it to discover its many facets and meanings. One of the most fantastic objects ever predicted by any theory is a black hole, which is a direct consequence of Einstein's work. The rest of this chapter is devoted to the theoretical analysis, search, and possible identification of black holes.

Holes in Space-time

As long ago as the eighteenth century, people had wondered about the existence of stars that were so

9.4 *Embedding diagrams showing the distortion of space by a massive body.*

massive that light could not escape from them. The famous French mathematician Marquis Pierre Simon de Laplace had postulated invisible stars that actually slow the velocity of light with their large gravity and become dark even if you are right next to them. Not until 1915 did Einstein's theory show that massive bodies can bend light and that gravity stretches (reddens) its wavelengths.

Another brilliant physicist from Germany, Karl Schwarzschild, was working with Einstein's theory when he discovered that if the mass of a star is concentrated at its center, the gravitational red shift becomes infinite, and the curvature of space increases to the point that it closes itself in, and off from, the universe outside. The point from which nothing can escape has become known as the Schwarzschild radius. Inside the radius even light is trapped. Outside the radius light can still escape from any emitting atoms, but the radiation may be extremely gravitationally red-shifted.

Sir Arthur Eddington, a distinguished British astrophysicist, extended Schwarzschild's work, postulating that a star may collapse indefinitely, space would curve around itself, and the star would disappear.

As compelling as the mathematical framework for disappearing stars was, as established by Schwarzschild and Eddington, the real research that put us on the

General Relativity and Black Holes

Black holes are only one phenomenon predicted by the application of Einstein's general theory of relativity. Einstein published the general theory in 1915, and the flurry of activity using this mathematical framework continues to this day.

Theorists have been finding ways of solving the complex field equations that form the basis of Einstein's work. Astronomy was quite naturally one of the fields of science that has benefited from all this research, since relativity relates to massive bodies, and things such as planets, stars, and in fact the entire universe are things with the most mass.

The general theory provides us with a new way of looking at the universe. Instead of massive bodies "pulling" on each other, as we previously viewed gravity's effect, Einstein explained gravity as a distortion of space and time imposed by massive bodies. We say that space is curved by the presence of mass.

Einstein himself worked with his equations, particularly regarding the dynamics of the universe as a whole. No one knew at the time that the universe is expanding, but Einstein realized that his theory predicted as much. Believing as he did that the universe is a static place, Einstein added to his equations a number that has been called the cosmological constant. This unusual fudge factor negates the part of the equations that predicts expansion of the universe, and its addition thus made Einstein's equations predict what he expected that they should.

A few years later, in the 1920s, Edwin Hubble at the Mount Wilson Observatory in California showed that the universe is expanding. Einstein removed the cosmological constant from his calculations, later saying that it was the biggest mistake of his life.

Black holes were first thought of mathematically when the general theory was applied to collapsing stars at the end of their lives. So condensed does the mass of the star become that its effect on space-time becomes incredibly great, and space curves so much that it actually closes around itself, preventing the escape of anything, even light.

Physicist John Wheeler coined the phrase *black hole* in the 1940s because anything that prevents the escape of light must be dark.

9.5 J. Robert Oppenheimer is often remembered as the father of the atomic bomb, but his pioneering theoretical work on neutron stars and black holes may be his greatest scientific contribution.

track of current black hole theory was related to dying stars and neutron degeneracy. J. Robert Oppenheimer had been working with his colleagues to show that neutron stars can exist, since neutrons can become densely packed and resist the further contraction of a collapsing star. Working with Hartland S. Snyder, he published a paper that showed that very massive dying stars can completely collapse, overcome neutron degeneracy, and disappear from view as their light is trapped by the soaring gravity of general relativity.

Almost 30 years elapsed before the work of Oppenheimer and his colleagues was taken seriously. It was considered an amusing speculation until the discovery of pulsars in 1967 suggested that neutron stars exist. Completely collapsed stars are only an extension of the theory. Thus black holes reemerged on blackboards, in computer programs, and, best of all, in the minds of many of the world's finest scientists. From the theoretical calculations of these scientists grew the "real" notion of black holes. The mental exercise of manipulating Einstein's equations stimulated one of the most exciting and captivating discoveries in the history of science.

Black Holes—What Are They?

The term *black hole* was coined in the 1940s by physicist John Wheeler, then of Princeton University. It refers to any object that is compressed enough to cause space to curve in on itself and cut it off from the outside world. We shall see that black holes may come in all sizes, but to appreciate their basic characteristics, let us describe the formation of the black hole from a very massive dying star.

It can be shown mathematically that if the remaining stellar core after a supernova has a mass three or more times that of the sun, it will become neither a white dwarf nor a neutron star. As this remnant contracts, the gravity above its surface increases very fast. In terms of general relativity, we might say that space-time is becoming increasingly distorted or curved. Figure 9.6 illustrates the effect of gravity on light from a collapsing star.

Eventually, gravity becomes so strong that not even light can escape, and although the star still exists, it has disappeared from view because no radiation leaves it. This boundary at which the star disappears is called the *event horizon*. Nothing can escape a black hole from within the event horizon.

For example, when a star with a mass of 10 solar masses collapses to 60 kilometers in diameter, a black hole forms because its event horizon is 60 kilometers across. Inside the event horizon, the dying star continues to collapse until it actually disappears into a geometric point called *singularity*. Figure 9.7 is an illustration of the geometry of a black hole, but we must remember for our discussion of nonstellar black holes later in this chapter that a black hole can exist even before a singularity forms, as it does when a dying star shrinks to its event horizon before becoming a singularity. The dimension of the event horizon of a black hole is dependent on the mass of the object in question. Within the event horizon, the curvature of space continues to increase as you approach the singularity. At the geometric point to which all of the mass of the dying star has been crushed, gravity is infinitely high and space-time is infinitely curved.

9.6 Below left: *As a massive star collapses, light escapes through an increasingly narrower cone until it can no longer escape.*

9.7 Below right: *The geometry of a black hole, showing the location of the singularity and event horizon.*

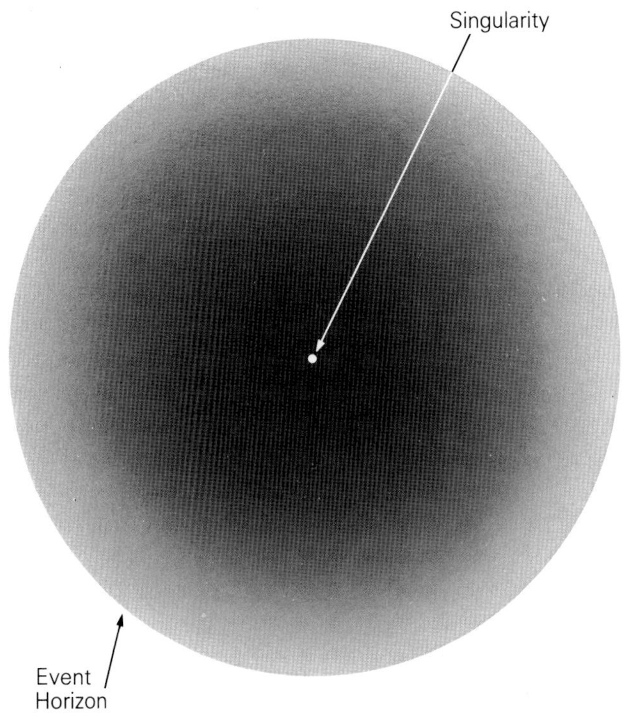

Another characteristic of a black hole is called the *photon sphere,* which is defined as the radius at which light will go into orbit around the event horizon. As the star in the center contracts, light emitted in the cone can escape. Light emitted outside the cone falls back to the star's surface, but light that is shone along the edge of the cone will go into orbit around the star. As the star collapses, the cone becomes narrower and narrower, but the photon sphere always has the same dimension from the time of its formation on, even after the star has completely collapsed into a singularity.

So far, we have been describing the characteristics of black holes that are not rotating, but this has only been for simplicity. In fact, black holes probably do rotate. After all, the star that collapsed was rotating from its early protostellar cloud of gas and dust.

In 1963 Roy P. Kerr solved the appropriate equations for rotating black holes and found that there are really two types of event horizons. Figure 9.8 shows a diagram of a rotating black hole. The outer event horizon is called the *stationary limit,* and between its boundary and that of the normal event horizon lies an interesting area called the *ergosphere. Ergon* is the Greek word for work, and the ergosphere gets its name because we might be able to extract energy from it. It is possible to escape from within the stationary limit, a notion we will explore in greater detail later in this chapter

Nonstellar Black Holes

Although the concept of black holes developed during the study of the life cycles of stars, it has become increasingly clear that black holes come in all sizes. The gifted British astrophysicist Steven Hawking has mathematically determined that conditions at the big bang, the cataclysmic explosion that started all space and time about 15 billion years ago, were such that amounts of matter about the size of mountains may have been compressed enough to become what he calls mini–black holes. Whereas the event horizon of a stellar black hole may be about 15 to 80 miles in diameter, depending on the mass of the original star, the event horizon of a mini–black hole would be about as large as an atomic particle (about one ten-trillionth of an inch).

Hawking has also discovered that mini–black holes violate the no-escape criterion of their larger relatives. Theory suggests that mini–black holes are leaking gamma radiation and subatomic particles back into space. As they "evaporate," they heat up and eventually explode with the power of millions of hydrogen bombs.

If mini–black holes are that small, supergiant black holes are the other extreme. Scientists now predict that supermassive black holes, say a billion times as massive as the sun, may be the energy sources that are causing some galaxies to explode. Quasars, the most distant and therefore the oldest objects we observe, may get

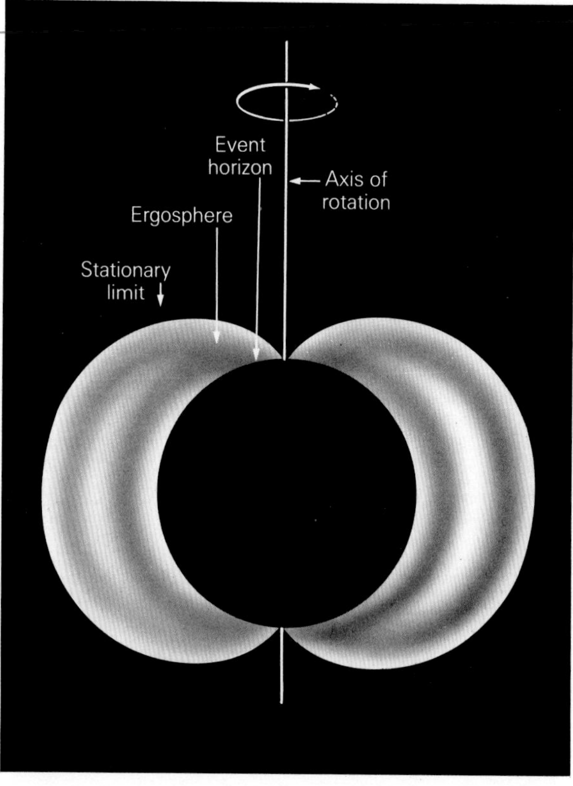

9.8 The geometry of a rotating black hole, showing the stationary limit, the ergosphere, and the event horizon.

their enormous energy from colossal black holes at their center.

On an even more philosophical plane, the entire universe may be inside a black hole. Since the discovery of receding galaxies in the early 1900s, astronomers have known that the universe is expanding, and scientists are trying to determine whether the universe will continue to expand forever or stop expanding and contract under its gravity and fall back upon itself. We call the universe "open" if it will continue expanding, and we say it is "closed" if there is enough mass to halt the outward flight of galaxies and make them collapse inward. We do not yet have the answer to whether the universe is open or closed.

If the universe is closed nothing can escape from it because its own gravity holds everything inside. Thus, we would consider it to be an enormous black hole from which nothing can escape.

The Search for Black Holes

If indeed black holes exist, they are by definition difficult to observe. Because no light escapes from them, we are cut off from the only certain way any information comes to us from outer space. The only way to identify the presence of a black hole is to observe the way it affects nearby objects that do emit radiation. Fortunately, there seem to be candidates doing just that.

Most of the stars in the sky exist in binary or multiple systems. In many observable systems, one of the stars probably has evolved into a compact object such as a black hole. What effect would the black hole have on its companion star? It would pull material from the atmospheric layers of the companion into its own region of strong gravity (of high curvature of spacetime). Scientists must look for signs of this accretion by a black hole. Some plausible examples have been found.

As a black hole exerts its strong force of gravity on its companion star, it tends to pull the visible component of the binary system into an egg shape because of tidal forces. As matter streams from the visible star toward the black hole, it spirals inward to the event horizon, forming what is called an *accretion disk*. Figure 9.9 is an artist's conception of a black hole at the center of the accretion disk. Material is pulled out of the visible star and spirals into the black hole, forming the accretion disk outside the event horizon.

Although bright stars are visible from earth, accretion disks would be too small to be recognized through optical telescopes. It turns out, however, that they emit propitious amounts of X-ray radiation. As the material in the accretion disk spirals toward the event horizon, collisions among atomic particles may heat the disk to 10 million° K, which is hot enough to emit intense streams of X rays. We can observe these X rays with satellites orbiting the earth.

Satellites pioneered the detection of X rays from celestial sources. In December 1970 the United States and Italy launched the Uhuru satellite, which contained a special X-ray telescope. In only a couple of years it compiled data on about 175 sources of X-ray emission.

Some of these X-ray sources exhibit pulses of emission that cannot be explained by hot accretion disks but rather by binary stars in which one component is a neutron star beaming radiation like a lighthouse beacon, described in Chapter 8. A few other candidates emit X rays in a more promising fashion. The X rays are constant except for occasional breaks in their flow caused by the visible companion star eclipsing the invisible component that emits the X rays. One of these candidates lies about 6,000 light-years away in the constellation Cygnus. Figure 9.10 indicates the location of this unusual X-ray source.

Case Study: Cygnus X-1

Cygnus X-1 is the notation given to the first X-ray source discovered in the constellation Cygnus, and it is very likely a black hole in orbit around a supergiant

9.9 An accretion disk forms around the black hole as it pulls matter off the companion star.

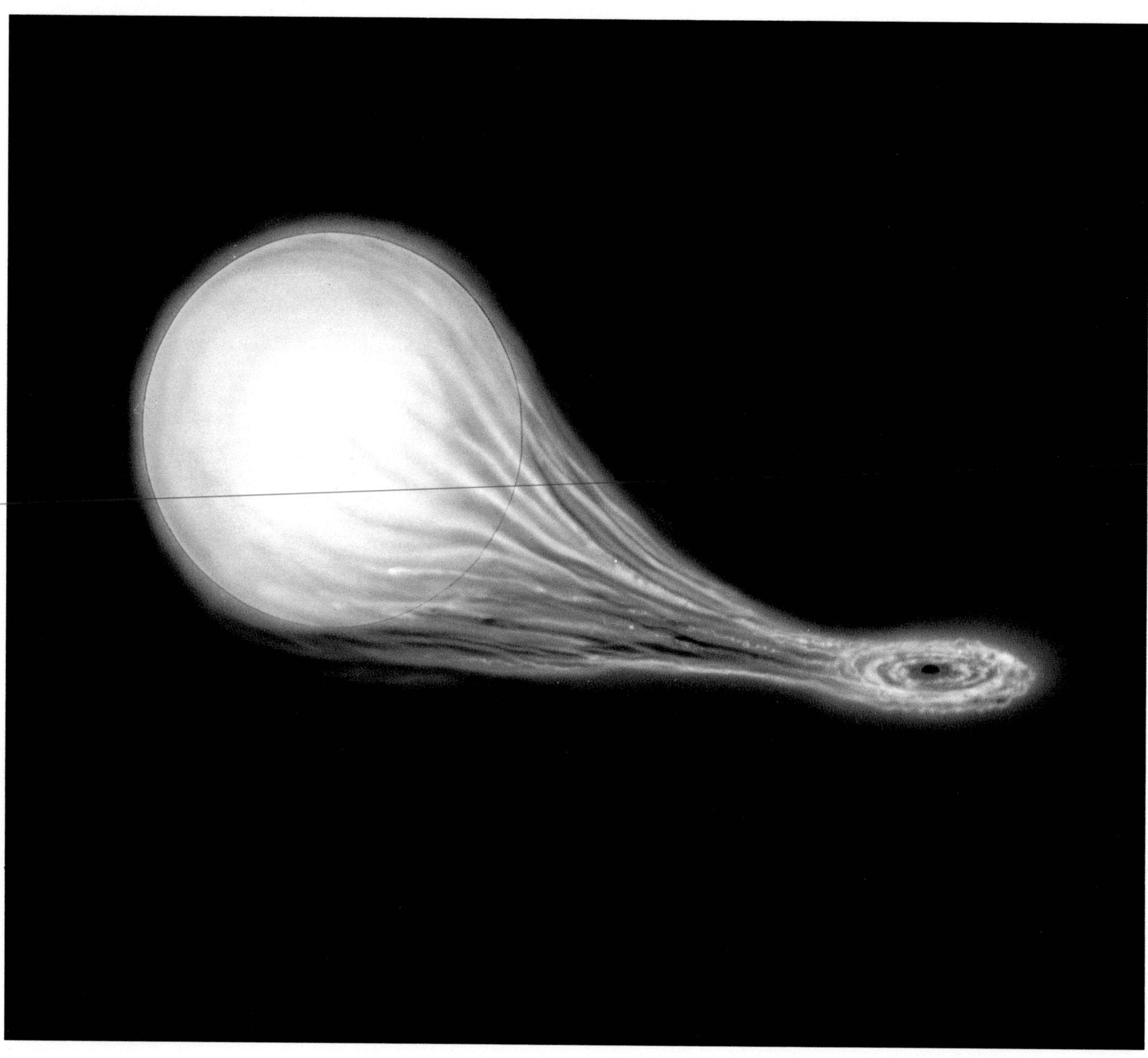

blue star. Its spectrum is characteristic of a close binary star system in that Doppler shifts indicate two objects orbiting a common center of mass. The visible star is a ninth-magnitude star with the ponderous designation HDE 226868. It is a blue supergiant of about $15M_{\odot}$. The Doppler shifts indicate a binary orbit with a fluctuation period of about 5.6 days, and we can deduce that the invisible companion has a mass of about $8M_{\odot}$. This is too massive to yield a neutron star, so it is probably a black hole.

Researchers have modeled Cygnus X-1 according to black hole theory and X-ray observations of the region. Most of the radiation comes from the inner 200 kilometers of the accretion disk, where temperatures soar to 10 million° K. Any ultraviolet radiation from the cooler outer regions of the disk would probably be indistinguishable from the ultraviolet glare of the blue supergiant star.

In addition to the steady X-ray emission of Cygnus X-1, occasional bright flare-ups occur more or less randomly. These are attributed to regional hot spots in the accretion disk that emit cones of radiation that beam additional energy in specific directions in space.

In the case of Cygnus X-1, the black hole scenario is likely because the invisible component is at least $4M_{\odot}$, but more likely to be as massive as $8M_{\odot}$. The case is not so clear for other black hole candidates.

Other Black Hole Observations

Uhuru recorded four particularly interesting binary X-ray emitters, but three of them are highly suspect and may or may not be black holes orbiting a visible star. In each case the orbit of the binary suggests that the invisible companion in question may have a mass two

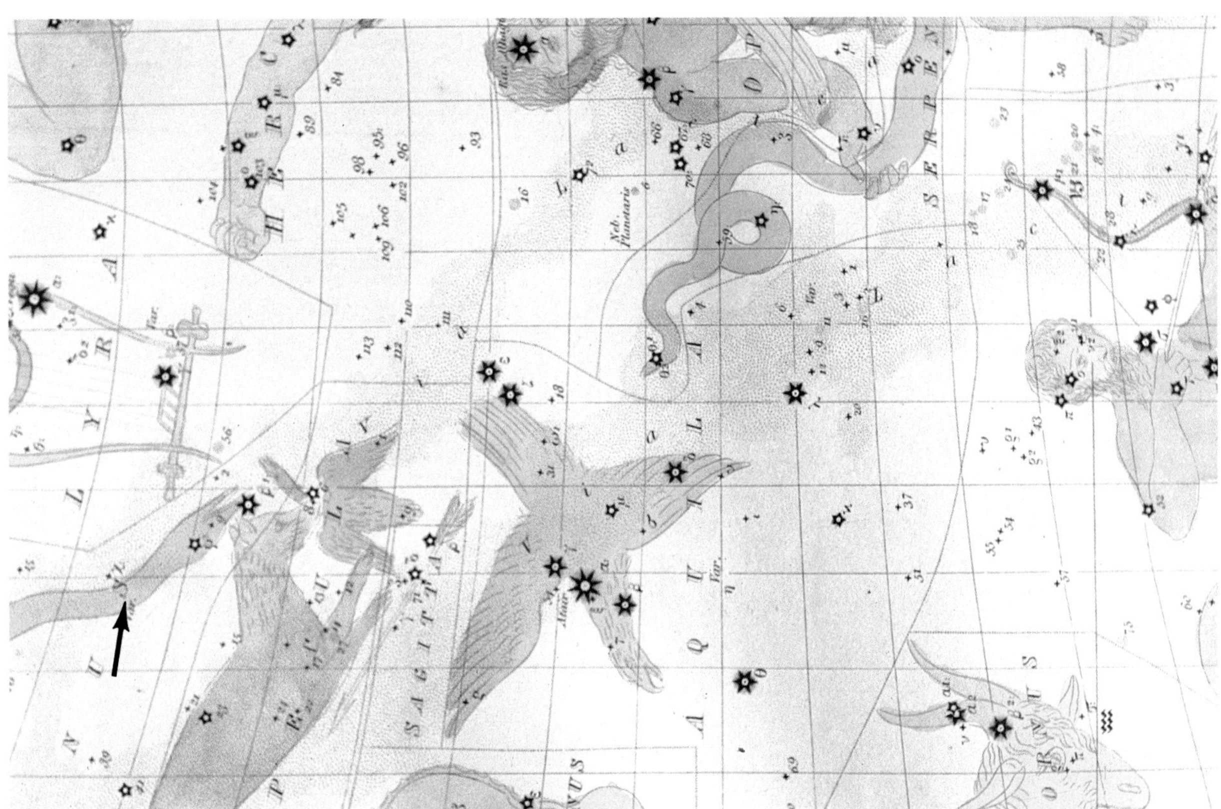

9.10 The constellation Cygnus and the location of the unusual X-ray source known as Cygnus X-1.

or three times that of the sun. This is just at the lower limit of a black hole's mass, and considering the error inherent in the determination of the mass, we have little confidence in assuring ourselves that black holes are involved at all.

In 1983, a second likely candidate for a black hole was discovered, but this time it appears to be in the Large Magellanic Cloud, one of the Milky Way Galaxy's satellite stellar systems. Named LMC X-1, it appears to be a binary system with an invisible component greater than $4M_{\odot}$.

Researchers continue to look for additional black holes, of both stellar and nonstellar origin, but clearly the difficulties are many, and a lone black hole may well be impossible to find. Gravity waves may yield some results, but no one has recorded any for certain at this time.

Fun with Black Holes

So exotic are black holes and the physics that they present that many entertaining and interesting possibilities have been postulated. Theoretically, an object can be fired into the ergosphere of a rotating black hole with astounding results. It will split in two, and while one half of the object moves toward the event horizon, the other half will escape the black hole with more energy than the initial whole object had. The gained energy probably comes from the black hole's rotation. Clearly, if we could do this experiment and harness the escaping object, we would be tapping a substantial source of energy. Some scientists have suggested setting up a colony outside the event horizon of a black hole so we could jettison all our garbage into the "bottomless pit."

The distortion of space-time by a massive body opens the mind to thoughts of travel through time and space. Black holes may be gateways to remote regions of our universe or even to other universes. Einstein and Nathan Rosen saw the mathematical possibilities of black hole subway systems, and if they do indeed link parallel or alternate universes, the connections are called Einstein-Rosen bridges.

Somewhere else, moreover, where matter would reappear, we have a *white hole,* which would be a cosmic gusher where material enters the universe. Wormholes are not observable entities, however, and calculations show that such a bridge pinches off in a very short time, so travel through is virtually impossible.

Black Holes and the Human Mind

Although Cygnus X-1 and LMC X-1 are generally considered to be probable black hole candidates, their study is still in its infancy. The number of binary systems in which a black hole may reside is staggering, but the difficulties in observing and verifying their existence are so great that we are left with only a handful of indirect clues on which to base our expectations.

It is not unreasonable to conclude, therefore, that the *conception* of a black hole might surpass the reality of black holes themselves. They are initially constructs of the human mind; they are intellectual monsters of our own fairyland. Whether we find that they exist or not, herein lies our great achievement: we thought of them.

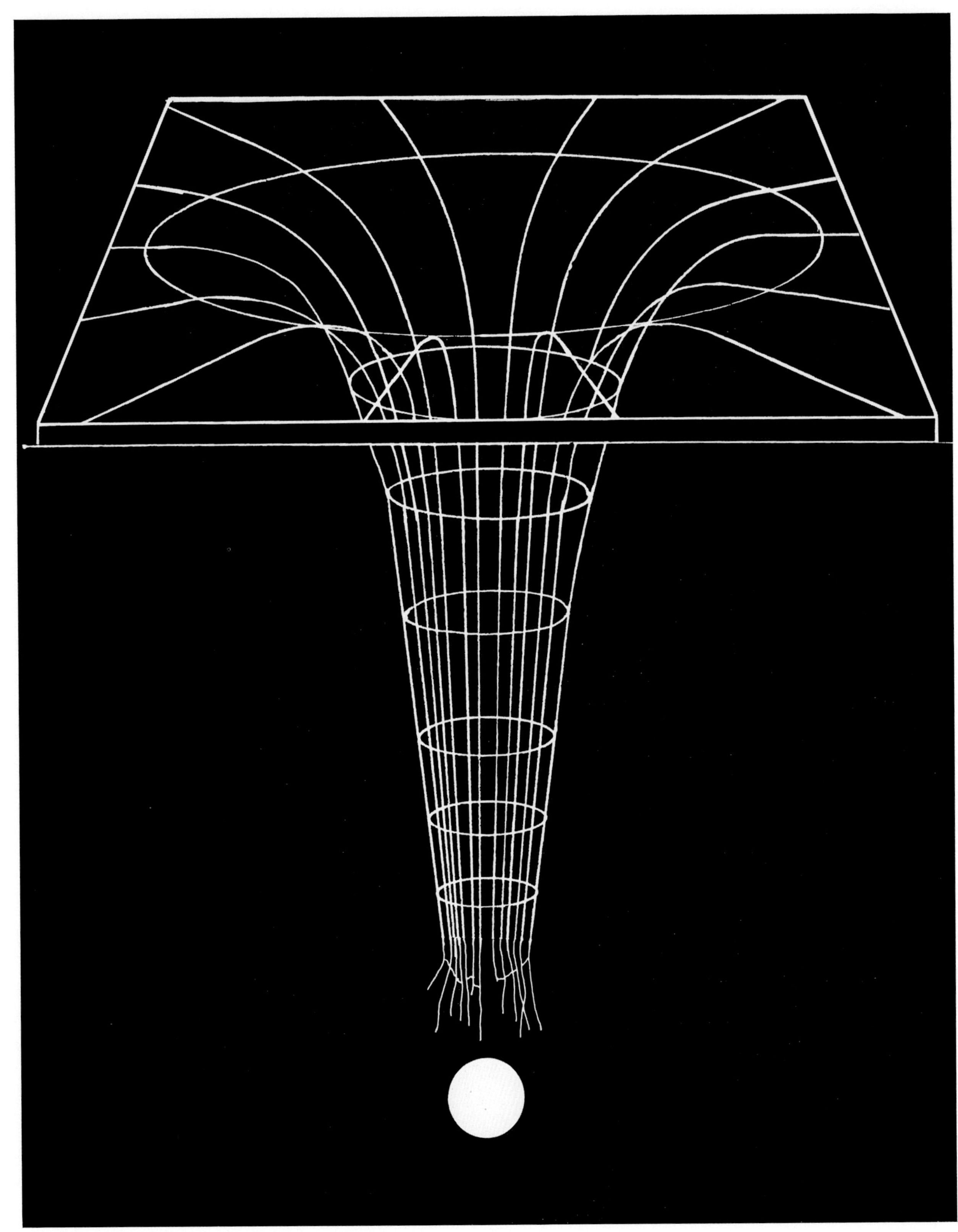

9.11 An embedding diagram illustrating the rip in the fabric of space-time caused by a massive object collapsing into a black hole.

10: STARS— WHERE LIFE BEGINS

The lives of stars have far-reaching ties to our society, to civilization, and even to the existence of life itself. To scientists, the universe is a laboratory of unimaginable extremes, displaying physical conditions that have never been duplicated on earth. During the lifetimes of stars, matter is pushed to its limits, from the cold dust clouds in the galaxy to the superdense, hot surfaces of white dwarf stars.

The relationship between humans and the stars lies much deeper than in our intellectual explorations. We are directly dependent on one star for survival. Our sun provides the earth with a climate that is suitable for sustaining life as we know it. The earth orbits about 93 million miles from the sun; at that distance, our planet resides within the sun's *ecosphere*. The ecosphere of a star is the region around the star where the temperature is neither too hot nor too cold to prevent the development and maintenance of life.

Venus orbits at the inner edge of the sun's ecosphere, and Mars lies near the outside boundary. Although the amount of sunlight is adequate for the existence of life on both worlds, their chemical constitution, their masses, and their planetary evolution have rendered them lifeless.

The sun provides us, directly and indirectly, with essentially all energy. The food chain of which we are the ultimate consumer begins with the synthesis of carbohydrates from water and carbon dioxide in the presence of sunlight and chlorophyll. This process, called photosynthesis, dominates life in the world of vegetation. We feed on plants and on animals that have also fed on plants. The energy from the sun, which has been changed and stored within flora and fauna, is released during digestion in our bodies.

Fossil fuels such as coal, oil, and natural gas are also end products of plant life. As we burn the fuels in our homes and cars, the sun's energy is released in the chemistry of combustion. We use the energy for warmth, electricity, and power.

Every star has an ecosphere, but not every ecosphere is a reasonable place to look for life. Red giants, being rather cool stars, have narrow ecospheres that are very near the star's surface. The probability of finding a planet orbiting within such a small region is very unlikely indeed.

Blue giant stars are young and hot. Their ecospheres are very wide, and planetary systems may be orbiting many of these stars. Blue giants, however, consume their nuclear fuels very fast and exist for only a few million years, thus living short lives on a stellar time scale. It is about 4.5 billion years since the earth formed from the solar cloud. It has taken 3.4 billion years for life to reach its present complexity. Blue giant stars themselves evolve more rapidly than life, and in most cases they would die long before the building blocks of life could form.

Double-star and multiple-star systems have complex and intertwined ecospheres, and planets orbiting the center of gravity of these systems would face changes in temperature and radiant energy. Clearly, multiple stars are unlikely candidates for nourishing life.

Variable stars also exhibit a changing flux of radiant energy so that the development of life on an orbiting planet is not possible. We face temperature variations on the earth because of the daily rotation of this planet about its axis, but they are small compared to variable stars. The sun is a star with a very consistent radiative flux. The amount of energy passing each second through a square centimeter, at the average distance of the earth from the sun, is equal to 135 milliwatts/cm^2. This value, called the *solar constant,* has been measured to an accuracy of about 1.5 percent, and recent results

10.1 Below left: *The sun's ecosphere is the shell around our star within which the temperature is suitable for the creation and evolution of life. Venus is on the inside edge of the ecosphere, and Mars orbits at the outside edge.*

10.2 Below center and right: *Relative sizes of stellar ecospheres depend on the mass and surface temperature of stars.*

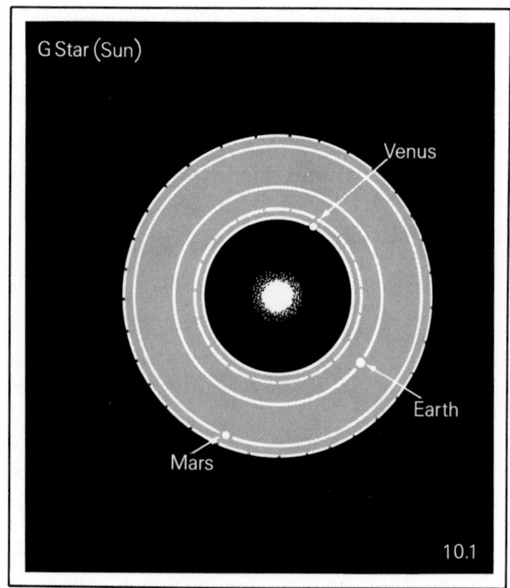

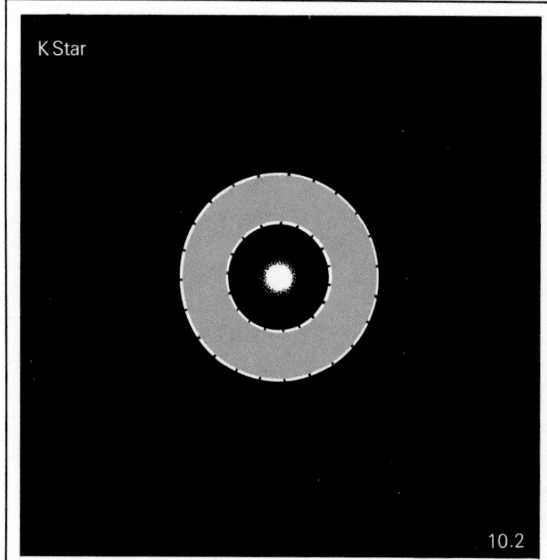

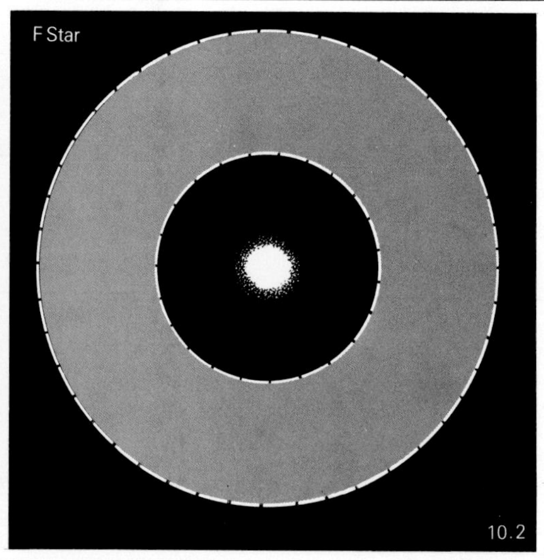

from the Solar Maximum Mission spacecraft indicate that short-term variations of about 0.2 percent actually do exist. Such fluctuations in the solar energy that reaches the earth may be caused by solar activity such as flares, but of far more danger to life is the possibility of a long-term variation in the solar constant. The earth's climate would be affected by such change. The sun may be a slowly varying star.

There are types of stars, however, whose variability is very extensive and predictable. Variable stars may have intensity variations on the order of an hour, a day, or even longer, and the energy output of some stars changes by several hundred times over very short intervals. The probability of finding life on planets orbiting variable stars is very small because of vast extremes in radiant energy.

Average yellow stars such as the sun thus appear to be the best candidates for having life-supporting planets. The Milky Way Galaxy, which is a great spiral configuration of stars in which our sun resides, contains approximately 400 billion stars. About 8 percent, or 32 million stars, are stable yellow stars similar to our sun. Of these candidates, we can only estimate the number of stars that have planets orbiting within the ecosphere. The best estimates place the number of inhabitable worlds at anywhere between 500,000 and 5 million. That may seem like a great number of places for intelligent beings to live. Nevertheless, the earth may be alone in supporting life.

The sun, however, does have small localized fluctuations of energy that may be dangerous to life on the earth. Fortunately, a layer of ozone in the earth's atmosphere absorbs the most dangerous parts of the electromagnetic spectrum, which are high-energy ultraviolet and X-ray radiations. Solar flares emit much more intense radiation in these parts of the spectrum than does the quiet sun. A prolonged period of solar activity or a long-term change in the sun's overall energy output could permanently alter the atmosphere and expose life on the surface to deadly, high-frequency radiation.

Ultraviolet light destroys living cells by chemical dissociation of the cells' constituent molecules. Some ultraviolet light does reach the surface; it is responsible for sunburns and suntans. Excess exposure to the sun results in blistering and skin diseases, so one can imagine the effect on life if all the ultraviolet light penetrated the atmosphere and reached the earth. Astronauts and future space colonists, however, are not protected by the atmosphere's ozone layer, so other precautions must be taken, such as special suits and visors. Nevertheless, the additional radiation from solar flares poses a danger to people and any living things we take into space. Solar physicists are working toward a better understanding of solar magnetic fields so that flares can be predicted and proper precautions taken to protect all life forms.

Life and the Shaping of a World

The conditions of the earth today are not the same as those at the dawn of life. Actually, life could not begin on a planet with characteristics similar to those with which we now live. The earth is in its present state because the evolution of life itself changed the planet forever.

Almost 4 billion years ago, the earth was a very different place. There was no oxygen in the air. Carbon dioxide, methane, and ammonia were major constituents of the atmosphere. Oxygen is highly corrosive, and its presence would have prevented complex molecules from forming. To survive the present conditions on earth, organic compounds have developed complex chemical means of protection. This protection, however, developed during the evolution of life and was not present at life's origin.

The oxygen in the atmosphere prevents solar ultraviolet radiation from reaching the surface of the earth. Ultraviolet rays are very hazardous to unshielded molecules, and without the ozone layer in the atmosphere (ozone is a molecule consisting of three oxygen atoms) absorbing the incoming ultraviolet radiation, life on the land would rapidly be destroyed.

The early earth needed the ultraviolet radiation to stimulate the generation of some complex molecules.

Certain chemical reactions require outside energy sources; solar ultraviolet radiation and lightning in the atmosphere provided the proper stimulus for these complex molecules to form. Free oxygen would have prevented that vital transfer of energy from the sun to the atomic reactions. Although the details of the origin of life are not well understood, it is thought that the necessary elements were present in the atmosphere of the young earth, needing only time for atoms to come together in the right quantities and arrangements. This is basically the thesis first proposed by the Soviet biochemist A. I. Oparin in 1924.

The molecules that led to the creation of life are long chains of atoms based on carbon. On geologic time scales, there was no hurry for atoms to dance into position, although the formation of large molecular chains may take less time than was once thought. In the early 1950s, Stanley Miller, then a graduate student at the University of Chicago, performed a significant experiment while studying with Harold Urey.

Urey had long argued that the early atmosphere was full of hydrogen, which eventually escaped from the earth's gravity. Miller put several simple molecules in a glass laboratory jar, including the hydrogen gas thought to be present in the young atmosphere. The other gases were water vapor (H_2O), ammonia (NH_3), and methane (CH_4). To simulate lightning, a probable energy source for the chemical reactions, Miller ignited electric discharges in the gas mixture. In a few days the glass of the jar was covered with a dark residue, which Miller analyzed and reported as consisting of complex molecules that were based on carbon. The sediment even included a few amino acids.

Other scientists have since extended this work, including researchers at the University of Maryland and Cornell University, and it turns out that only a few hours are required to produce organic molecules. Although amino acids are quite relevant to the origin of

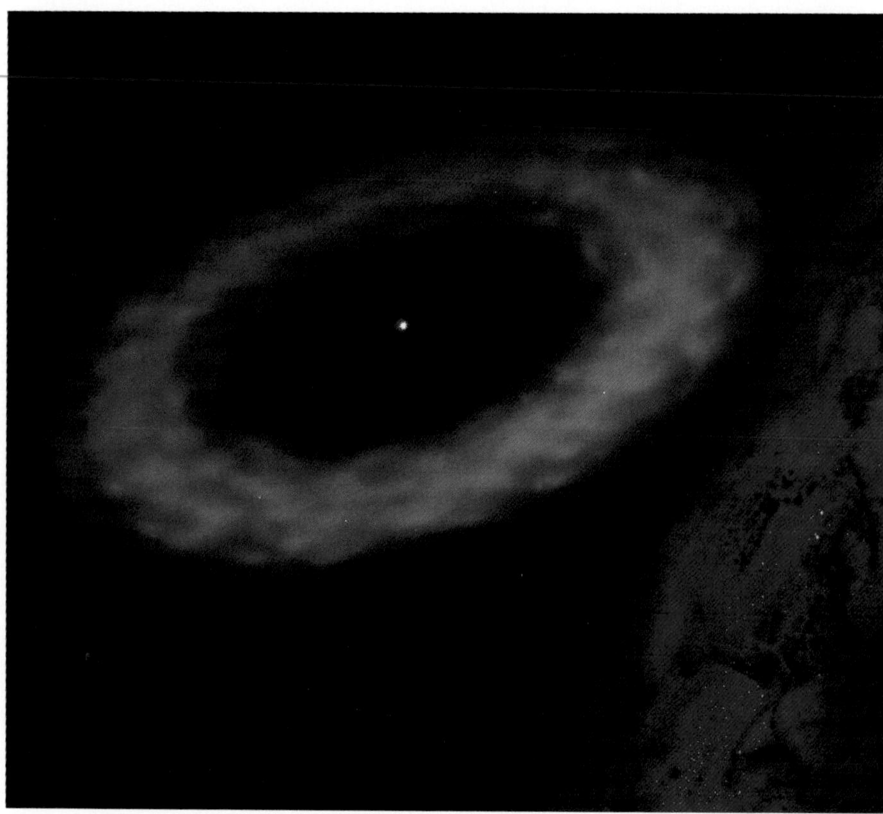

10.3 This artist's concept illustrates the ring of material discovered by the Infrared Astronomical Satellite (IRAS) around the star Vega.

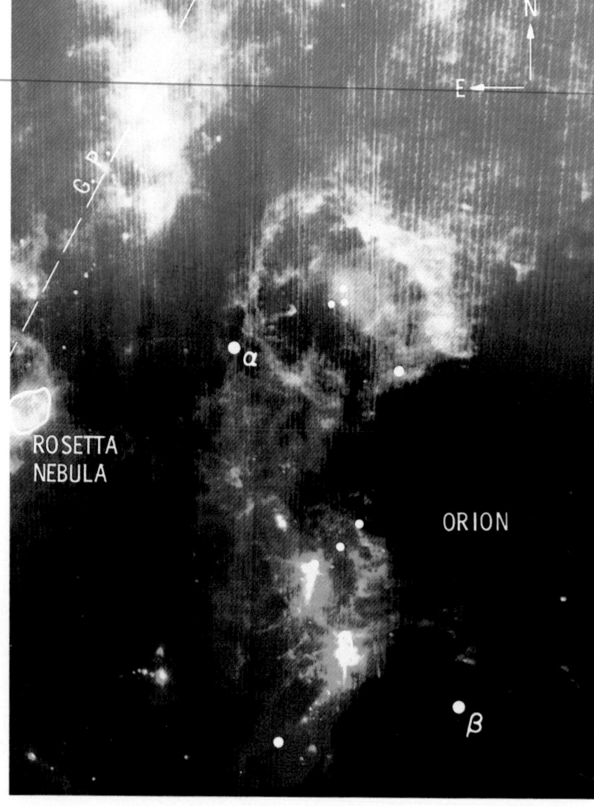

10.4 This false-color image of the region of space around the constellation Orion was produced from data from IRAS. Here, the infrared radiation indicates the presence of warm gas and dust clouds where stars are being born. Some of this material is left over from star formation and may eventually collapse to form solar systems.

10.5 An artist's rendition of IRAS in orbit over Western Europe.

life, these experiments are a long way from forming living organisms, but at least scientists have succeeded in making a first step. Independent research has also succeeded in putting amino acids together to form molecules resembling proteins, so thread by thread the tapestry of life is being woven in laboratories.

Life did form and evolve from chains of organic molecules. This may have taken place in the oceans, where water currents washed nourishment across tiny creatures. Plant life developed and utilized carbon dioxide while expelling oxygen as a waste product. The face of the earth changed dramatically as this oxygen entered the atmosphere and blocked the sun's ultraviolet radiation. Plant life grew safely on land.

The sky turned blue as free nitrogen, which makes up some 70 percent of the atmosphere, and free oxygen became the primary constituents of the air. Animal life developed, also protected from ultraviolet light and requiring oxygen to breathe, and the face of the land changed forever. At last, some 3.5 billion years after the first living things emerged, humans rose to dominate the earth. Human beings are made of carbon, oxygen, iron, phosphorus, and a host of other elements. Where did these elements come from? Most of the matter in the universe is hydrogen; helium is the second most abundant element. Table 7 lists the relative abundances of the most prevalent atoms found spectroscopically in the sun. Most of these are familiar elements we find on the earth, such as magnesium, silicon, and aluminum.

As we look into space, we see stars similar to the sun in that they are full of these heavy atoms. We also see stars that are different, exhibiting only hydrogen and helium in their spectra. Why does this difference exist? It is related to the origin of the various elements.

To trace the origin of the elements, we must start at the beginning of the universe, at the big bang. The big bang theory is currently the generally accepted explanation of the creation of the universe. In this theory the universe began with a colossal explosion, when everywhere at once space and time were created. From that explosion the universe has expanded, galaxies have formed, and intelligent life on earth (and elsewhere?) has developed to ponder its own beginnings.

Scientists are able to trace back to a time fractions of a second after the big bang by using equations and physical principles that apply to the current state of the universe. Computers are very helpful in processing the vast amounts of information derived from these calculations, and scientists are able to make theoretical models of the early universe.

According to these calculations, the temperature of the universe immediately after the big bang was trillions of degrees, and only the simplest forms of matter existed. In this context, we can think of heat as the energetic motions of the elementary particles. They were so energetic at this temperature that it was not possible for them to be bound together in larger, stable configurations. As the universe expanded, it cooled. In only a minute and a half, the temperature had decreased to about a billion degrees. The density of matter was very high, so deuterons (the combination of a neutron and a proton) formed. We call the process of formation of elements *nucleosynthesis*. The nuclei of heavier elements, including lithium, helium, and isotopes of hydrogen, also formed as neutrons and protons combined in heavier groups. This is the process of fusion, which requires high temperatures (so the particles are moving very rapidly) and high densities (so there is a great probability that particles frequently collide). With the appropriate physical conditions, such as those in the early universe and in the centers of stars, elementary particles are literally crushed together to a point where nuclear forces hold them together, overcoming the repulsion of electrostatic forces. Scientists believe that the development of fusion reactors on the earth may help solve the world's future energy problems, but the conditions needed for sustained fusion have not yet been duplicated in laboratories.

After only a few minutes, the temperature dropped to only 100 million° K. This is even cooler than the interior of our sun. In terms of the creation of elements, therefore, cosmic nucleosynthesis stopped. Approximately 75 percent of the mass in the universe was hydrogen. The rest was helium, free protons, neutrons, and electrons. Isotopes of hydrogen—deuterium, and tritium, and perhaps a small amount of lith-

Table 7
Solar Abundances of the Most Common Elements

	Symbol	Atomic Number
For each 1,000,000 atoms of hydrogen there are:	H	1
63,000 atoms of helium	He	2
690 atoms of oxygen	O	8
420 atoms of carbon	C	6
87 atoms of nitrogen	N	7
45 atoms of silicon	Si	14
40 atoms of magnesium	Mg	12
37 atoms of neon	Ne	10
32 atoms of iron	Fe	26
16 atoms of sulfur	S	16
3 atoms of aluminum	Al	13
2 atoms of calcium	Ca	20
2 atoms of sodium	Na	11
2 atoms of nickel	Ni	28
1 atom of argon	Ar	18

ium—may have formed shortly after the big bang.

If only the lightest elements, which are still the most abundant in the universe, formed in the big bang, where did the heavier elements come from? It appears now that nucleosynthesis took place in two distinct epochs. First, the lightest elements formed during the big bang, and second, the heavier elements were created in stars and supernovae several billion years later.

Humans—A Supernova Remnant

In 1957, scientists first realized that nucleosynthesis occurs during certain nuclear reactions in stellar interiors. In Chapter 5, we saw the various processes believed to supply stars with energy—the proton-proton reaction, the carbon-nitrogen-oxygen (CNO) reaction, and the triple alpha process. In each reaction, atoms of certain elements are combined to form heavier elements. Helium is a product of the proton-proton reaction, as well as of the big bang, so the cosmic abundance of helium has changed from that of the early universe due to stellar nucleosynthesis. The CNO cycle also yields some of the heavier elements, and the triple alpha process produces carbon from helium atoms. The work of E. Margaret Burbidge, Geoffrey Burbidge, William Fowler, and Fred Hoyle in 1957 led to an understanding of the production of even heavier elements in stellar interiors.

For elements more massive than helium to be created in the nuclear fires of a stellar core, the interior must become very hot. The stellar interior of massive stars undergoes a series of stages, including nuclear burning, collapse, and reignition of fusion. This may happen several times in some very large stars until iron is formed in the core.

The unique character of iron nuclei prevents iron atoms from being turned into any heavier elements in the center of stars. While all fusion reactions that lead to the production of elements lighter than or including iron release energy and make stars shine, to produce elements that are more massive than iron, energy has to be *supplied* to the atoms. This is done, as explained in Chapter 5, by neutron capture, but the high temperatures in a stellar core are not sufficient for continuous neutron capture, so energy production is effectively snuffed out when iron dominates the star's interior.

At this point in the lives of massive stars, the final collapse begins because there is no energy flowing outward to support the star against its own huge gravity. As described in Chapter 8, this last collapse is catastrophic. As the mass of the star is condensed to a smaller and smaller volume, the temperature of the core heats up to 100 billion° K. At these temperatures and high internal densities, every nuclear reaction possible takes place, and all elements heavier than iron up to uranium are formed.

The material in the star rebounds in an enormous supernova explosion, and all the elements produced during the star's lifetime, and those produced in the

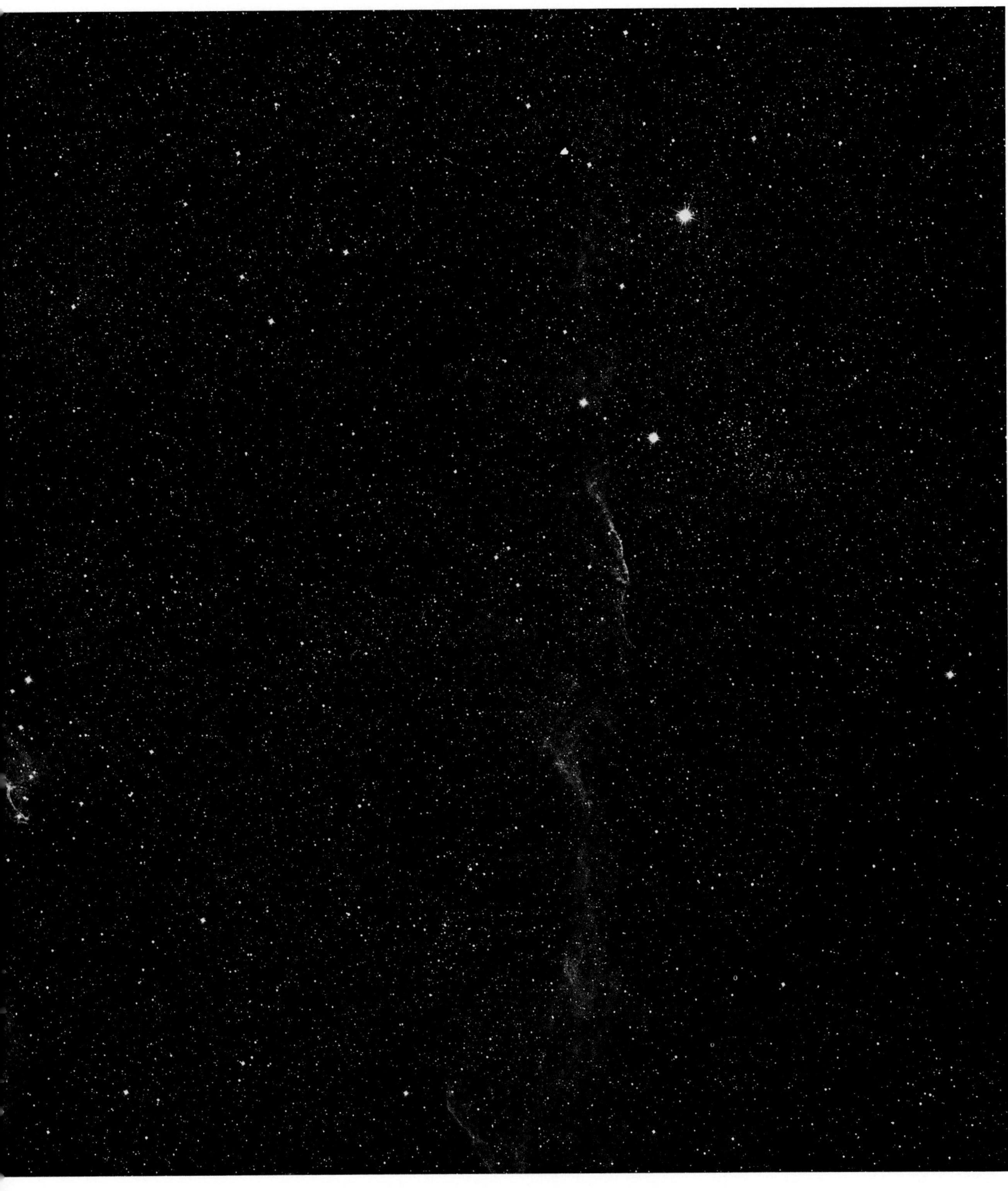

10.6 The beautiful nebulosity associated with the Vela supernova and pulsar is expanding into space and is rich in heavy elements that will eventually replenish the interstellar medium with material for new stars.

Table 8
Searches for Extraterrestrial Intelligence

Date	Observer(s)	Site	Antenna Size (m)	Search Frequency (MHz)	Frequency Resolution (Hz)	Objects	Total Hours
1960	Drake (OZMA)	NRAO	26	1,420–1,420.4	100	2 stars	400
1966	Kellerman	CSIRO	64	many, between 350 and 5,000	—	1 galaxy	—
1968	Troitski, Gershtein, Starodubtsev, Rakhlin	Zimenkie, UAAE	13	926–928, 1,421–1,423	13	12 stars	11
1970	Troitski, Bondar, Starodubtsev	Gorki, Crimea, Murmansk	dipole	1,863, 927, 600	—	all-sky	700+
1971	Verschuur (OZPA)	NRAO	91 43	1,419.8–1,421, 1,410–1,430	490	9 stars	13
1972	Palmer, Zuckerman (OZMA II)	NRAO	91	1,413–1,425, 1,420.1–1,420.7	64,000 4,000	674 stars	500
1972	Kardashev, Gindilis	Eurasian network	dipole	1,337–1,863	—	all-sky	—
1973	Dixon, Ehman, Raub, Kraus	OSURO	53	1,420.4 relative to galactic center	10 & 1 kHz	all-sky	—
1974	Bridle, Feldman	ARO	46	22,235.8	30,000	500 stars	140
1974	Wishnia	Copernicus	1	searched for UV laser lines		3 stars	—
1975–1976	Drake, Sagan	NAIC	305	1,420, 1,667, 2,380	1,000	4 galaxies	100
1975–1979	Israel, De Ruiter	WRST	1,500 (baseline)	1,415	4×10^6	50 star fields	400
1976	U. C. Berkeley (SERENDIP)	HCRO	26	1,410–1,430, 1,653–1,673	2,500	all-sky	—
1976	Clark, Black, Cuzzi, Tarter	NRAO	43	8,522–8,523	5	4 stars	7

Date	Observer(s)	Site	Antenna Size (m)	Search Frequency (MHz)	Frequency Resolution (Hz)	Objects	Total Hours
1977	Black, Clark, Cuzzi, Tarter	NRAO	91	1,665–1,667	5	200 stars	100
1977	Drake, Stull	NAIC	305	1,664–1,668	0.5	6 stars	10
1977	Wielebinski, Seiradakis	MPIFR	100	1,420	$2 \times 10'$	3 stars	2
1978	Horowitz	NAIC	305	1,420 ± 500 Hz	0.015	185 stars	80
1978	Cohen, Malkan, Dickey	NAIC HRO CSIRO	305 36 63	1,665–1,667 22,235.08 1,612.231	9,500 65,000 4,500	25 globular clusters	40 20 20
1978	Knowles, Sullivan	NAIC	305	130–500	1	2 stars	5
1979	Cole, Ekers	CSIRO	64	5,000	1×10^6	F, G, & K stars nearby	50
1979	Freitas, Valdes	Leuschner Observatory	0.8	searched photos for e.t. probes at L_4 & L_5			30
1979	JPL, U.C. Berkeley (SERENDIP II)	DSS 14	64	S & X band	19,500	listens for signals while tracking NASA spacecraft	400+
1979	Tarter, Black	NAIC	305	1,420.4 ± 2	5	200 stars	35
1981	Clark, Cuzzi			1,666 ± 2	600		
1981	Lord, O'Dea	U. Mass.	14	115,000	20,000 125,000 4×10^8	north galactic rotation axis	50
1981	Israel, Tarter	WRST	3,000 (baseline)	1,420	4×10^6 1×10^7	85 star fields	600
1981	Biraud, Tarter	Nancy, France	40 × 240	1,665–1,667	97.5	300 stars	80+
1981	Shostak	WRST	3,000	1,420.4 relative	1,200	galactic center	4

final collapse, are hurled out into space at tremendous velocities. These very atoms, expelled in the star's explosive death, enrich the interstellar medium. For billions of years, these heavy atoms drift in space and eventually, by gravitational collapse, form new generations of stars that exhibit the heavy elements in their spectra. The sun is such a star, as are all Population I stars (see Chapter 2). Population II stars are those that form from hydrogen clouds that have not mingled with heavy elements. We might think of them as first-generation stars—stars that have formed from the original matter of the universe. The sun is a second-generation star made from recycled atoms, as are the planets, trees, and human beings.

Life Beyond the Earth

Many familiar molecules have formed in nebulae, including methyl alcohol and formaldehyde, so it is clear that chemical principles with which we deal on earth are valid throughout the universe. When our solar

10.7 The Viking lander searched Mars's soil for evidence of life during what may be considered one of the greatest human adventures.

systems collapsed out of a large cloud of gas and dust, the heavy atoms from supernovae eventually formed the rocky worlds and ourselves. Organic chemistry, chemistry based on the carbon atom, eventually led to life and humans. If the same organic chemistry is at work in the universe everywhere we look, we are led to ask the most profound question, Are we alone in the universe?

The question of life elsewhere in the universe can be treated only in terms of probabilities since we have no evidence that life exists anywhere but on the earth. We must calculate the probability that appropriate stars with solar systems stay on the main sequence long enough for matter to evolve into living things. We must calculate the probability of finding planets around those stars, and we must estimate the number of these planets that have conditions suitable for life. Once we have calculated these probabilities, we must face the greatest uncertainty: On how many of these suitable planets does life actually arise?

This method of analysis was developed by Cornell astronomer Frank Drake and extended by several other scientists. Additional probabilities were added to estimate the number of civilizations that would choose to

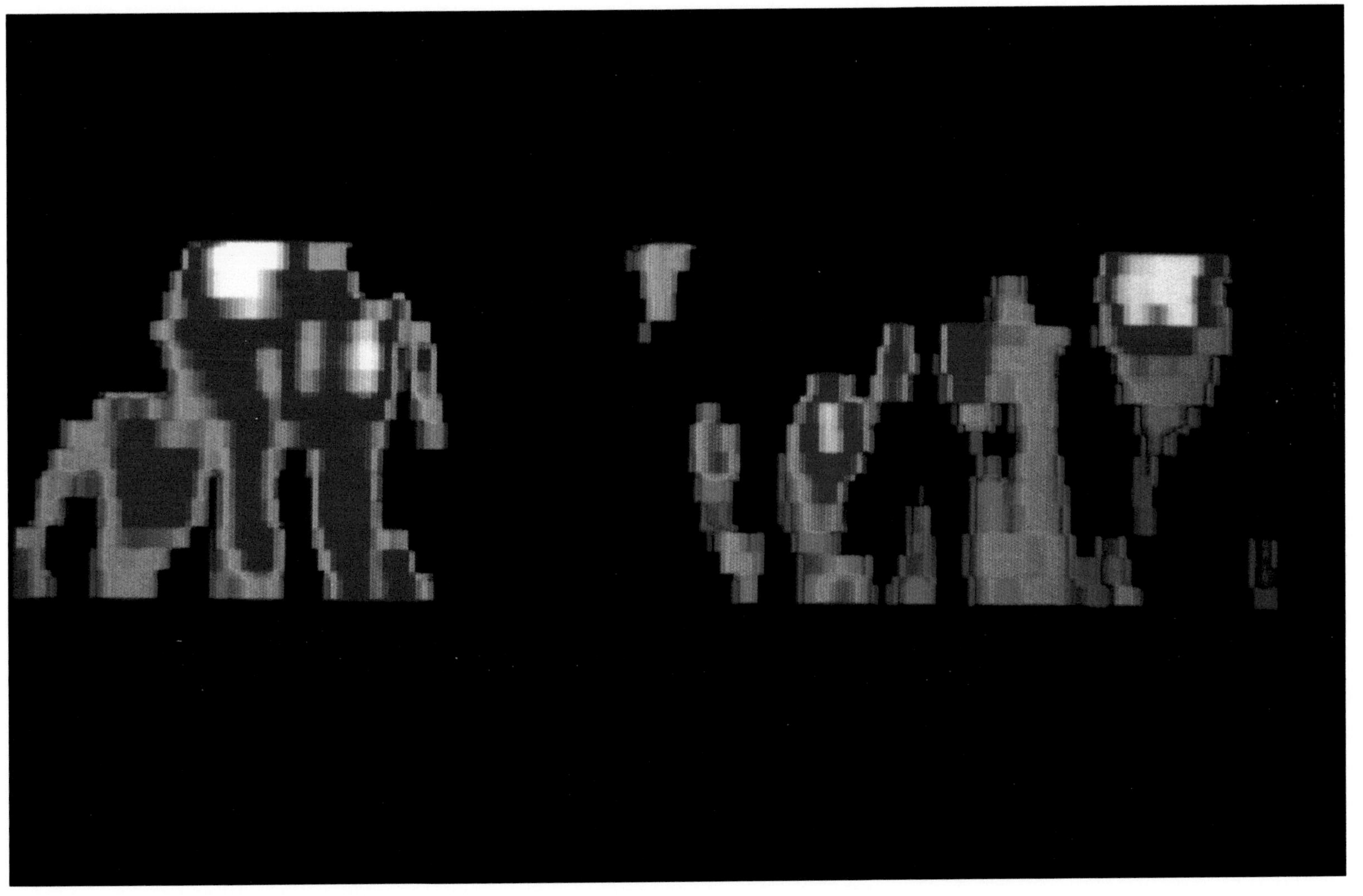

10.8 *The Large Magellanic Cloud, a nearby irregular galaxy, is highly populated with warm regions of star formation. White areas in this IRAS image have the highest temperatures.*

communicate with other species. Drake summed up his entire analysis in 1961 with a simple equation, where N is the number of civilizations in our galaxy that might be able to communicate with each other. It is: $N = Rf_pN_ef_lf_if_cL$. R is the rate of star formation in the Milky Way Galaxy; f_p is the fraction of these stars that have planets; N_e is the number of planets per solar system that are suitable for life; f_l is the fraction of those planets on which life actually arises; f_i is the fraction of these life forms that develop intelligence; f_c is the number of intelligent species who have developed technology and the desire to communicate; and L is the lifetime of such a civilization.

Depending on our selection of values for each letter, we can predict hundreds of civilizations in the galaxy, or we can predict that our species is unique. Nevertheless, we know that the processes that led to life on our planet are indeed at work throughout the universe wherever stars are dying and being born.

The Search for Life Among the Stars

There are only two ways to discover life forms outside our earth. They are to send satellites to nearby planets to search directly for life and to listen for the radio transmission of technological societies.

Of the planets in our solar system, only Mars exhibits characteristics that may be favorable for life, but we have sent the Viking lander to look in the sands of the red planet for microorganisms. There is no evidence that life ever evolved there.

Other planets are too hot or too cold, and even Saturn's moon Titan, which may be covered with clouds of organic material, is probably unsuitable for life because of the extreme cold a billion miles from the sun. Voyager I and Voyager II have both passed by Titan during their visit to Saturn.

The other method commonly used to search for extraterrestrial intelligence is to attempt to tune in on radio-frequency broadcasts of alien civilizations. This naturally assumes that any life forms broadcasting such signals must have an evolved intelligence that is familiar with the transmission and reception of radio waves.

In the past two decades, there have been at least 35 searches using radio telescopes located around the world. Each search has focused on specific target stars and used frequencies at which an advanced civilization might transmit. Table 8 shows these searches, the corresponding frequencies and targets, and the length of observation. To date, these observing programs have been fruitless, but they have only scratched the surface of the potential sites for inhabited planets. A far more extensive program is required to adequately scan the sky looking for life.

Many astronomers favor such a project and have organized what is called the Search for Extraterrestrial Intelligence (SETI). This is an informal international organization of people who are committed to systematically scanning the skies for radio manifestations of other civilizations.

One specific proposal is to build an array of more than 1,000 radio telescopes, each 100 meters in diameter, that would combine to be a fantastically sensitive receiver of radio signals. The array would cover about 100 square kilometers. The telescopes would fill a large circle, and since it would be an "eye" on the sky, it has been named Project Cyclops. The cost, however, is prohibitive—about $5 billion.

The construction of Cyclops will depend on a major national commitment to the search for extraterrestrial intelligence, a commitment not likely to be made in the near future, but research in scientific fields ranging from stellar nucleosynthesis to protein formation continues to unveil the processes that led to life on earth and perhaps elsewhere in the universe.

10.9 Do we look to other galaxies for signs of life, or must we hope to find it in our own giant city of stars? Perhaps the universe is teeming with intelligent civilizations. Perhaps we are alone.

11: THE FUTURE OF THE UNIVERSE

The Astronomical Enterprise

One of the joys of astronomy is the interdisciplinary character of this, the oldest science. Perhaps because astronomy is truly universal, it embodies all other endeavors of the human mind, from the soaring heights of religion and philosophy to the complex world of biochemistry. In this book we have seen the marriage of several fields of physics. Atomic physics is involved in radiative processes such as the formation of spectral lines, and nuclear physics governs energy generation, neutrino formation, and the construction of neutron stars and white dwarfs. When we consider black holes as wormholes, not only are we using general relativity theory, but we must begin thinking about the way the universe is, the very fabric of space and time.

Other fields of astronomy are equally involved in utilizing the knowledge and techniques of other sciences. Planetary exploration is a combination of both geology and meteorology. The structure of planets, their volcanoes and quakes, has been photographed, and in some cases seismographic equipment has been deposited on the surface of alien worlds. The atmospheres of Venus, Mars, and the gaseous cloud tops of Saturn and Jupiter reveal wind patterns and cyclones that may help us understand our own weather system. Lightning has been detected in Jupiter's upper atmosphere by our robot explorers Voyager I and Voyager II.

The search for life in the cosmos uses our knowledge of biochemistry and biology. On Mars in the 1970s a remote laboratory called Viking scratched in the dry, ancient sands of the red planet in search of microbes, or at least a clue that they could exist there.

We have beamed radio signals into space in the hope that someone out there might receive them. We have listened with giant ears in the hopes of receiving transmissions from other intelligent life forms. We have traced the universe back to just a split second after the

11.1 The Great Nebula in Andromeda is a relatively nearby galaxy very much like the Milky Way. Both galaxies, along with 19 others, formed from the same huge cloud of gas that came from the big bang.

big bang, and we have looked into the future at the death of the sun and darkening of the universe billions of years from now. These are all elements of human achievement, of the creative mind synthesizing ideas and expanding our horizons of knowledge and insight.

This too is a joy of astronomy: to be able to think about the grand view, the big picture, and to think of the earth not as a platform from which we view the universe but as part of the universe, a small part of something much bigger.

Perhaps, however, the greatest joy of all is that the stars are available to anyone on a clear night. The beauty of a sky after sunset is breathtaking, from the appearance of the first star to the myriad pinpoints of light in the night sky. Astronomy is for everyone, from the romantic to the philosopher, from the geologist to the cosmologist. It is the vehicle for us to probe the grand questions of the cosmos.

The Formation of Galaxies

The generally accepted theory describing the origin of the universe is the big bang theory, which explains how the universe flashed into existence at once, and time and space were created at that moment. From this violent beginning, the universe was flooded with light and all of the elementary particles that eventually came together to form atoms.

In this newly born universe, the temperature was trillions of degrees, and only the simplest forms of matter could exist. The elementary particles (protons, neutrons, and electrons) filled space so densely that the universe was opaque to its own radiation. As the universe expanded, it gradually cooled. After about a minute and a half had elapsed, the temperature was only about 1 billion° K, cool enough to allow the formation of deuterons (the combination of a neutron and a proton), and nucleosynthesis began. The nuclei of lithium, helium, and deuterium formed as neutrons and protons combined in heavier groups.

Over the next million years, the universe continued to expand and cool. Suddenly, at a temperature of about 3,000° K, hydrogen atoms formed from protons and electrons. Electrons are quite a bit lighter than protons, so at the high temperatures of the early universe, the electrons moved too fast to be trapped by electrostatic attraction of the oppositely charged protons. At the low temperature of 3,000° K, the electrons were finally moving slowly enough to become bound to the proton. The formation of hydrogen atoms drastically changed the nature of the universe. Light emitted at the initial event and by hot particles could not travel very far without being absorbed and reemitted millions of times by the matter. With the advent of hydrogen atoms, which freely formed throughout space, came the first chance that light could travel great distances. Atoms emit and absorb radiation at special wavelengths, the arrangement of which is inherent and unique to each element. Since a large number of electrons and protons were in bound systems absorbing only certain wavelengths of radiation, most wavelengths of light were free to permeate space.

Up to this point in the life of the universe, matter was uniformly distributed, but inhomogeneities in density began to grow until density fluctuations became so great that gravitational attraction among particles began to dominate the physical processes that existed within large clouds of matter. Such clouds are protogalaxies, and they collapse under their own gravity much as protostars form from nebulae in interstellar space.

The mass of a protogalactic cloud is so great that the collapse from a gas cloud must be at very great speeds. Such rapid collapse causes turbulence that fragments the cloud into numerous smaller regions that each begin collapsing toward their centers. Each of these fragments of the original cloud can be called a protogalaxy, and mathematical computations show that fragmentation of enormous gas clouds does in fact lead to mass concentrations similar to the mass in galaxies we now observe.

A protogalaxy survives additional collapse without further fragmentation only because it begins to radiate energy, the loss of which lets the interior cool and contract further. If the heat were to build up inside a protogalaxy, the pressure of atoms would not permit the galactic material to become more dense and compact. The cloud would then dissipate if it could not cool itself through radiation.

As a protogalaxy continues its collapse, it eventually fragments into protostars that of course heat up and become stars by the processes described in Chapter 4, where nebulae collapse to form stars.

The First Stars

The primary distinguishing feature of the first stars that formed in our galaxy must have been the obvious lack of elements heavier than helium. As we have seen in previous chapters, only hydrogen and helium existed in large quantities as a result of the big bang, so those atoms alone populated the gas clouds that formed protogalaxies and fragmented into stars.

Most of the first stars that formed probably were 10 or more times as massive as the sun, because only a great mass was capable of gravitationally containing the hot gas that must have existed in the protostars, which were mostly hydrogen. Heavier elements would help a collapsing protostar cool, but the first stars formed at high temperatures and masses.

Imagine the spectacle of a very young galaxy in which hot massive stars shone thousands of times more brightly than our sun and died in supernova explosions in only a few million years. Remember that the more massive a star is, the more rapidly it consumes its nuclear fuel and dies.

We have already noted how supernovae enrich the interstellar medium with heavier elements, which are generated in stellar cores as they are born and during the final explosion of the star itself. The first stars that formed in a galaxy were the first to form heavy elements and spread them out into interstellar space.

Several generations of stars in galaxies such as ours may have gradually enriched the interstellar medium with successive supernovae. We cannot tell where in the series lies the sun, but its spectrum of heavy elements makes it clear that our nearest star is not one of the first stars.

Star Formation Today

If the fragmentation of protogalaxies undergoing collapse led to the first stars, we might well ask what leads to the birth of stars in the current epoch of star formation.

We see more and more evidence of nearby regions

11.2 Radio astronomy is only slightly more than 50 years old, but today large radio telescopes are scanning the skies for faint signals from celestial objects and other life forms.

in space and even in other galaxies where stars are forming. Large gas and dust clouds begin collapsing due to gravity. The friction among atomic particles heats up the cloud as it shrinks, and eventually the temperature rises to the point at which nuclear reactions begin in the center of the new star. Figure 11.3 is an infrared image of our galaxy showing hot spots where stars are forming

There is no reason, however, that nebulae must begin collapsing. They may sit there for eons with no hint of star formation or they may dissipate on stellar winds from nearby stars. Yet many nebulae are stellar nurseries. Astronomers have determined that one mechanism that triggers star formation is the same phenomenon that distributes the heavy elements into space—a supernova explosion.

The shock wave from these colossal detonations travels through space and may disturb the stability of nebulae. Once the gas and dust clouds have been compressed by the pressure of the shock wave, gravitational collapse may begin and the cloud may fragment into several protostars. Thus the death of one star may trigger the birth of many, as well as alter their chemistry.

The presence of heavy elements is significant in the current epoch of star formation because they take the

11.3 This image of the center of our galaxy was produced from observations made by IRAS. The bulge in the band of color is the center of the galaxy. The yellow and green knots and blobs scattered along it are giant clouds of gas and dust heated by nearby stars.

shape of dust grains in interstellar space before being dissociated at higher stellar temperatures. The presence of grains helps collapsing clouds to remain cool because the grains radiate into space much of the internal energy of the cloud. Thus less massive stars, such as the sun, can freely form. Low-mass stars live lives billions of years long, and only once they have formed (after a reasonable percentage of heavy elements has been accumulated) does a galaxy take on a shape that may last billions of years.

Star Formation and the Morphology of Galaxies

When the first stars formed in the Milky Way Galaxy, from a distant point outside the protogalaxy an observer probably could have seen a spectacular fireworks display. The galaxy may still have been collapsing from its protogalactic cloud, and bright, hot, massive stars were flashing into existence from the available hydrogen. In brief periods of only a few million years, these same stars burst out of existence, and new stars formed from their debris.

The heavy elements allowed smaller, longer-lasting stars to form, and gradually our own galaxy took the shape we currently see. It is a vast spiral conglomeration of stars. The shape of spiral galaxies long puzzled astronomers, and many explanations have been devised to account for the existence of spiral arms. The measurement of the rotation of other spiral galaxies has demonstrated that the farther from the center a star is, the more slowly it is traveling around the galactic core. This is called differential rotation. Remember that the sun rotates more rapidly at the equator than at the poles—this is also differential rotation. We would thus expect that the spiral arms of a galaxy will wrap up and disappear in just a few galactic rotations. This is not what we observe. The Milky Way Galaxy alone has probably rotated some 50 or 60 times during its existence, but the spiral shape is still evident today. The sun also has probably traveled around the center 20 times in its 5-billion-year lifetime. Why does the spiral structure persist?

The currently accepted explanation of spiral arms is related in part to current star formation in galaxies. It is called the density wave theory and was first proposed in the 1920s, shortly after the discovery of the expansion of the universe. A Swedish astronomer named Bertil Lindblat suggested that spiral arms in galaxies are manifestations of patterns that move through galaxies among the stars. He imagined that some sort of density wave passes through galaxies and bunches stars together in the familiar spiral pattern. In the 1960s these notions were elaborated by the work of two American astrophysicists, Frank Shu and C. C. Lin. They showed that the gravitational interaction among stars bunches them together and correlates their individual orbits in an organized way.

For example, Figure 11.5a shows a group of elliptical orbits of stars as they pass around the center of a galaxy. Figure 11.5b shows the same number of ellipses, but the individual orbits are somehow correlated so that a clear spiral shape emerges where there are regions of stars that are closely bunched (Figure 11.5c).

The accumulation of stars along spiral arms has an important effect on the gas and dust of the interstellar medium. Where there are increased numbers of stars, there is increased gravitational attraction on the interstellar medium. This pulls the gas and dust toward the spiral arms, and a shock wave forms that moves through the galaxy with the spiral density wave. This shock front compresses the interstellar medium into stellar precursors, and eventually emission nebulae and new stars form at the edge of the spiral arms. In fact the sun has moved in and out of spiral arms many times. This is possible because the sun orbits the galactic nucleus more slowly than do the spiral density waves.

Photographs of some galaxies seem to show that emission nebulae do exist at the edges of spiral arms where compression has occurred. The bright regions at the edge of the spiral arms in Figure 11.6 are emission nebulae where stars are being born such as those we see in our own solar neighborhood.

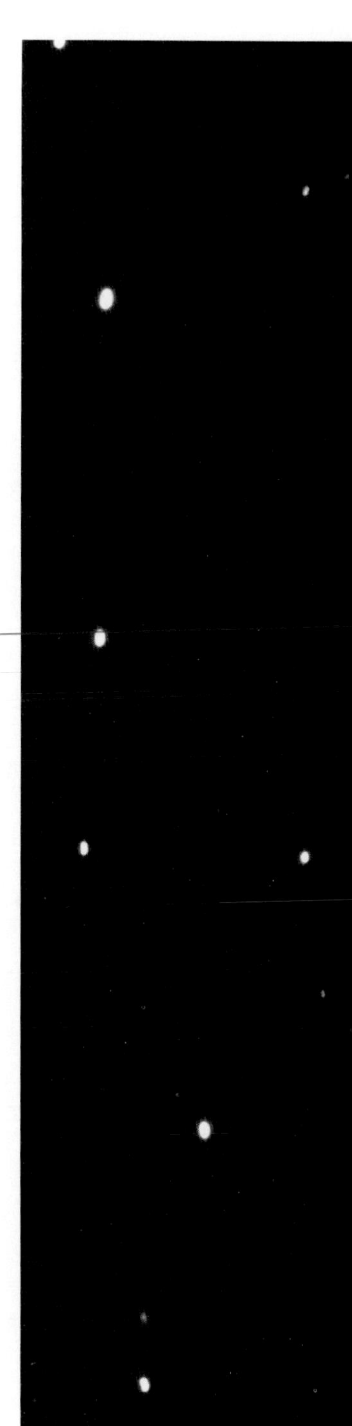

11.4 *This large spiral galaxy, cataloged NGC 4565, is viewed edge-on. Note the dark lane of dust that runs along the plane of the galaxy.*

Thus, both supernova explosions and density waves are very important in the formation of new stars, but only after the initial stars collapsed from protogalactic gas. Stars that are forming currently, however, are being born from the greatly enriched interstellar medium. The heavy elements are mostly distributed in nebulae as dust grains that help the collapsing clouds cool and prevent the formation of massive hot stars. New stars are generally cooler and longer-lived than the first stars.

The Future of Star Formation

Although we can observe stars forming in our own and other galaxies, the future of star formation is dependent on some fundamental properties of the universe. Although cosmology is not a topic of this book, a brief review of our notions about the future of the universe will prove helpful in considering the future of the stars.

We have already mentioned that the universe is expanding and has been doing so for between 10 and 20 billion years, since the big bang created all space and time. A great question remaining before us is, What is the future of the universe? It will either continue to expand forever or it will stop expanding and contract upon itself.

The mass of the universe will determine its future. If the mass is large enough, the gravity of the entire universe will halt the expansion and cause the matter to collapse inward. The universe will reverse course, and as it does the density and temperature will become extremely high, matching conditions of the early universe to the point where matter is ripped apart into subatomic particles.

It is possible that another big bang will occur at the end of the contraction and matter will explode outward again. Conversely, the universe might end with the contraction. The notion of a succession of big bangs is known as the oscillating universe theory. Our current universe would then be the result of the most recent of a series of bangs.

If there is enough mass in the universe to cause a contraction, we term the universe closed. On the other hand, if there is not enough mass to gravitationally halt the universe's expansion, we say that the universe is open.

It is a difficult task to make accurate estimates of the total mass of the universe. Only a few years ago, scientists first got an idea of how much molecular hydrogen is in interstellar space. This amount adds up to quite a lot of mass. We cannot be certain how much mass is invisible to us in black holes since we cannot see them. Scientists believe they have discovered a few black holes in our galaxy, but only by observing their effect on nearby matter that we can see. These observations are rare. We simply cannot determine the mass of the universe based on how much we see.

Physicists have developed methods that indirectly tell us the average density of matter in space. One technique employs the abundances of light elements such as hydrogen, helium, and lithium. The light elements were formed shortly after the big bang, and thus their abundances give us information about conditions at that time in the universe. There should have been as much mass then as there is now, according to the conservation laws. The one uncertainty we encounter is just how much of each element has been formed or consumed in the fusion process at the center of stars. This hinders our attempts at accuracy.

Theoretical studies, however, have indicated that the abundance of deuterium is almost entirely a result of the big bang, and not stellar in origin. Deuterium is an isotope of hydrogen. Hydrogen has one proton as the nucleus. Deuterium has a proton and a neutron, making it more massive than hydrogen. By observing deuterium emissions with a radio telescope, we can determine its abundance relative to normal hydrogen. The ratio of the two is a sensitive indicator of the conditions in the universe at the time of the isotope's creation.

Deuterium has been discovered in various molecules in place of normal hydrogen, and both radio and ultraviolet emissions of deuterium atoms have been recorded. Although there does not appear to be evidence in the deuterium observations of sufficient mass to close the universe, astronomers now believe that

11.5 This illustration shows that a group of elliptical orbits can lead to a spiral structure if they are arranged in the proper fashion. Only the position of the orbits changes in this sequence. No real spiral structure exists.

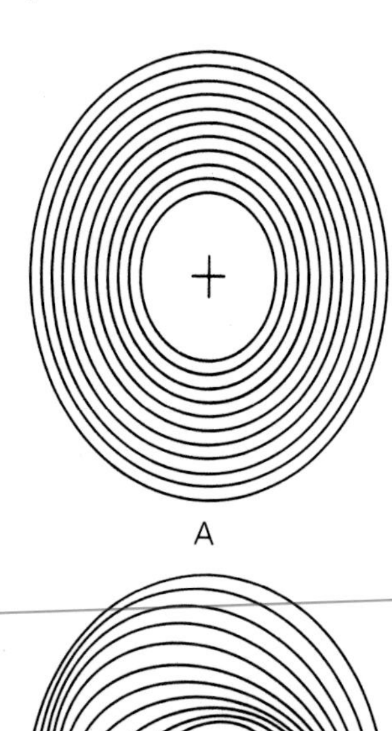

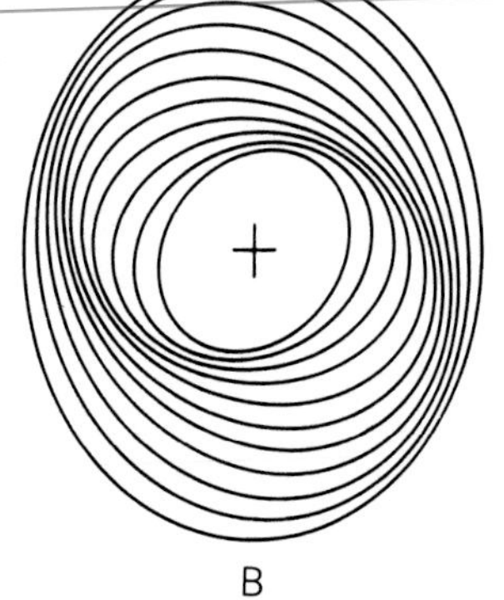

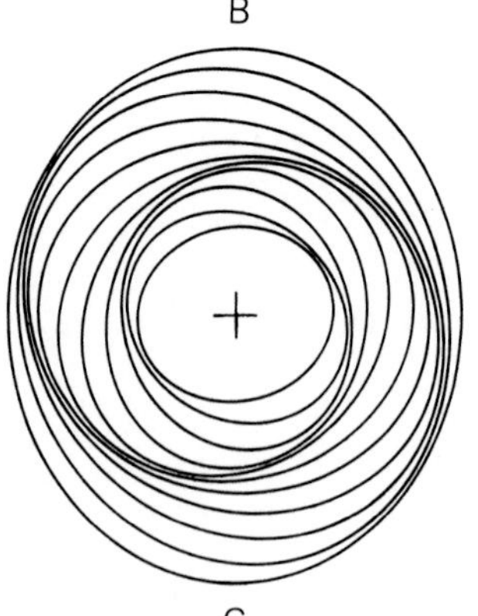

11.6 The Andromeda Galaxy (M31) as recorded in visible light (above) and by IRAS (below). The infrared photograph shows warm regions in the spiral arms where stars are forming. Up close, these areas would appear rich in HII regions and protostars. The galaxy as seen in white light is shown on the right.

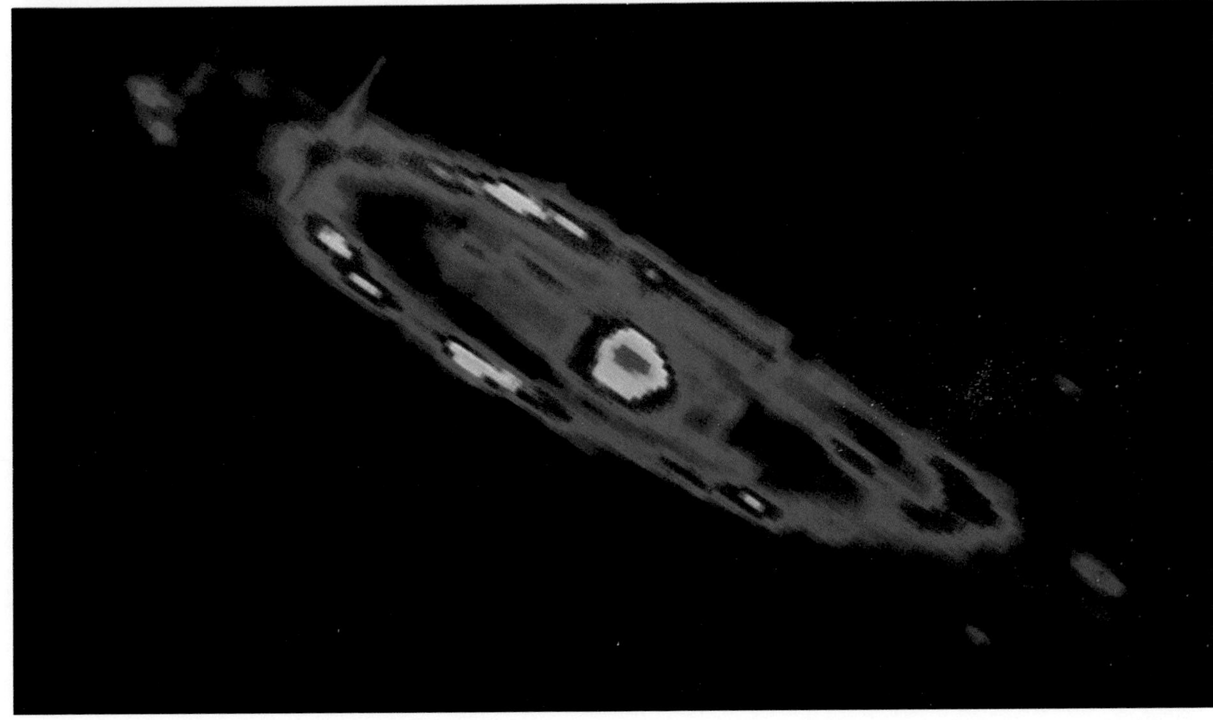

there is much mass hidden within clusters of galaxies and in invisible halos around galaxies.

What does all this mean for star formation? If the universe continues to expand forever, eventually star formation will come to an end, and galaxies will grow cold and dark. If, on the other hand, the universe is closed, the expansion will someday stop, and as the universe plunges headlong back toward its origins, it will heat up as it grows smaller, and stars will continue to form out of gas and dust until the moment when all the matter in the universe is crushed out of existence into the biggest black hole of all. Perhaps a new universe will rise from the corpse of the old.

A Sense of the Future

We do not know all there is to know about the life and death of stars. We will see new vistas from satellites as

11.7 Around the world, astronomers are using telescopes, computers, satellite technology, and, above all, their brains to probe the mysteries of the cosmos. At one time, this dome at the Harvard College Observatory housed the largest telescope in the world. Today, the 15-inch refractor is a reminder of the old methods of the astronomer.

we probe the inner recesses of dark clouds in space, and astronomers will continue to look for the telltale signs of black holes in orbit about visual stars.

Even though there is much to learn, we have witnessed tremendous strides in understanding the cosmos. Some techniques are still in their infancy, such as observation of gamma rays, but astronomers have used every part of the electromagnetic spectrum to garner information about celestial objects. As we have discussed in this book, the general story appears complete, with plenty of details still to be added.

In the final analysis, it is the need to know that keeps astronomers looking up, literally and figuratively. It is the tradition and future of humans to question the existence of primordial lights in the sky, but learning about them does not make their simple beauty fade nor diminish the joy in each of us when we look up into the night. Astronomers have echoed these feelings through the years, but perhaps Walt Whitman said it best.

When I heard the learn'd astronomer,
When the proofs, the figures, were ranged in columns before me,
When I was shown the charts and diagrams, to add, divide,
and measure them,
When I sitting heard the astronomer where he lectured
with much applause in the lecture room,
How soon unaccountable I became tired and sick,
Till rising and gliding out I wander'd off by myself,
In the mystical moist night-air, and from time to time,
Look'd up in perfect silence at the stars.

There is joy in learning, too. In the future, astronomers will continue to ask questions, the answers to which will be revealed by human ingenuity and skill at thinking. Do black holes really exist? Will the universe expand forever? Where are the solar neutrinos we expect to record? These questions and others have a bearing not only on our understanding of the universe and the life and death of stars, but ultimately on our understanding of ourselves and our destiny within the cosmos.

Picture Acknowledgments

Chapter 1
1.1, 1.9: Photograph by Jay M. Pasachoff
1.3: Palomar Observatory
1.7, 1.8: Yerkes Observatory
1.12: Kitt Peak National Observatory
1.13: Celestron International

Chapter 2
Picture on page 22: Celestron International
2.3: Palomar Observatory
2.5, 2.12, 2.13: NASA
2.6: Photograph by Robert Boyle
2.7, 2.10: Celestron International

Chapter 3
Picture on page 40: Celestron International
3.3, 3.4, 3.7, 3.9, 3.10, 3.15: Celestron International
3.17: Painting by Valentino M. Gonzales
3.18, 3.19: Photograph by Jay M. Pasachoff
3.20: Steward Observatory

Chapter 4
Picture on page 60: NASA
4.1, 4.2: NASA
4.3: Harvard College Observatory
4.4: Photograph by Jay M. Pasachoff
4.5, 4.7, 4.8, 4.9: Celestron International
4.10: Lick Observatory
4.11: Steward Observatory

Chapter 5
Picture on page 72: Celestron International
5.3: Celestron International
5.16: Harvard College Observatory

Chapter 6
Picture on page 88: Harvard College Observatory
6.6, 6.13, 6.19: Photograph by Jay M. Pasachoff
6.7, 6.8: Celestron International
6.9: Princeton University
6.12, 6.18b: Daystar Filter Corporation
6.13, 6.19: Photograph by Jay M. Pasachoff
6.15: Sacramento Peak Observatory
6.16: Big Bear Solar Observatory
6.17, 6.18a, 6.18c: Harvard College Observatory
6.20: NASA
6.21: Painting by Valentino M. Gonzales

Chapter 7
Picture on page 108: Celestron International
7.7, 7.8: Palomar Observatory
7.9, 7.10, 7.11, 7.16: Celestron International

Chapter 8
Picture on page 124: Photograph by Jay M. Pasachoff
8.5, 8.6, 8.7: Celestron International
8.8: NASA
8.11, 8.20: Palomar Observatory
8.13: Courtesy Bell Laboratories
8.14: Photograph by Jay M. Pasachoff
8.15: Smithsonian Institution
8.19: Painting by Valentino M. Gonzales

Chapter 9
Picture on page 142: Valentino M. Gonzales
9.9: Painting by Valentino M. Gonzales

Chapter 10
Picture on page 156: NASA
10.3, 10.4, 10.5, 10.7, 10.8: NASA

Chapter 11
11.1: Photograph by Jay M. Pasachoff
11.2: Lick Observatory
11.3: NASA
11.4: Celestron International
11.6: Celestron International
11.7: Photograph by Donald Alan Cooke

APPENDIXES

Appendix 1
Additional Reading

General Reading

Friedman, Herbert. *The Amazing Universe.* Washington, D.C.: National Geographic Society, 1975. National Geographic's survey of modern astronomy.

Mitton, Simon, ed. *The Cambridge Encyclopedia of Astronomy.* New York: Crown Publishers, 1977.

Shapley, Harlow, and H. E. Howarth, eds. *A Source Book in Astronomy.* New York: McGraw-Hill, 1929. Reprints of fundamental articles.

———, ed. *Source Book in Astronomy 1900–1950.* Cambridge, Mass,: Harvard University Press, 1960. Reprints of fundamental articles.

Struve, Otto, and Velta Zebergs. *Astronomy of the Twentieth Century.* New York: Macmillan, 1962.

Advanced Books

Avrett, Eugene H., ed. *Frontiers in Astrophysics.* Cambridge, Mass.: Harvard University Press, 1976.

Harwit, Martin. *Astrophysical Concepts.* New York: John Wiley & Sons, 1973.

Shu, Frank H. *The Physical Universe.* Mill Valley, Calif.: University Science Books, 1982.

Textbooks in Astronomy

Abell, G. O. *Exploration of the Universe.* 4th ed. Philadelphia: Saunders College Publishing, 1982.

Hoyle, F. *Astronomy and Cosmology: A Modern Course.* San Francisco: Freeman, 1975.

Pasachoff, J. M. *Contemporary Astronomy.* 2nd ed. Philadelphia: Saunders College Publishing, 1981.

Shu, F. H. *The Physical Universe: An Introduction to Astronomy.* St. Paul, Minn.: West Publishing Co., 1983.

Zeilik, M. *Astronomy: The Evolving Universe.* 2nd ed. New York: Harper & Row, 1979.

Life in the Universe

Drake, F. *Intelligent Life in Space.* New York: Macmillan, 1962.

Goldsmith, D., and T. Owen. *The Search for Life in the Universe.* Menlo Park, Calif.: Benjamin/Cummings, 1980.

Sagan, C. *The Cosmic Connection.* New York: Anchor Press/Doubleday, 1973.

Shklovskii, I. S., and C. Sagan. *Intelligent Life in the Universe.* New York: Dell, 1966.

Monthly Non-Technical Magazines on Astronomy

Astronomy, 625 East St. Paul Avenue, P.O. Box 92788, Milwaukee, Wis. 53202.

The Griffith Observer, 2800 East Observatory Road, Los Angeles, Calif. 90027.

Mercury, Astronomical Society of the Pacific, 1290 Twenty-fourth Avenue, San Francisco, Calif. 94122.

Sky and Telescope, 49 Bay State Road, Cambridge, Mass. 02238.

Magazines and Annuals Carrying Articles on Astronomy

Discover, Time-Life Building, New York, N.Y. 10020.

National Geographic, Washington, D.C. 20036.

Natural History, Membership Services, Box 4300, Bergenfield, N.J. 07621.

Science Digest, P.O. Box 10076, Des Moines, Iowa 50350.

Science 82, 83, 84, etc., P.O. Box 10790, Des Moines, Iowa 50340.

Science News, 1719 N Street, N.W., Washington, D.C. 20036. Published weekly.

Stars and the Sun

Aller, Lawrence H. *Atoms, Stars, and Nebulae.* Rev. ed. Cambridge, Mass.: Harvard University Press, 1971.

Eddy, John A., with Rein Ise, ed. *A New Sun: The Solar Results from Skylab.* NASA SP-402, 1979, GPO 033-000-00742-6.

Fire of Life, The Smithsonian Book of the Sun. Smithsonian Exposition Press, W. W. Norton Co., 1981.

Golden, Frederick. *Quasars, Pulsars, and Black Holes.* New York: Scribner's, 1976.

Jastrow, Robert. *Red Giants and White Dwarfs.* 2nd ed. New York: W. W. Norton Co., 1979.

Noyes, Robert W. *The Sun.* Cambridge, Mass.: Harvard University Press, 1982.

Payne-Gaposchkin, Cecilia. *Stars and Clusters.* Cambridge, Mass.: Harvard University Press, 1979.

Shipman, Henry L. *Black Holes, Quasars, and the Universe.* 2nd ed. Boston: Houghton Mifflin, 1980.

Sullivan, Walter. *Black Holes.* New York: Anchor Press/Doubleday, 1979.

Galactic Astronomy and Cosmology

Ferris, Timothy. *Galaxies.* San Francisco: Sierra Club, 1981.

———. *The Red Limit.* New York: William Morrow & Co., 1977. Written for the general reader.

Fowler, William A. *Nuclear Astrophysics.* Philadelphia: American Philosophical Society, 1967.

Gamow, George. *One, Two, Three...Infinity.* New York: Bantam Books, 1971.

Kaufmann, William J. *The Cosmic Frontiers of General Relativity.* Boston: Little, Brown, 1977.

Silk, Joseph. *The Big Bang.* San Francisco: W. H. Freeman & Co., 1979.

Weinberg, Steven. *The First Three Minutes.* New York: Basic Books, 1977.

Appendix 2
Messier Catalog

M	NGC	Right Ascension 1980.0 h m	Declination ° ′	Apparent Magnitude	Description
1	1952	5 33.3	+22 01	11.3	Crab Nebula in Taurus
2	7089	21 32.4	−00 54	6.3	Globular cluster in Aquarius
3	5272	13 41.3	+28 29	6.2	Globular cluster in Canes Venatici
4	6121	16 22.4	−26 27	6.1	Globular cluster in Scorpio
5	5904	15 17.5	+02 11	6	Globular cluster in Serpens
6	402	17 38.9	−32 11	6	Open cluster in Scorpio
7	6475	17 52.6	−34 48	5	Open cluster in Scorpio
8	6523	18 02.4	−24 23		Lagoon Nebula in Sagittarius
9	6333	17 18.1	−18 30	7.6	Globular cluster in Ophiuchus
10	6254	16 56.0	−04 05	6.4	Globular cluster in Ophiuchus
11	6705	18 50.0	−06 18	7	Open cluster in Scutum
12	6218	16 46.1	−01 55	6.7	Globular cluster in Ophiuchus
13	6205	16 41.0	+36 30	5.8	Globular cluster in Hercules
14	6402	17 36.5	−03 14	7.8	Globular cluster in Ophiuchus
15	7078	21 29.1	+12 05	6.3	Globular cluster in Pegasus
16	6611	18 17.8	−13 48	7	Open cluster and nebula in Serpens
17	6618	18 19.7	−16 12	7	Omega Nebula in Sagittarius
18	6613	18 18.8	−17 09	7	Open cluster in Sagittarius
19	6273	17 01.3	−26 14	6.9	Globular cluster in Ophiuchus
20	6514	18 01.2	−23 02		Trifid Nebula in Sagittarius

M	NGC	Right Ascension h m	1980.0 Declination ° ′	Apparent Magnitude	Description
21	6531	18 03.4	−22 30	7	Open cluster in Sagittarius
22	6656	18 35.2	−23 55	5.2	Globular cluster in Sagittarius
23	6494	17 55.7	−19 00	6	Open cluster in Sagittarius
24	6603	18 17.3	−18 27	6	Open cluster in Sagittarius
25	IC4725	18 30.5	−19 16	6	Open cluster in Sagittarius
26	6694	18 44.1	−09 25	9	Open cluster in Scutum
27	6853	19 58.8	+22 40	8.2	Dumbbell Nebula; planetary nebula in Vulpecula
28	6626	18 23.2	−24 52	7.1	Globular cluster in Sagittarius
29	6913	20 23.3	+38.27	8	Open cluster in Cygnus
30	7099	21 39.2	−23 15	7.6	Globular cluster in Capricornus
31	224	0 41.6	+41 09	3.7	Andromeda Galaxy (Sb)
32	221	0 41.6	+40 45	8.5	Elliptical galaxy in Andromeda; companion to M31
33	598	1 32.8	+30 33	5.9	Spiral galaxy (Sc) in Triangulum
34	1039	2 40.7	+42 43	6	Open cluster in Perseus
35	2168	6 07.6	+24 21	6	Open cluster in Gemini
36	1960	5 35.0	+34 05	6	Open cluster in Auriga
37	2099	5 51.5	+32 33	6	Open cluster in Auriga
38	1912	5 27.3	+35 48	6	Open cluster in Auriga
39	7092	21 31.5	+48 21	6	Open cluster in Cygnus
40	—	—	—	6	Double star in Ursa Major
41	2287	6 46.2	−20 43	6	Open cluster in Canis Major
42	1976	5 34.4	−05 24		Orion Nebula
43	1982	5 34.6	−05 18		Orion Nebula; smaller part
44	2632	8 38.8	+20 04	4	Praesepe; open cluster in Cancer
45	—	3 46.3	+24 03	2	The Pleiades; open cluster in Taurus
46	2437	7 40.9	−14 46	7	Open cluster in Puppis
47	2422	7 35.6	−14 27	5	Open cluster in Puppis
48	2548	8 12.5	−05 43	6	Open cluster in Hydra
49	4472	12 28.8	+08 07	8.9	Elliptical galaxy in Virgo
50	2323	7 02.0	−08 19	7	Open cluster in Monoceros
51	5194	13 29.0	+47 18	8.4	Whirlpool Galaxy; spiral galaxy (Sc) in Canes Venatici
52	7654	23 23.3	+61 29	7	Open cluster in Cassiopeia
53	5024	13 12.0	+18 17	7.7	Globular cluster in Coma Berenices
54	6715	18 53.8	−30 30	7.7	Globular cluster in Sagittarius
55	6809	19 38.7	−31 00	6.1	Globular cluster in Sagittarius
56	6779	19 15.8	+30 08	8.3	Globular cluster in Lyra
57	6720	18 52.9	+33 01	9.0	Ring Nebula; planetary nebula in Lyra
58	4579	12 36.7	+11 56	9.9	Spiral galaxy (SBb) in Virgo
59	4621	12 41.0	+11 47	10.3	Elliptical galaxy in Virgo
60	4649	12 42.6	+11 41	9.3	Elliptical galaxy in Virgo
61	4303	12 20.8	+04 36	9.7	Spiral galaxy (Sc) in Virgo
62	6266	16 59.9	−30 05	7.2	Globular cluster in Scorpio

M	NGC	Right Ascension h m	1980.0 Declination ° ′	Apparent Magnitude	Description
63	5055	13 14.8	+42 08	8.8	Spiral galaxy (Sb) in Canes Venatici
64	4826	12 55.7	+21 48	8.7	Spiral galaxy (Sb) in Coma Berenices
65	3623	11 17.8	+13 13	9.6	Spiral galaxy (Sa) in Leo
66	3627	11 19.1	+13 07	9.2	Spiral galaxy (Sb) in Leo; companion to M65
67	2682	8 50.0	+11 54	7	Open cluster in Cancer
68	4590	12 38.3	−26 38	8	Globular cluster in Hydra
69	6637	18 30.1	−32 23	7.7	Globular cluster in Sagittarius
70	6681	18 42.0	−32 18	8.2	Globular cluster in Sagittarius
71	6838	19 52.8	+18 44	6.9	Globular cluster in Sagitta
72	6981	20 52.3	−12 39	9.2	Globular cluster in Aquarius
73	6994	20 57.8	−12 44		Open cluster in Aquarius
74	628	1 35.6	+15 41	9.5	Spiral galaxy (Sc) in Pisces
75	6864	20 04.9	−21 59	8.3	Globular cluster in Sagittarius
76	650	1 40.9	+51 28	11.4	Planetary nebula in Perseus
77	1068	2 41.6	−00 04	9.1	Spiral galaxy (Sb) in Cetus
78	2068	5 45.8	+00 02		Small emission nebula in Orion
79	1904	5 23.3	−24 32	7.3	Globular cluster in Lepus
80	6093	16 15.8	−22 56	7.2	Globular cluster in Scorpio
81	3031	9 54.2	+69 09	6.9	Spiral galaxy (Sb) in Ursa Major
82	3034	9 54.4	+69 47	8.7	Irregular galaxy (Irr) in Ursa Major
83	5236	13 35.9	−29 46	7.5	Spiral galaxy (Sc) in Hydra
84	4374	12 24.1	+13 00	9.8	Elliptical galaxy in Virgo
85	4382	12 24.3	+18 18	9.5	Elliptical galaxy (S0) in Coma Berenice
86	4406	12 25.1	+13 03	9.8	Elliptical galaxy in Virgo
87	4486	12 29.7	+12 30	9.3	Elliptical galaxy (Ep) in Virgo
88	4501	12 30.9	+14 32	9.7	Spiral galaxy (Sb) in Coma Berenices
89	4552	12 34.6	+12 40	10.3	Elliptical galaxy in Virgo
90	4569	12 35.8	+13 16	9.7	Spiral galaxy (Sb) in Virgo
91	—	—	—		M58?
92	6341	17 16.5	+43 10	6.3	Globular cluster in Hercules
93	2447	7 43.6	−23 49	6	Open cluster in Puppis
94	4736	12 50.1	+41 14	8.1	Spiral galaxy (Sb) in Canes Venatici
95	3351	10 42.8	+11 49	9.9	Barred spiral galaxy (SBb) in Leo
96	3368	10 45.6	+11 56	9.4	Spiral galaxy (Sa) in Leo
97	3587	11 13.7	+55 08	11.1	Owl Nebula; planetary nebula in Ursa Major
98	4192	12 12.7	+15 01	10.4	Spiral galaxy (Sb) in Coma Berenices
99	4254	12 17.8	+14 32	9.9	Spiral galaxy (Sc) in Coma Berenices
100	4321	12 21.9	+15 56	9.6	Spiral galaxy (Sc) in Coma Berenices
101	5457	14 02.5	+54 27	8.1	Spiral galaxy (Sc) in Ursa Major
102	—	—	—		M101?
103	581	1 31.9	+60 35	7	Open cluster in Cassiopeia
104	4594	12 39.0	−11 35	8	Sombrero Nebula; spiral galaxy (Sa) in Virgo

M	NGC	Right Ascension h m	1980.0 Declination ° ′	Apparent Magnitude	Description
105	3379	10 46.8	+12 51	9.5	Elliptical galaxy in Leo
106	4258	12 18.0	+47 25	9	Spiral galaxy in (Sb) Canes Venatici
107	6171	16 31.8	−13 01	9	Globular cluster in Ophiuchus
108	3556	11 10.5	+55 47	10.5	Spiral galaxy (Sb) in Ursa Major
109	3992	11 56.6	+53 29	10.6	Barred spiral galaxy (SBc) in Ursa Major

Positions and magnitudes based on a table in the *Observer's Handbook* 1980 of the Royal Astronomical Society of Canada.

Appendix 3
Basic Constants

Physical constants

Speed of light	c	=	299 792 458 m/s
Constant of gravitation	G	=	$6.6726 \pm 0.0005 \times 10^{-11}$ m³/kg/s²
Planck's constant	h	=	6.6262×10^{-27} erg · s
Boltzmann's constant	k	=	1.3806×10^{-16} erg/kelvin
Stefan-Boltzmann constant	σ	=	5.66956×10^{-5} erg/cm² · deg⁴ · s¹
Wien displacement constant	$\lambda_{max} T$	=	0.289789 cm·K = 28.9789×10^{6} Å·K
Mass of hydrogen atom	m_H	=	1.6735×10^{-24} gm
Mass of neutron	m_n	=	1.6749×10^{-24} gm
Mass of proton	m_p	=	1.6726×10^{-24} gm
Mass of electron	m_e	=	9.1096×10^{-28} gm
Rydberg's constant	R	=	1.09677×10^{5}/cm

Mathematical constants

$\pi = 3.1415926536$

$e = 2.7182818285$

Astronomical constants

Astronomical unit*	1 A.U.	=	$1.495\,978\,70 \times 10^{11}$ m
Solar parallax*	$\pi_\odot$	=	8.794148 arc sec
Parsec	$pc_\odot$	=	206 264.806 A.U.
		=	3.261633 light years
		=	3.085678×10^{18} cm
Light year	ly	=	9.460530×10^{17} cm
		=	6.324×10^{4} A.U.
1 day		=	86400 s
Sidereal year		=	365.256366 ephemeris days
		=	3.155815×10^{7} s
Mass of sun*	$M_\odot$	=	1.9891×10^{33} gm
Radius of sun*	$R_\odot$	=	696000 km
Luminosity of sun	$L_\odot$	=	3.827×10^{33} erg/s
Solar constant	S	=	135.3 mW/cm²

Appendix 4
Greek Alphabet

	Upper Case	Lower Case
alpha	Α	α
beta	Β	β
gamma	Γ	γ
delta	Δ	δ
epsilon	Ε	ϵ
zeta	Ζ	ζ
eta	Η	η
theta	Θ	θ
iota	Ι	ι
kappa	Κ	κ
lambda	Λ	λ
mu	Μ	μ
nu	Ν	ν
xi	Ξ	ξ
omicron	Ο	ο
pi	Π	π
rho	Ρ	ρ
sigma	Σ	σ
tau	Τ	τ
upsilon	Υ	υ
phi	Φ	ϕ
chi	Χ	χ
psi	Ψ	ψ
omega	Ω	ω

Appendix 5
The Constellations

Latin Name	Abbreviation	Translation	Latin Name	Abbreviation	Translation
Andromeda	And	Andromeda	Lacerta	Lac	Lizard
Antlia	Ant	Pump	Leo	Leo	Lion
Apus	Aps	Bird of Paradise	Leo Minor	LMi	Little Lion
Aquarius	Aqr	Water Bearer	Lepus	Lep	Hare
Aquila	Aql	Eagle	Libra	Lib	Scales
Ara	Ara	Altar	Lupus	Lup	Wolf
Aries	Ari	Ram	Lynx	Lyn	Lynx
Auriga	Aur	Charioteer	Lyra	Lyr	Harp
Boötes	Boo	Herdsman	Mensa	Men	Table (mountain)
Caelum	Cae	Chisel	Microscopium	Mic	Microscope
Camelopardalis	Cam	Giraffe	Monoceros	Mon	Unicorn
Cancer	Cnc	Crab	Musca	Mus	Fly
Canes Venatici	CVn	Hunting Dogs	Norma	Nor	Level (square)
Canis Major	CMa	Big Dog	Octans	Oct	Octant
Canis Minor	CMi	Little Dog	Ophiuchus	Oph	Ophiuchus (serpent bearer)
Capricornus	Cap	Goat	Orion	Ori	Orion
Carina	Car	Ship's Keel	Pavo	Pav	Peacock
Cassiopeia	Cas	Cassiopeia	Pegasus	Peg	Pegasus (winged horse)
Centaurus	Cen	Centaur	Perseus	Per	Perseus
Cepheus	Cep	Cepheus	Phoenix	Phe	Phoenix
Cetus	Cet	Whale	Pictor	Pic	Easel
Chamaeleon	Cha	Chameleon	Pisces	Psc	Fish
Circinus	Cir	Compass	Piscis Austrinus	PsA	Southern Fish
Columba	Col	Dove	Puppis	Pup	Ship's Stern
Coma Berenices	Com	Berenice's Hair	Pyxis	Pyx	Ship's Compass
Corona Australis	CrA	Southern Crown	Reticulum	Ret	Net
Corona Borealis	CrB	Northern Crown	Sagitta	Sge	Arrow
Corvus	Crv	Crow	Sagittarius	Sgr	Archer
Crater	Crt	Cup	Scorpius	Sco	Scorpion
Crux	Cru	Southern Cross	Sculptor	Scl	Sculptor
Cygnus	Cyg	Swan	Scutum	Sct	Shield
Delphinus	Del	Dolphin	Serpens	Ser	Serpent
Dorado	Dor	Swordfish	Sextans	Sex	Sextant
Draco	Dra	Dragon	Taurus	Tau	Bull
Equuleus	Equ	Little Horse	Telescopium	Tel	Telescope
Eridanus	Eri	River Eridanus	Triangulum	Tri	Triangle
Fornax	For	Furnace	Triangulum Australe	TrA	Southern Triangle
Gemini	Gem	Twins	Tucana	Tuc	Toucan
Grus	Gru	Crane	Ursa Major	UMa	Big Bear
Hercules	Her	Hercules	Ursa Minor	UMi	Little Bear
Horologium	Hor	Clock	Vela	Vel	Ship's Sails
Hydra	Hya	Hydra (water monster)	Virgo	Vir	Virgin
Hydrus	Hyi	Sea serpent	Volans	Vol	Flying Fish
Indus	Ind	Indian	Vulpecula	Vul	Little Fox

INDEX